get crafty

get crafty

over 160 beautiful, easy-to-make projects – step by step

lucy painter

southwater

This edition is published by Southwater

Distributed in the UK by
The Manning Partnership
251–253 London Road East
Batheaston
Bath BA1 7RL
tel. 01225 852 727
fax 01225 852 852

Published in the USA by
Anness Publishing Inc.
27 West 20th Street
Suite 504
New York
NY 10011
fax 212 807 6813

Distributed in Canada by
General Publishing
895 Don Mills Road
400–402 Park Centre
Toronto, Ontario M3C 1W3
tel. 416 445 3333
fax 416 445 5991

Distributed in Australia by
Sandstone Publishing
Unit 1, 360 Norton Street
Leichhardt
New South Wales 2040
tel. 02 9560 7888
fax 02 9560 7488

Southwater is an imprint of Anness Publishing Limited
Hermes House, 88–89 Blackfriars Road, London SE1 8HA
tel. 020 7401 2077; fax 020 7633 9499

Publisher: Joanna Lorenz
Project Editor: Christopher Fagg
Editor: Harriette Lanzer
Designers: Patrick McLeavey, Hannah Attwell, Dean Hollowood

Previously published as *New Craft Collection*

10 9 8 7 6 5 4 3 2 1

Acknowledgements *Projects* Ofer Acoo, Madeleine Adams, Dinah Alan-Smith, Deborah Alexander, Michael Ball, Evelyn Bennett, Amanda Blunden, Petra Boase, Penny Boylan, Janet Bridge, Al Brown, Louise Brownlow, Esther Burt, Judy Clayton, Gill Clement, Lilli Curtiss, Sophie Embleton, Lucinda Ganderton, Louise Gardam, Lisa Gilchrist, Andrew Gilmore, Dawn Gulyas, David Hancock, Jill Hancock, Lesley Harle, Stephanie Harvey, Bridget Hinge, Labeena Ishaque, Sameena Ishaque, Paul Jackson, Mary Maguire, Rachel Howard Marshall, Abigail Mill, Terence Moore, Izzy Moreau, Jack Moxley, Oliver Moxley, Cleo Mussie, Sarbjitt Natt, Cheryl Owen, Emma Petitt, Lizzie Reakes, Kim Rowley, Deborah Schneebeli-Morrell, Debbie Siniska, Isabel Stanley, Thomasina Smith, Adele Tipler, Kellie-Marie Townsend, Karen Triffitt, Liz Wagstaff, Sally Walton, Stewart Walton, Emma Whitfield, Josephine Whitfield, Melanie Williams, Dorothy Wood
Photography Steve Dalton, James Duncan, Michelle Garrett, Lucy Mason, Gloria Nicol, Debbie Patterson, Peter Williams

Contents

Introduction

This book contains over 160 step-by-step projects using a variety of exciting crafts, both traditional and new. You can select a project at any level of skill, from the simplicity of paper cut-outs to the more detailed art of soldering tin. Or, use a needlework craft to create soft furnishings for the home and complement them with some beautiful painted glassware. Children, in particular, will love the salt dough ideas, and anyone wanting to cheer up walls and furniture should look no further than the stamping projects.

Whatever your preferred style of craft, you're bound to find inspiration in this collection. You could also try out a craft new to you and discover hidden talents. Just pick your project, experiment with the materials, follow the clear instructions and enjoy the result.

Using Templates

There are easy-to-use templates at the back of the book for a lot of the projects. For tracing templates, you will need tracing paper, a pencil, card or paper and a pair of scissors. The templates can be traced on to tracing paper and cut out to use as pattern guides. If a pattern is to be used a number of times, the template tracing should be transferred to thin card. To do this, trace the template on to tracing paper, using a pencil, then place the tracing paper face down on the card. Re-draw the motif on the back of the tracing and it will appear on the card.

To enlarge the templates to the required size, either use a grid system or a photocopier. For the grid system, trace the template and draw a grid of evenly spaced squares over your tracing. To scale up, draw a larger grid on to another piece of paper. Copy the outline on to the second grid by taking each square individually and drawing the relevant part of the outline in the larger square.

Papercrafts and Papier-mache

Experiment with paper to create some memorable gifts, such as this charming Sunburst Bowl.

Stencilling, Stamping and Printing

A marvellously easy and effective method to make individual pieces, such as this Mexican Citrus Tray.

Embroidery

Embroider beautiful effects on to fabrics, as is illustrated in this Underwater Picture.

Applique, Patchwork and Cross Stitch

Follow the step-by-step instructions to make exciting projects, such as this pretty Seashell Beach Bag.

Modelling and Salt Dough

Get stuck into the wonderful texture of salt dough and clay, and create some amazing end results, such as these Salt and Pepper Pots.

WOOD, WIRE AND TINWORK

This section includes fun ideas such as this wood Grasshopper on a Stick, as well as exciting wire and tin projects.

DECORATING GLASS AND CERAMICS

Re-vamp old china and glass and your crockery cupboard will soon be transformed with projects such as this Fruit Bowl.

PAPERCRAFTS AND PAPIER-MACHE

Working with paper is a truly satisfying and creative craft, and the bonus is that it can also be good for the environment, if you recycle old and used papers in your projects. There is such a wealth of colours, textures and sizes available in paper that the scope for producing wonderful decorations and gifts really is endless.

The projects in this book should inspire you to experiment with paper whatever your tastes and ability. Steps are provided to take you through the process of creating a traditional paper cut-out, which you can easily adapt to make as simple or intricate as you like. Or, if you prefer a more weighty project, you could get involved in the art of papier-mâché – and explore the delights you can make from the simplest of materials.

MATERIALS AND EQUIPMENT

Paper comes in many different weights, textures, patterns and colours. Before you embark on the projects here, explore some possible paper sources. Art and hobby shops, printers, office stationers and specialist suppliers are all good starting points. And don't forget to look around your own home – you'll be amazed at how many pieces of paper and card you have got already. You just need to view the material in a different light, and recognize that those old newspapers on the coffee table can be transformed into an exciting new creation.

A craft knife and a cutting mat or a pair of paper scissors are vital when working with paper, and so too is masking tape as it won't tear the paper. Paper glue or spray adhesive are also useful to have at hand if you want to attach pieces of paper to each other.

Painting and colouring your paper projects presents no problem, and there is a wide range of crayons, pens, paints and varnishes available that are suitable for paper. Just check the manufacturer's instructions before you apply the material to paper, and if you like, you can always do a test run on a scrap of paper first, just to make sure.

RIGHT *The equipment necessary for papercrafts is very simple and straightforward.*

Working with different papers

There are so many varieties of paper available that you will have to let your personal taste dictate what you use for your projects. Here are a few of the more exciting papers you could try.

Tissue and crepe paper are cheap papers sold at stationers and craft suppliers. Tissue paper needs to be layered to build up intense colour. Crepe paper is thicker and crinkly and its only drawback is that adhesive tape doesn't stick to it well.

Hand-printed paper is the perfect way to personalize gift wrap. All you need is plain paper and a spark of inspiration. Potato cuts, rubber stamps, stencils, rollers or brushstrokes will all produce unique patterned papers. Use lightweight paper, or cheap brown wrapping paper for the best results.

Corrugated card gives projects a unique texture and depth, and it is also very cheap to buy.

Natural papers are environmentally friendly handmade papers usually imported from the East; the selection really is enormous. It is possible to buy paper made from banana skins or recycled Bombay newsprint inlaid with rose petals. The colours are often hotter and spicier than home-produced papers, so it is well worth seeking out a specialist paper outlet and stocking up for future use.

LEFT *Papers are available in every kind of colour and texture from art suppliers and craft shops.*

BASIC TECHNIQUES

Tearing newspaper

Sheets of newsprint are laid and have a definite grain, usually running from the top to the bottom of the newspaper.

1 If you try to tear a sheet of newspaper against the grain – from side to side – it is impossible to control.

2 If newspaper is torn along the grain it is possible to produce very regular strips, as wide or narrow as you need.

Making papier-mâché pulp

MATERIALS

5 sheets newspaper
45 ml/3 tbsp PVA (white) glue
20 ml/ 4 tsp wallpaper paste
10 ml/2 tsp plaster of Paris
10 ml/2 tsp linseed oil

1 Tear the newspaper into pieces about 2.5 cm/1 in square and put them in an old saucepan with water to cover. Simmer for about half an hour.

2 Spoon the paper and any water into a blender or food processor and liquidize it. Pour it into a suitable container with a lid.

3 Add the PVA (white) glue, wallpaper paste, plaster of Paris and linseed oil. Stir vigorously and the pulp is ready to use.

Preparing the surface for papier-mâché painting

The surface of the papier-mâché should be primed before painting to conceal the newsprint and to provide a good ground for decoration.

MATERIALS

fine sandpaper
paintbrush
white emulsion (latex) paint

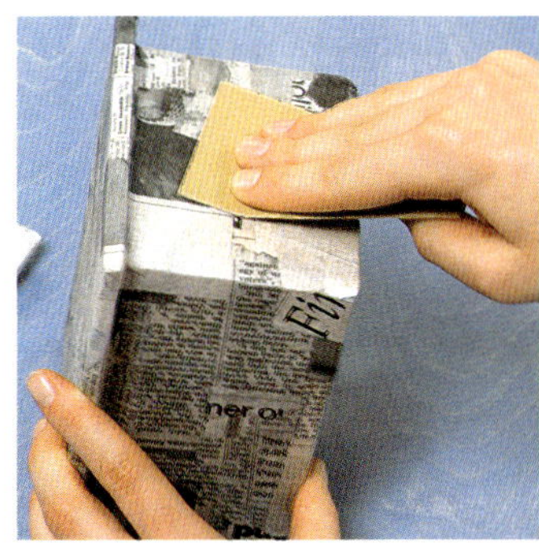

1 Gently smooth the surface of the papier-mâché using fine sandpaper.

2 Apply a coat of white emulsion (latex) paint and leave the object to dry.

3 Rub down the dry paint lightly using fine sandpaper, and apply a second coat of paint. Once this has dried, the papier-mâché may be decorated.

Paper Cut-outs

Gemini – the twins – is the chosen motif for this effective paper card decoration: the two halves of the card are identical in design, yet one is the negative image of the other. These cut-outs are a traditional skill in Poland, where they are usually deftly cut freehand using a pair of scissors.

You Will Need

Materials

tracing paper
thin card or paper in two colours, plus a large sheet for backing
all-purpose glue

Equipment

pencil
craft knife
cutting mat
scissors

1 Trace the template from the back of the book, enlarging if necessary. Attach the tracing to the wrong side of one piece of coloured card with a few dabs of glue.

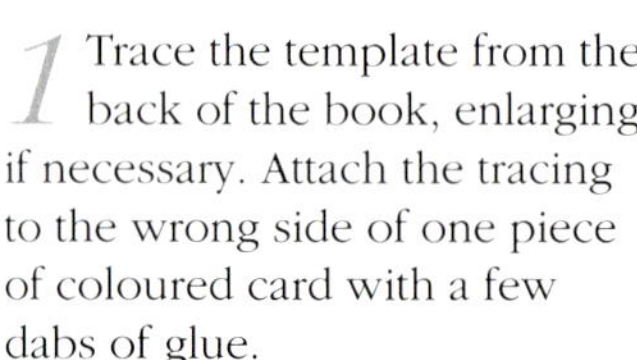

2 Using a craft knife, cut out through the template and reserve all the shapes.

3 Remove the tracing paper, turn the card over and then back it with some card in a contrasting colour.

4 Cut the backing card twice the size of the cut-out card and fold down the centre. Stick a piece of the contrast card or paper to one side of the fold and arrange cut-out pieces on it to match the original design. Stick the cut-out card on the opposite side.

DECOUPAGE ROSE EGGS

Re-use old wrapping paper when you are making these patterned eggs.

YOU WILL NEED

MATERIALS

rose scrapbook motifs or rose-decorated wrapping paper
PVA (white) glue
wooden or blown eggs
clear nail varnish

EQUIPMENT

small scissors
paintbrush

1 Cut out a selection of small rose motifs. You may find other motifs you can use, such as butterflies or forget-me-nots. Look out for interesting shapes and cut them out carefully around the outlines.

2 Using PVA (white) glue, stick the cut-out flowers to the wooden or blown eggs, making sure you overlap the edges to give a densely patterned surface. Make sure that all the wood or shell is covered.

3 Once the glue is dry, coat the eggs with three or four coats of clear nail varnish, allowing each coat to dry thoroughly before adding the next one.

Christmas Tree Star

Persuade the fairy to take a well-earned rest this year, and make a magnificent gold star to take pride of place at the top of the Christmas tree.

You Will Need

Materials	Equipment
tracing paper	*pencil*
thin card or paper	*scissors*
corrugated card	*craft knife*
newspaper	*cutting mat*
PVA (white) glue	*metal ruler*
gold spray paint	*bowl*
gold relief or puff paint	*paintbrush*
gold glitter	
thin gold braid	

1 Trace the template from the back of the book, enlarging if necessary, then transfer it to thin card or paper. Cut it out and draw around it on the corrugated card. Cut it out using a craft knife and metal ruler. Tear the newspaper into small strips. Thin the PVA (white) glue with some water and brush it on to both sides of the newspaper, coating it thoroughly. Stick it on the star, brushing it down with more glue to get rid of any air bubbles. Work all over the star in a single layer, covering the edges and points neatly. Allow the star to dry thoroughly, then apply a second layer.

2 If the star begins to buckle, place it under a heavy weight. When it is thoroughly dry, spray both sides of it gold and allow to dry.

3 Draw the design on one side of the star in gold relief paint and sprinkle it with glitter while it is still wet. Allow to dry thoroughly before repeating the design on the other side. Attach thin gold braid with which to hang the star from the top of the Christmas tree.

PAPIER-MACHE PLATE

For this papier-mâché plate, the colour is incorporated into the paper pulp before it is moulded. This would be a wonderful project for a whole family to do together, with each person making his or her own sign for the plate.

YOU WILL NEED

MATERIALS

acrylic paints
paper pulp (see Basic Techniques)
strong card
PVA (white) glue
crepe paper
wallpaper paste
tracing paper
thin card or paper
chalk or white pencil
black emulsion (latex) paint and gold paint (optional)

EQUIPMENT

fork
pencil
plate
craft knife
cutting mat
paintbrush (optional)

1 Using a fork, mash acrylic paint into the paper pulp until the colour is evenly mixed. Cut out two circles of card the same size, using an old plate as a template. Cut a smaller circle from one and glue the rim to the front of the other circle and the centre to the back. Cover with crepe paper soaked in wallpaper paste.

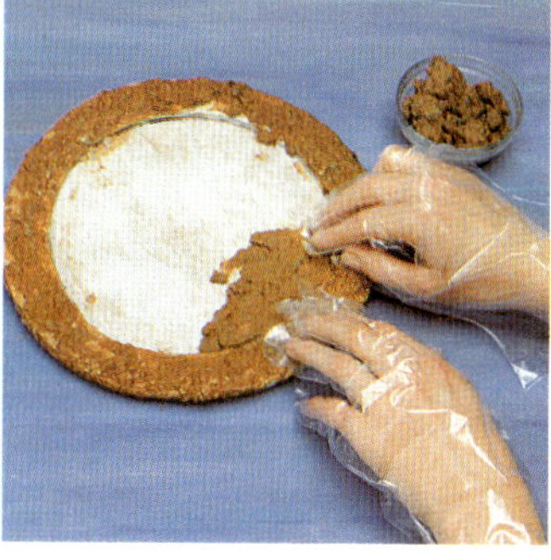

2 Press coloured pulp on to the edge of the plate, building it up in thin layers, and adding more when dry. Trace the template from the back of the book, enlarging if necessary. Transfer to thin card or paper. Cut it out and draw around it with chalk or white pencil on to the plate. Build up the body with pulp, covering the outline.

3 Add finer details such as legs and claws with more thin layers of paper pulp. Allow to dry thoroughly. To add some definition, take a dry brush with some black emulsion (latex) paint and wipe lightly over the scorpion and the rim of the plate. Repeat with gold paint.

Gilded Bookmark

Look for pictures of old engravings and heraldic devices for this découpage: the clearly defined images will photocopy perfectly and look great once they've been cunningly aged with tea. Use stiff card so that the bookmark isn't too bulky.

You Will Need

Materials
stiff card
acrylic gesso
acrylic paints: red, orange and green
gold paint
tea bags
photocopied images
PVA (white) glue
velvet ribbon

Equipment
craft knife
cutting mat
metal ruler
paintbrush
bowl
scissors

1 Using a craft knife and metal ruler, cut a rectangle of card 15 x 5 cm/6 x 2 in, and cut off the corners diagonally.

2 Paint it with acrylic gesso. Mix a red oxide colour using red, orange and green acrylics and paint this all over the bookmark. When dry, cover with gold paint, leaving some of the red oxide showing through.

3 Make a very strong solution of tea and paint the photocopies with this to create an aged appearance. Allow to dry, then cut out.

4 Stick on the cut-outs with PVA (white) glue and varnish with diluted PVA (white) to seal. Glue a length of velvet ribbon to the back of the bookmark.

GARLAND TRAY CUT-OUTS

The simple leaf design for this pretty découpage tray is folded and cut out like a row of dancing paper dolls. When drawing the design, make sure that your outline continues to the folds so that your paper garland stays in one piece when it is opened out.

YOU WILL NEED

MATERIALS	EQUIPMENT
wooden tray	*paintbrushes*
yellow emulsion (latex) paint	*pencil*
large sheet of green paper	*scissors*
PVA (white) glue	*scrap paper*
clear gloss acrylic varnish	

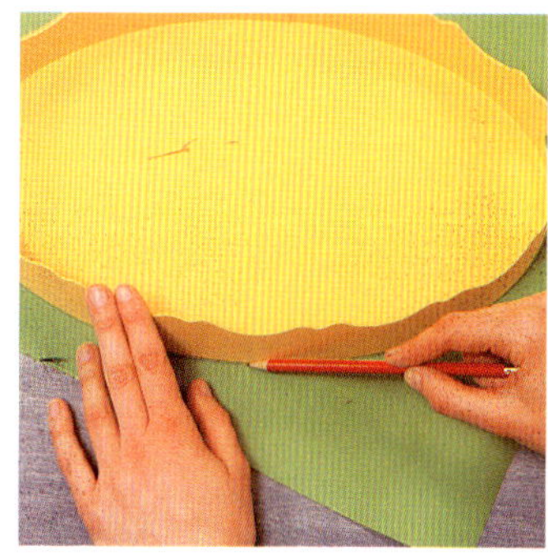

1 Paint the tray with two coats of yellow emulsion (latex) paint and allow to dry. Place the tray on the green paper and draw around it. Cut out the shape just inside the line.

2 Fold the paper in half, then in half again. Draw a series of connecting leaf shapes on to scrap paper and cut them out. When you are happy with the design, draw around it on to the green paper, making sure that it reaches the folded edges. Cut along the pencil line.

3 Open out the garland carefully and glue it on to the tray. Allow to dry.

4 Protect the tray with up to four coats of varnish.

BEAMING SUN WALL PLAQUE

A cheerful sunny face looking down at you is sure to cheer you up, so put this wall plaque where it will do you most good – perhaps over the breakfast table! The plaque is made from sandwiched layers of corrugated card and mounted on card in the same way, so it is very easy to make. There is also an alternative idea, using papier-mâché pulp to mould the face.

YOU WILL NEED

MATERIALS	EQUIPMENT
corrugated card	*pair of compasses*
PVA (white) glue	*pencil*
masking tape	*craft knife*
white undercoat paint	*scissors*
acrylic paints: red, yellow and blue	*paintbrushes*
matt varnish	

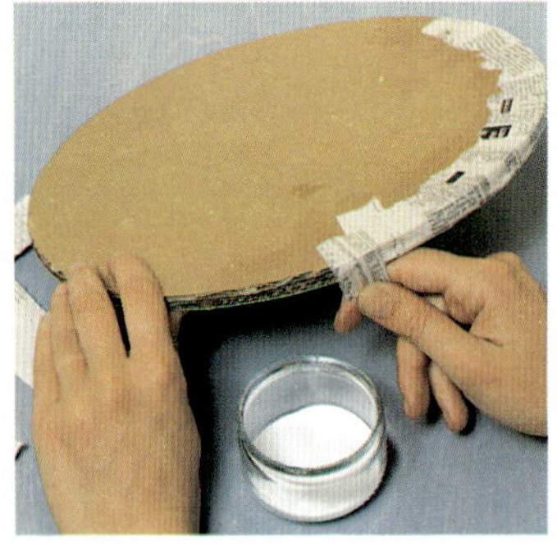

1 Draw and cut out five equal circles of card to the size required. Glue together three circles. Bind the edges with masking tape.

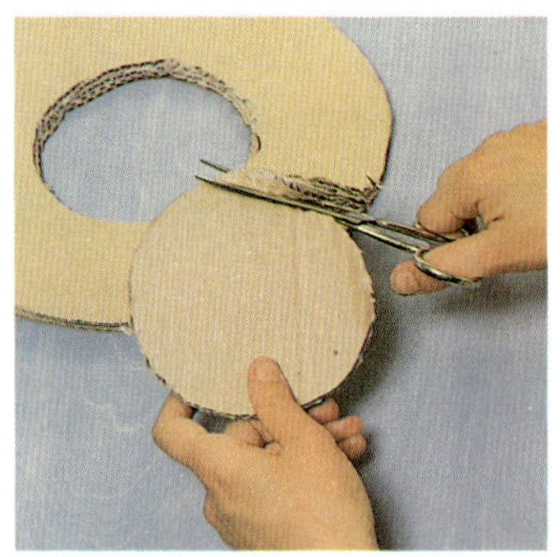

2 Glue the remaining two circles together and cut out a circle from the centre. Trim this smaller circle so that there will be a gap all around it when it is replaced.

3 On the circle with the hole, draw the rays of the sun and cut them out. Bind the edges inside and out and also the edges of the small circle.

4 Glue the prepared sun rays and the face on to the backing circle, centralizing the face in the slightly larger area left for it.

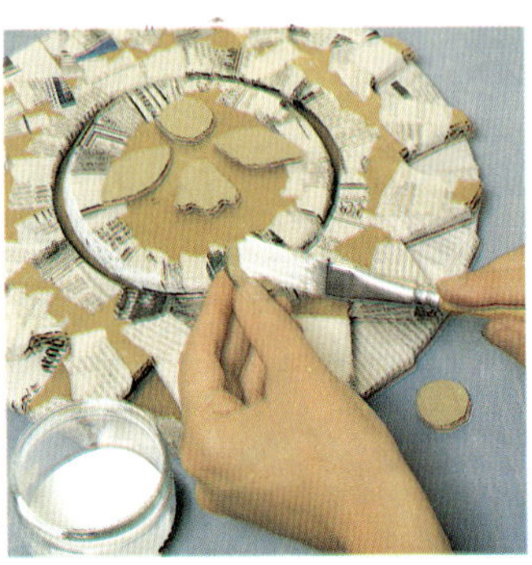

5 Draw the features on card freehand and cut them out. Glue them on to the face.

6 Prime the whole of the plaque with white undercoat and allow to dry.

7 Decorate with acrylic paints. When dry, apply two coats of varnish.

8 Alternatively, make the sun shape from papier-mâché pulp (see Basic Techniques), moulding it by hand on the backing circle. Use fine string to delineate the features and give relief detail to the rays. Coat the face in primer and paint as before.

Decorative Napkin Ring

This practical project recycles old card to create something special for the dinner table. You could decorate the ring with a design of your choice, or use this stylish heraldic motif.

You Will Need

Materials

tracing paper
thick card
poster tube
newspaper
wallpaper paste
acrylic gesso
acrylic paints: blue, red, yellow, light gold, black and white
gloss acrylic varnish

Equipment

hard and soft pencils
craft knife
cutting mat
bowl
fine and medium paintbrushes
glue gun or epoxy resin glue

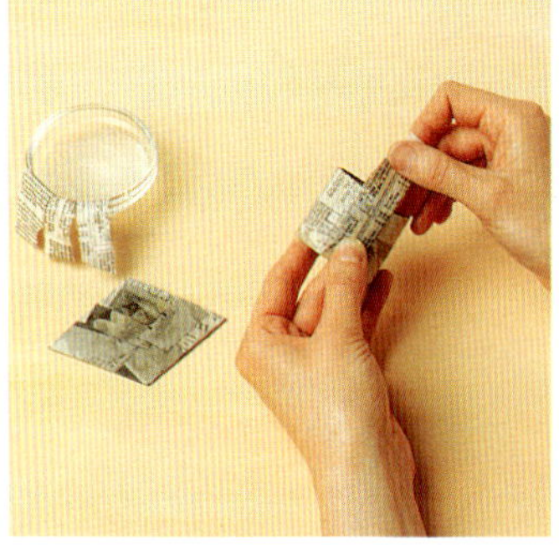

1 Trace the template from the back of the book, enlarging if necessary. Cut out a card diamond. Cut a 4 cm/1½ in section from the poster tube. Coat strips of newspaper with wallpaper paste. Cover the ring, with the edges, with several layers. Cover the diamond with about ten layers.

2 When the papier-mâché is dry, prime it with three coats of acrylic gesso. Transfer the traced design on to the diamond by rubbing over the back with a soft pencil, then drawing over the outlines.

3 Paint the background diamonds in blue and red and the lion and fleur-de-lys in yellow. Highlight the design in light gold paint and outline the shapes in black. Pick out details in red and white. Paint the ring with two coats of blue. Seal the diamond and ring with acrylic varnish and, when dry, glue the two parts together.

Orange Bowl

Hoard your old magazines so that you can assemble a good collection of orange and yellow papers for this papier-mâché bowl. It is designed to look like half an orange – plain on the outside and beautifully textured inside.

You Will Need

Materials

petroleum jelly
newspaper
wallpaper paste
old magazine pages that are predominantly orange and yellow
orange wrapping paper
gloss varnish
gold paint

Equipment

large bowl
scissors
medium and fine paintbrushes

1 Coat the inside of the bowl with a layer of petroleum jelly. Soak strips of newspaper in wallpaper paste. Cover the inside of the bowl with at least ten layers of strips. Allow to dry thoroughly, then gently ease the bowl from the mould.

2 Tear the magazine pages into long, narrow triangles and paste them around the inside of the bowl so that they taper towards the bottom.

3 Cover the outside of the bowl with torn strips of plain orange and yellow wrapping paper, carefully overlapping the edges.

4 Leave the bowl to dry thoroughly, then trim the top edge with scissors. Coat the bowl with a protective layer of varnish. Paint a thin line of gold paint along the top edge to complete the bowl.

Sunburst Bowl

This spectacular sun seems to burst out of the bowl towards you. Use all your creativity to make the design as exuberant as possible. Papier-mâché gives you the ability to make graceful vessels without the skill and equipment needed for making ceramics. This bowl is ideal for fruit, nuts or small display items, but you might well want to leave it empty to show it off.

You Will Need

Materials

petroleum jelly
newspaper
paper pulp (see Basic Techniques)
PVA (white) glue
white undercoat paint
gouache or acrylic paints: yellow, blue and red
gold "liquid leaf" paint or gold gouache paint
fixative spray
gloss varnish

Equipment

bowl
medium and fine paintbrushes
paint-mixing container
pair of compasses
pencil

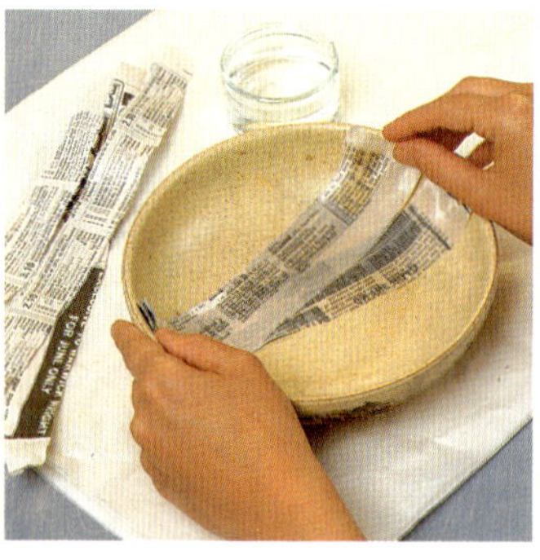

1 Coat the inside of the bowl with a layer of petroleum jelly. Dip strips of newspaper in water, then lay them over the inside of the bowl.

2 Press the paper pulp into the mould so that it is about 1 cm/½ in thick. Allow to dry in an airing cupboard, for about five days.

3 Release the dried paper pulp from the mould and cover it in strips of newspaper dipped in PVA (white) glue. Allow to dry thoroughly.

4 Give the bowl two coats of white undercoat, allowing each coat to dry.

5 Use the pair of compasses to locate the sun shape accurately, then draw a small circle for the centre and a larger one to contain the rays. Draw the rays freehand.

6 Fill in the yellow and gold areas first of all. Then paint the rim in gold. Fill in the blue background, leaving a white band below the gold rim.

7 Paint the red border and allow to dry. Seal the bowl with fixative spray and protect it with a coat of varnish.

TWISTED PAPER FRAME

This frame is made from unravelled twisted paper, which is available from most gift shops. It is simple to make, and provides the ideal frame for your favourite photo or picture.

YOU WILL NEED

MATERIALS	EQUIPMENT
card	*plate and saucer*
twisted paper	*pencil*
PVA (white) glue	*scissors*
emulsion (latex) paints: white and gold	*craft knife*
fabric star motifs	*cutting mat*
backing card (optional)	*old toothbrush*
	paint-mixing containers

1 Draw around the plate on to the card. Place the saucer in the centre of the circle and draw around it. Cut out the outer circle with scissors and then the inner circle using a craft knife, so you are left with a card ring.

2 Unwind the twisted paper and wind it carefully around the ring until it is fully covered. Stick the end down with PVA (white) glue.

3 Dip an old toothbrush into the white paint and run your finger along the bristles so that a fine spray of paint lands on the card frame. Repeat with the gold paint.

4 Stick the star motifs all over the frame with PVA (white) glue. If you like, stick a card backing circle on the back, leaving a gap in which to insert a picture.

PAPIER-MACHE JUG

This jug looks like a modern Italian ceramic, with its elegant shape and brilliant colours, but in fact it is made from papier-mâché shaped round a blown-up balloon. A sunflower moulded from paper pulp makes a relief decoration.

YOU WILL NEED

MATERIALS

balloon
newspaper
wallpaper paste
thin card
masking tape
round margarine container
fine string
paper pulp (see Basic Techniques)
acrylic paints: blue, yellow, red and green
clear varnish

EQUIPMENT

scissors
medium and fine paintbrushes
paint-mixing container

1 Blow up the balloon and tie a knot in it. Soak strips of newspaper in wallpaper paste, and cover the balloon with at least eight layers of them. Allow to dry. Cut slits in the top of the balloon at the knot end and remove the balloon. Cut out a V-shape in one side. Cut a piece of card to form a spout and tape in position.

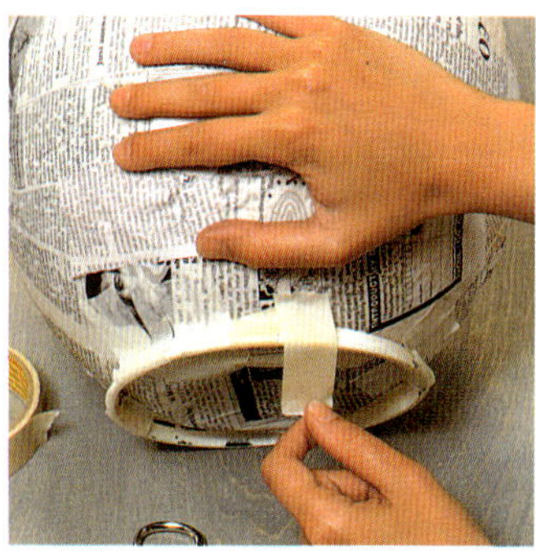

2 Tape the rim of a margarine container to the bottom for the base. For the handle, roll up some glued newspaper sheets and curve them to fit the jug. Allow to dry. Cover the handle with string, leaving about 1–2.5 cm/½ –1 in at each end uncovered. Cut two slits in the side and insert the handle.

3 Model the paper pulp on the side of the jug in the shape of sunflowers and leaves. Allow to dry overnight. Paint the background, flowers and details and allow to dry, before giving the jug a coat of varnish.

Papier-mache Frame

This frame provides a beautiful three-dimensional background to a picture or painting. You can experiment as much as you like with the frame: try using softer colours instead of the strong ones here, or replace the heart motifs with a design of your choosing to create a truly individual frame.

You Will Need

Materials

- *tracing paper*
- *card*
- *masking tape*
- *wire*
- *newspaper*
- *wallpaper paste*
- *white emulsion (latex) paint*
- *self-hardening clay*
- *poster paints: royal-blue, violet and yellow*
- *clear varnish*
- *photo or picture*
- *PVA (white) glue (optional)*

Equipment

- *pencil*
- *craft knife*
- *cutting mat*
- *paintbrushes*
- *clay modelling tool*

1 Trace the template from the back of the book, enlarging if necessary. Cut out the centre square. Score along the dotted lines using a craft knife, taking care not to cut right through.

2 Fold each flap inwards along the scored edges and tape the frame together with masking tape.

3 Fix a piece of wire to the back, using masking tape.

4 Tear the newspaper in small squares, measuring about 2.5 x 2.5 cm/ 1 x 1 in. Dip them in wallpaper paste and stick them on to the frame until both the front and the back of the frame are well covered.

5 Prime the covered frame with a coat of white paint and allow to dry. Apply a second coat of paint to make sure that the surface is opaque. Allow to dry thoroughly.

6 Form heart shapes out of clay by hand and push these on to the front of the frame for decoration. Fix the hearts in place by smoothing down the sides with a clay modelling tool.

7 Paint the frame with poster paints and allow to dry. Seal with a coat of varnish. Once dry, stick your chosen photo or picture on to the card (set aside in step 1) and glue or tape it in place.

CRACKLE-GLAZED PRINT

Antique prints are expensive, but with this technique you can create your own thoroughly original design very cheaply. Use a photocopier to enlarge or reduce motifs and practise arranging them until you have a design that appeals.

YOU WILL NEED

MATERIALS

selection of black and white cupid prints
spray adhesive
tea bags and instant coffee
PVA (white) glue
hardboard or card
acrylic medium
clear acrylic gloss varnish
burnt umber acrylic paint

EQUIPMENT

scissors
large soft Chinese paintbrush
household and fine paintbrushes
paint-mixing container

1 Cut out the prints and lightly coat them on the back with spray adhesive. Arrange the prints until you are happy with the result. By using spray adhesive, you can reposition the designs as many times as you like. Photocopy the final result.

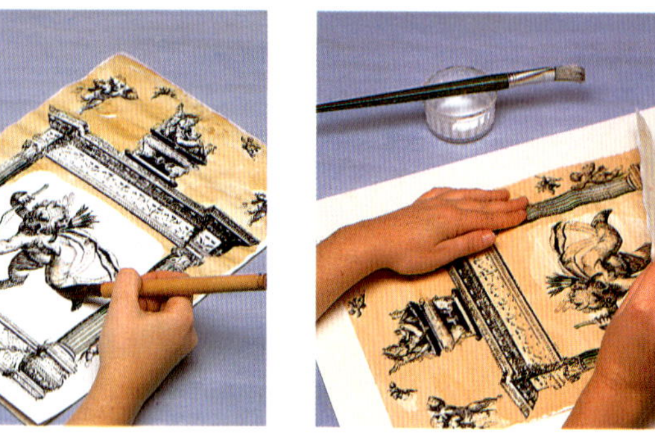

2 Make a "cocktail" of one tea bag and three teaspoons of coffee and let it cool. Apply to the print with a Chinese paintbrush. You can experiment with brews of different strengths and apply the mixture several times, to create depth. Allow to dry.

3 Mix equal parts of PVA (white) glue and water and apply the mixture to the back of the print with a household paintbrush. Smooth the print on to the hardboard or card backing. (You can also apply the print directly to a wall or a piece of furniture.) Brush the PVA (white) mixture on top of the print and backing and allow to dry.

4 Cover the print and backing with acrylic medium in the same way. This may cause the paper to wrinkle, but don't worry: once dry, the wrinkles will vanish.

5 Coat with acrylic varnish, to give a shiny finish and add an antique look.

6 Mix burnt umber acrylic paint into the varnish and paint cracks with a fine paintbrush. Add more shadows and blend them in softly. Finally, apply another coat of acrylic varnish and allow to dry.

WATER BEARER'S SHRINE

Aquarius, the water bearer, carries the waters of creation and symbolizes death and renewal. An original tribute to him is this charming wall plaque.

YOU WILL NEED

MATERIALS	EQUIPMENT
thin card or paper	*pencil*
corrugated card	*craft knife*
masking tape	*cutting mat*
paper pulp (see Basic Techniques)	*bowl*
newspaper	*paintbrushes*
wallpaper paste	
PVA (white) glue	
white acrylic primer	
gouache paints: pale blue, dark blue, orange and red	
gloss varnish	
gold enamel paint	
epoxy resin glue	
mirror-hanging plate	

1 Draw templates for the shrine, its sides and figure, and transfer them to corrugated card. Cut them out and assemble them using masking tape. Make a small rectangular "step" from card and fix it to the figure's back.

2 Apply paper pulp to the front of the figure to give a rounded shape. When dry, cover the figure and plaque in several layers of newspaper strips soaked in wallpaper paste. Allow to dry.

3 Paint on a coat of PVA (white) glue followed, when dry, by a coat of white acrylic primer. Decorate the plaque and figure with gouache paints.

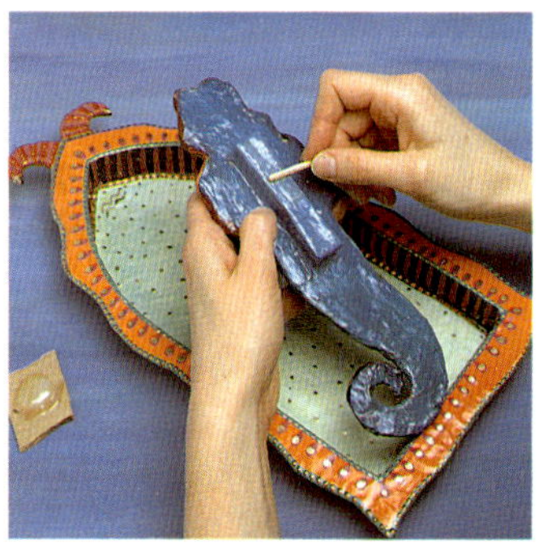

4 Varnish, then, when dry, highlight the details with gold enamel paint. Use epoxy resin glue to secure the figure in place and fix a mirror-hanging plate to the back.

GOLD-RIMMED BOWL

This attractive bowl is delicately hand-painted and decorated with gold paint. Its cheerful, sunny design will brighten up any dull corner. Use it purely as decoration, or to hold trinkets, nuts or sweets.

YOU WILL NEED

MATERIALS

petroleum jelly
newspaper
paper pulp (see Basic Techniques)
PVA (white) glue
white undercoat paint
gold "liquid leaf" paint
acrylic paints: white, yellow, ochre, turquoise and brown
paper tissue
fixative spray
gloss varnish

EQUIPMENT

bowl
scissors
large, medium and fine paintbrushes
pair of compasses
pencil
paint-mixing container

1 Apply a coat of petroleum jelly to the inside of the bowl. Line it with strips of wet newspaper. Put the paper pulp into the bowl in an even layer about 1 cm/½ in deep. Allow to dry in an airing cupboard for about five days. Release the bowl from the mould. Dip strips of newspaper in PVA (white) glue and cover the bowl.

2 Give the bowl two coats of white undercoat. Use a pair of compasses to help you centralize the flower motif. Draw the flower freehand.

3 Paint the rim with gold "liquid leaf". Decorate the bowl with the acrylic paints. Mix white into all the colours to lighten them and, before the paint dries, dab some off with a paper tissue so that the undercoat shows through in places. Allow to dry. Spray with fixative spray, then give the bowl a coat of varnish.

Mirrored Keepsake Box

This box is made from an old poster tube decorated with mirror shards. It is an original idea for storing jewellery.

You Will Need

Materials

section of poster tube
card
masking tape
PVA (white) glue
newspaper
4 marbles
wallpaper paste
epoxy resin glue
chemical metal filler
(i.e. car-body repair filler)
mirror fragments
white acrylic primer
selection of gouache paints
glossy varnish
gold enamel paint

Equipment

pencil
scissors
pair of compasses
small and fine paintbrushes
paint-mixing containers

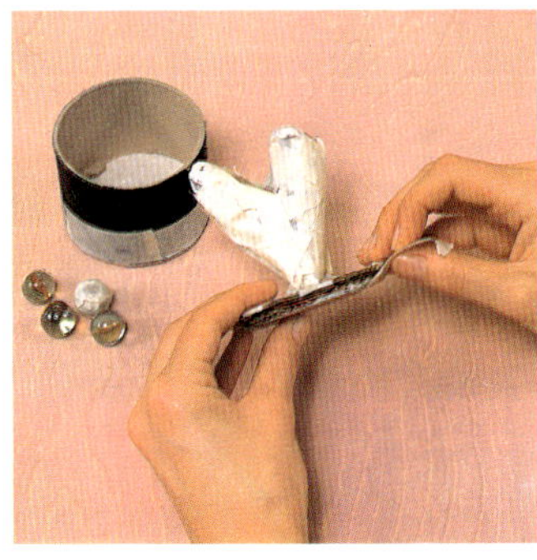

1 Draw around the poster tube end on card, cut it out and tape it to the tube. Cut out a slightly larger lid and another circle 1 cm/½ in less in diameter. Glue together. Bend a roll of newspaper into a heart shape and tape it to the lid. Cover the marbles with masking tape.

2 Cover the box, lid and marbles with several layers of newspaper strips soaked in wallpaper paste. When dry, glue the marbles to the box base with epoxy resin glue. Mix up the filler, spread it on to the lid, and carefully push in the mirror fragments.

3 Paint the box, excluding the mirror pieces, with PVA (white) glue. When dry, prime the box and paint the design with gouache paints.

4 Coat the box with several layers of glossy varnish, and allow to dry thoroughly. Add detail in gold enamel.

Floating Leaves Mobile

Featherlight paper leaves will flutter delicately in the merest whiff of air. Use a variety of textures for the cut-outs – look out for handmade paper incorporating leaves and flower petals.

You Will Need

Materials

thick silver florist's wire
tracing paper
thin card or paper
selection of coloured and textured papers
matching sewing thread

Equipment

wire-cutters
round-nosed pliers
pencil
scissors
needle

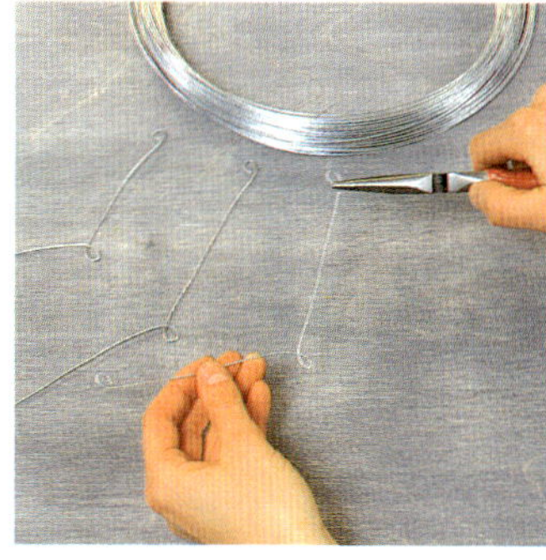

1 Cut two lengths of wire 20 cm/8 in and one length 30 cm/12 in. Twist each piece of wire in the middle to make a loop. Make a small loop, pointing downwards, at each end of each length.

2 Trace the templates from the back of the book, enlarging if necessary. Transfer them to card or paper and cut out. Draw round them on coloured and textured papers, then cut out the shapes.

3 Use a needle to attach an assortment of leaves on to a length of thread to hang from each wire loop.

4 Use thread to hang the two shorter wires from the ends of the longer one. Tie the leaves to each wire loop. Fasten a length of thread to the top loop to hang the mobile.

DECORATED BOX

This mirror box has a wonderful corrugated texture. The mirror is hidden behind doors, which can be closed when not in use.

YOU WILL NEED

MATERIALS

corrugated card
PVA (white) glue
newspaper
masking tape
white undercoat paint
gouache paints: red, blue, orange, yellow and white
gloss varnish
gold "liquid leaf" paint
mirror
epoxy resin glue
2 small brass door hinges

EQUIPMENT

craft knife
cutting mat
metal ruler
pencil
fine paintbrushes
paint-mixing container

1 Cut out the box pieces from corrugated card. The back is 26 cm/10 in high and 13 cm/5 in wide at the base. The sides are 3.5 cm/1½ in deep. Create a recess 3.5 cm/1½ in deep and 8 cm/3 in square, for the mirror to sit in. Cut a 13 cm/5 in flat square frame for the outside of the recess. Cut a 7 cm/2¾ in square piece of card in half for the doors. Cut out the petals for the sides of the box. Cut out the sunflowers and the stems, bulking out the middles by gluing on scrunched-up newspaper with PVA (white) glue. Assemble the box, using masking tape. Leave off the doors.

2 Cover the box with layers of newspaper soaked in diluted PVA (white) glue. Allow to dry. Paint with undercoat.

3 Paint all the pieces with gouache paints. When dry, apply several coats of varnish. Add details in gold and glue on the mirror. Pierce three holes in the shelf and glue in the sunflowers with epoxy resin glue. Glue the hinges and doors in position.

LOVE TOKEN BOWL

This delightful container for a Valentine's gift uses a simple but very decorative technique.

YOU WILL NEED

MATERIALS

petroleum jelly
newspaper
paper pulp (see Basic Techniques)
PVA (white) glue
white acrylic primer
tracing paper
masking tape
gouache or acrylic paints: blue, white, red, yellow and gold
clear gloss varnish

EQUIPMENT

bowl
medium and fine paintbrushes
pencil
scissors
paint-mixing container

1 Coat the inside of the bowl with a layer of petroleum jelly, followed by strips of newspaper. Press a layer of paper pulp into the bowl. When dry, release from the bowl. Cover the pulp with newspaper strips dipped in PVA (white) glue.

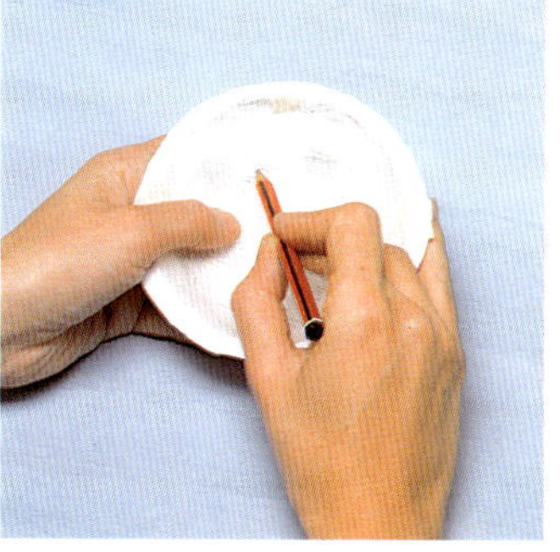

2 When dry, cover with white primer. Trace the template from the back of the book, enlarging if necessary. Snip the edges so the template can be taped flat inside the bowl, and transfer the outline.

3 Paint the background pale blue, dabbing on lighter shades for a mottled effect.

4 Paint the design, mixing the colours to achieve subtle shades. Paint the rim gold. When dry, give the bowl a coat of varnish.

Wall Plaque

Although the heart and farm animal motifs call to mind folk art, the strong pastel colours used to paint this plaque give it a more contemporary feel. It would be at home in a light, modern interior.

You Will Need

Materials

galvanized wire, from a coat hanger
card, 13 x 13 in/5 x 5 in
masking tape
newspaper
wallpaper paste
white emulsion (latex) or poster paint
self-hardening clay
acrylic or poster paints: pink, mauve, blue, green and yellow
clear varnish

Equipment

scissors
medium and small paintbrushes
clay-modelling tools
paint-mixing containers

1 Shape a hook from the wire and tape it on to the back of the card with masking tape.

2 Tear the newspaper into small strips. Dip them into the wallpaper paste and cover both sides of the card with a layer of newspaper.

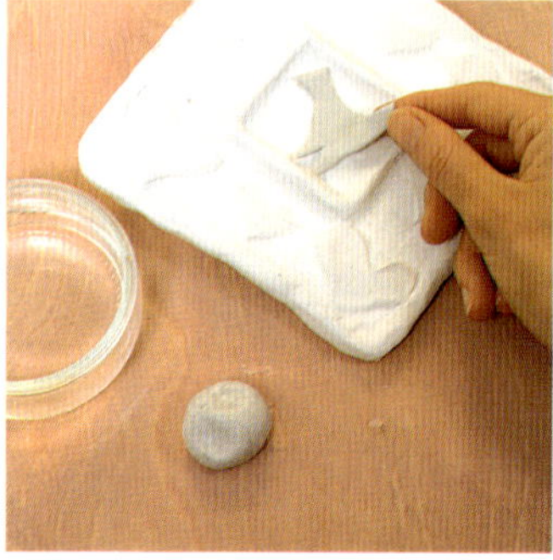

3 Prime both sides of the plaque with white paint and allow to dry. Mould decorative borders, heart shapes and a central chicken motif in the self-hardening clay. Allow to dry thoroughly.

4 Decorate with the paints and allow to dry. Finish with a coat of varnish.

Scherenschnitte

Intricately cut paper designs existed for many centuries in the Middle and Far East before they became popular in Europe and America. This papercraft technique is also known by the German term "Scherenschnitte" as it was particularly practised in Switzerland and Germany.

You Will Need

Materials
- *tracing paper*
- *paper*
- *thin black paper*
- *spray adhesive*
- *mounting paper*

Equipment
- *pencil*
- *craft knife*
- *metal ruler*
- *cutting mat*

1 Trace the template from the back of the book, enlarging if necessary. Transfer it to paper. Fold the thin black paper in half.

2 Cut along the centre edge of the design using a craft knife and a metal ruler.

3 Give the reverse side of the tracing a very light coat of spray adhesive and stick it to the back of the black paper. Cut out the shapes using the tip of the craft knife. Move the paper around as you cut, so that you always cut at the easiest angle.

4 Very carefully, separate the black paper from the tracing, making sure that the picture does not tear. Unfold the picture and display it on mounting paper.

CARDBOARD GIFT BOXES

It is simple to transform a flat sheet of thin card into an attractive gift box to make an ideal receptacle for that special present. Stamp rows of scampering dogs diagonally on to your box before folding it to add a frivolous touch, or select your own motif for an individualized look. The box can be scaled up or down, depending on the size you require, and the surface can be decorated with different designs to suit the occasion.

YOU WILL NEED

MATERIALS

thin coloured card
piece of paper (optional)
stamp pad
double-sided tape

EQUIPMENT

pencil
ruler
craft knife
cutting mat
rubber stamp
set square (optional)
blunt knife

1 Follow the design from the back of the book, scaling it up or down to the required size, but taking care to keep the proportions the same.

2 Cut out the box from coloured card using a ruler and craft knife to ensure that you make neat and accurate lines for it.

3 Using a straight-edged piece of paper or a ruler as a guide, stamp rows of motifs diagonally across the card.

4 Make sure that you extend the pattern over the edges by stamping partial motifs at the ends of each alternate row.

5 On the wrong side of the card, hold a set square or ruler against the fold lines and score along them with a blunt knife. Make sure that you do not break the surface of the card at all.

6 Fold along the score lines, making sure that all the corners are square. Apply double-sided tape to the joining edges, then peel off the backing paper and press the sides of the box together.

7 Continue folding and sticking the card in this way, ensuring that all the edges fit together neatly. Finally, fold in the end pieces to complete the card box.

CREPE PAPER BAGS

These bags can be decorated with any motif – use stickers of cartoon characters, cars, animals or planes to decorate gift bags for children's parties.

YOU WILL NEED

MATERIALS

bright crepe paper
contrasting thread
metallic stick-on stars
gold or silver cord

EQUIPMENT

pinking shears
sewing machine, with zigzag attachment

1 Decide on the size of your bag and, using pinking shears, cut out two rectangles from the crepe paper.

2 Set the sewing machine to a large zigzag stitch. Place the triangles together and sew along the three edges.

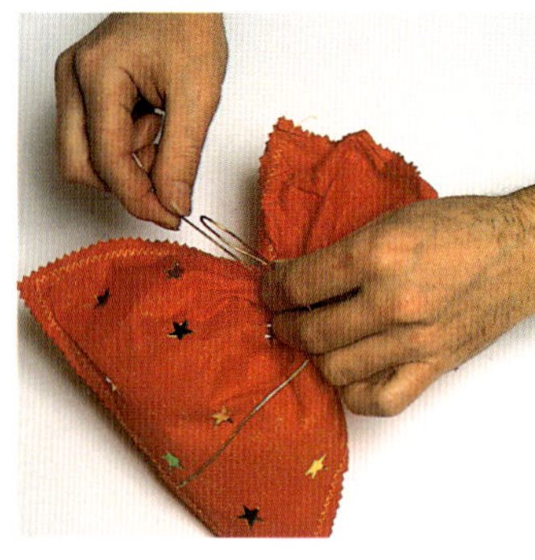

3 Place the stars randomly over the bag, then fill it with your gifts, and tie up the bag with gold or silver cord.

CARRIER BAGS

It really is great fun making bags, and they can be used for all sorts of objects – buttons, sweets, jewellery and, of course, for presenting gifts.

YOU WILL NEED

MATERIALS

tracing paper
stiff coloured paper
double-sided tape
cord or ribbon

EQUIPMENT

pencil
blunt knife or scissors
ruler
hole punch

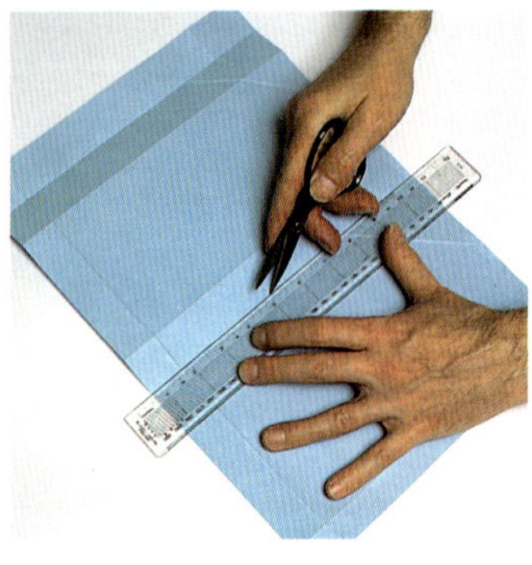

1 Trace the template from the back of the book, enlarging if necessary. Transfer it to stiff paper. The dotted lines indicate mountain folds and the dashed lines are valley folds. Use a blunt knife or scissors and a ruler to score along the fold lines. Cut out the shape.

2 Stick the bag together using double-sided tape along the seams. Using the hole punch, carefully make two sets of holes opposite each other on the top seam.

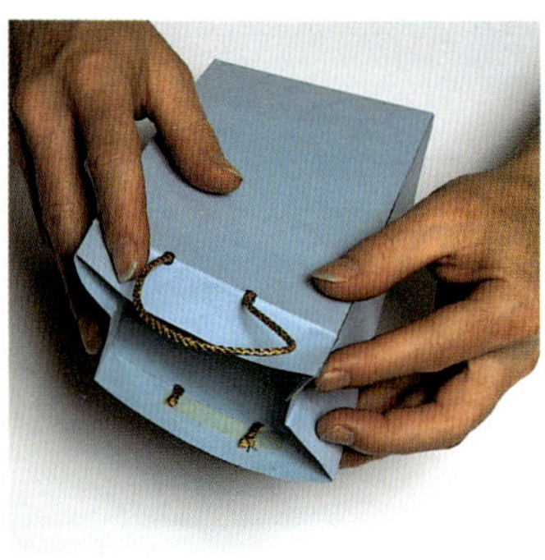

3 Place a square of tape below each hole. Thread the cord or ribbon through the holes, peel off the backing paper and press together to hold the handles in place between the bag and the overlapping seam.

Stencilling, Stamping and Printing

In this section you can find projects which, in their different ways, all involve transferring an image or motif to a surface, which can be anything from paper to plaster, floors to fabric. Stamping – whether using commercial stamps or the home-made kind – is probably the easiest method there is of transforming a plain surface. You can use the techniques to cover large areas, such as the walls of a room, or small, such as notepaper or gift wrapping.

In addition to stamping, there are exciting print projects for linocuts and potato prints, and a great selection of stencilling ideas from cork tiles to curtains. All the projects are easily adaptable to suit your needs and will inspire you to make up your own motifs and patterns!

BASIC STAMPING TECHNIQUES

Stamping is a simple and direct way of making a print. The variations, such as they are, come from the way in which the stamp is inked and the type of surface to which it is applied. It is a good idea to experiment and find a method and effect that you find most pleasing.

RIGHT *Printing is fun as well as decorative. Here is a selection of the materials you may find yourself using.*

FAR RIGHT *You can buy ready-made commercial stamps, or make them yourself from plastic foam, linoleum blocks – and, of course, the humble potato.*

Stamping with a brush
The advantage of this technique is that you can see where the colour has been applied. This method is quite time-consuming, so use it for smaller projects. It is ideal for inking an intricate stamp with more than one colour.

Stamping with a foam roller
This is the very best method for stamping large areas, such as walls. The stamp is evenly inked and you can see where the colour has been applied. Variations in the strength of printing can be achieved by only re-inking the stamp after several printings.

Stamping with a stamp pad
This is the traditional way to ink rubber stamps, which are less porous than foam stamps. The method suits small projects, particularly printing on paper. Stamp pads are more expensive to use than paint, but they are less messy and produce very crisp prints.

Stamping by dipping in paint
Spread a thin layer of paint on to a plate and dip the stamp into it. This is the quickest way of stamping large decorating projects. As you cannot see how much paint the stamp is picking up, you will need to experiment.

Stamping with fabric paint
Spread a thin layer of fabric paint on to a plate and dip the stamp into it. Fabric paints are quite sticky and any excess paint is likely to be taken up in the fabric rather than to spread around the edges. Fabric paint can also be applied by brush or foam roller, and is available with integral applicators.

Stamping with several colours
A brush is the preferred option when using more than one colour on a stamp. It allows greater accuracy than a foam roller because you can see exactly where you are putting the colour. Two-colour stamping is very effective for giving a shadow effect or a decorative pattern.

BASIC STAMPING TECHNIQUES

Potato

Commercial

Foam

Lino

Surface applications

The surface on to which you stamp or stencil your design will greatly influence the finished effect. This page gives hints and tips for best results.

Rough plaster
You can roughen your walls before stamping or stencilling by mixing the filler to a fairly loose consistency and spreading it randomly on the wall. When dry, roughen it with coarse sandpaper, using random strokes.

Fabric
As a rule, natural fabrics are the most absorbent, but to judge the painted effect, experiment first on a small sample. Fabric paints come in a range of colours, but to obtain the subtler shades, you may need to combine the primaries with black or white. Card behind the fabric will protect your work surface.

Tiles
Wash tiles in hot water and detergent to remove any dirt or grease, and dry thoroughly. If the tiles are already on the wall, avoid printing in areas which require a lot of cleaning. The paint will only withstand a gentle wipe with a cloth. Loose tiles can be baked to add extra strength and permanence to the paint. Always read the manufacturer's instructions before you do this.

Smooth plaster or lining paper
If you are using a stamp, ink it with a small foam roller to achieve the crispest print. Re-create perfect repeats by re-inking with every print, or give a more hand-printed effect by making several prints between inkings.

Wood
Rub down the surface of any wood to give the paint a better "key" to adhere to. Some woods are very porous and absorb paint, but you can intensify the colour by over-printing later. If you stamp or stencil on wood lightly, the grain will show through. Seal your design with matt varnish.

Glass
Wash glass in hot water and detergent to remove any dirt or grease, and dry it thoroughly. It is best to print on glass for non-food uses, such as vases. Practise on a spare sheet of glass first. As glass has a slippery, non-porous surface, you need to apply your print with a direct on/off movement.

STENCILLED SPRIG CURTAIN

This regular repeat pattern is easy to achieve by ironing the curtain fabric to mark a grid before you start to stencil. Alternatively, the leaf motif could be stencilled randomly across the fabric for a more informal look. Wash and iron the fabric before you start work.

YOU WILL NEED

MATERIALS

tracing paper
thin card or paper
cotton voile, to fit window
newspaper
masking tape
spray adhesive
fabric paints: green, blue, brown and pink
matching sewing thread
curtain wire

EQUIPMENT

pencil
craft knife
cutting mat
iron
thick and thin stencil brushes
paint-mixing container
sewing machine

1 Trace the template from the back of the book, enlarging it to 17 cm/6½ in high. Transfer it to thin card and cut it out. Fold the fabric into 20 cm/8 in vertical pleats and 25 cm/10 in horizontal pleats, then iron it lightly to leave a grid pattern. Cover your work surface with newspaper and tape the fabric down so that it is fairly taut.

2 Spray the back of the stencil with adhesive and place it in the first rectangle. Mix the paints to achieve subtle shades. Paint the leaves in green, adding blue at the edges for depth. Paint the stem in brown and the berries in a brownish pink. Repeat the design in alternate rectangles.

3 Turn the stencil upside-down and paint the top leaf in the centre of the plain rectangles pink. Add a darker shade at the tip and mark the stalk in brown. Fix the paints according to the manufacturer's instructions. Hem the sides and lower edge of the curtain. Make a 2.5 cm/1 in channel at the top and insert the curtain wire.

Suns and Moons Napkin

Transform plain napkins by decorating them with golden suns and blue moons. To achieve the best result, cut the stencils carefully and register them accurately, with the help of the cross-points you draw on the napkin.

You Will Need

Materials

tracing paper
2 sheets of thin card, size of the napkins
spray adhesive
napkins
fabric paints: gold and blue

Equipment

pencil
ruler
craft knife
cutting mat
iron
fabric marker
sponge or stencil brush

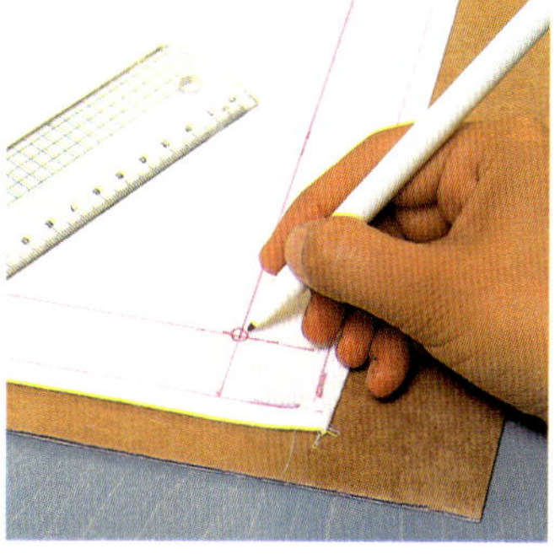

1 Trace the template from the back of the book, enlarging it if necessary. Rule grids on the card to help you position the motifs. Transfer the motifs on to the thin card; you will need to make one stencil for the suns and one for the moons. Cut out the stencils.

2 Spray adhesive on the sun stencil. Iron a napkin and lay it on the stencil, smoothing it outwards from the centre. With a fabric marker, draw the registration marks on the napkin, parallel to the edges. The lines should cross at the centre of the corner sun motif.

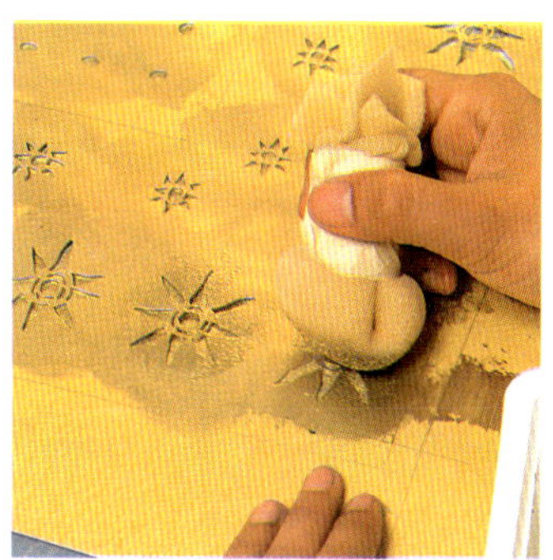

3 Spray adhesive on the reverse of the sun stencil and register the stencil on the cross-points. Using a sponge or stencil brush, apply the gold paint. Remove the stencil, then allow to dry. Repeat with the moon stencil and blue paint, registering the stencil as before. Fix the paints according to the manufacturer's instructions.

STYLISH LAMPSHADE

Unusual lampshades can be very expensive, so the solution is to take a plain lampshade and apply some surface decoration that will transform it from a utility object into a stylish focal point. The design, which resembles a seedpod, is easy to cut from high-density foam and it makes a bold, sharp-edged print that is highly effective.

YOU WILL NEED

MATERIALS

tracing paper
card
spray adhesive
high-density foam
thinned emulsion (latex) paints: cream-yellow and pale blue
plain lampshade

EQUIPMENT

pencil
craft knife
cutting mat
2 plates
small rubber roller

1 Trace the template on this page, enlarging it if necessary. Transfer it to a piece of card and cut it out. Lightly spray the shape with adhesive and place it on the foam. Cut around the outline, going all the way through the foam. Then cut around the centre detail to a depth of about 1 cm/½ in. Undercut and scoop this section away before cutting away the background.

2 Spread some cream-yellow paint on to a plate and coat a small roller evenly. Use it to apply a coat of paint to the foam stamp.

3 Make the first print a partial one, using only the top end of the stamp. Continue to print at random angles, leaving plenty of spaces for the second colour. Wash the stamp to remove all traces of yellow.

4 Spread some pale blue paint on to a second plate and coat the roller evenly. Use it to apply a coat of paint to the foam stamp.

5 Stamp pale blue shapes at random angles in between the cream-yellow ones. Be sure to make some partial prints so that the pattern continues over the edges.

CREEPY CRAWLY HANDKERCHIEF

A handkerchief full of little bugs sounds alarming, but these prints adapted from nineteenth-century folk art woodcuts are anything but! If the handkerchief has a self-weave pattern, use it as a guide for the prints; if not, scatter them about but make sure they are evenly spaced over the fabric. Practise first on a spare piece of fabric.

YOU WILL NEED

MATERIALS

lino tile, 15 x 15 cm/6 x 6 in
tracing paper
fabric paints in various colours
fabric paint medium
laundered white handkerchief

EQUIPMENT

lino tools
craft knife
pencil
paintbrush

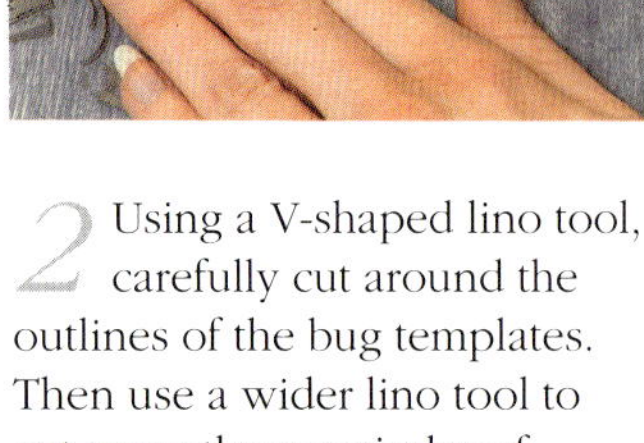

1 Cut the lino tile into six pieces, each measuring 5 x 7.5 cm/2 x 3 in. Trace the templates from the back of the book and transfer them to the lino pieces.

2 Using a V-shaped lino tool, carefully cut around the outlines of the bug templates. Then use a wider lino tool to cut away the remainder of the background.

3 Apply fabric paints to the blocks. Using a paintbrush, blend the colours to achieve interesting paint effects. Dilute the paint as necessary with fabric medium.

4 Place the block on the fabric, press evenly over the back and lift it up carefully to avoid smudging the print. Fix the paints according to the manufacturer's instructions.

SEASHORE SPONGEWARE SET

Imagine the effect of a whole tea-set of this seashore design, set out on shelves or a dresser. Painting your own is an inexpensive way of transforming plain, white china, and the end result is unique.

YOU WILL NEED

MATERIALS

cellulose kitchen sponge
all-purpose glue
corrugated card
ceramic paints: dark blue and dark green
paper towels
white china
white spirit

EQUIPMENT

ballpoint pen
scissors
plate
rag
fine black magic marker
stencil brush
cosmetic sponge (optional)

1 Draw your crab shape freehand on the sponge. Cut the crab out and glue it to a small square of corrugated card. Trim the card as close to the crab as possible. Pour a small amount of dark blue ceramic paint on to a plate. Lightly press the sponge into the paint and blot off any excess paint with paper towels. Gently apply even pressure to stamp the crab on to the china. Carefully lift off the sponge, in a single movement. Repeat the pattern as often as necessary for your design. Remove any mistakes with white spirit on a rag. Fix the paint according to the manufacturer's instructions.

2 With the magic marker, draw the border freehand around the bottom of the mug. Fill in the waves using a stencil brush and fix the paint again.

3 Alternatively, use the cosmetic sponge to sponge the border around the mug. Use both the blue and green paints, to give depth to the border. Fix the paint.

CHECKERBOARD POTATO PRINT

Potato prints are one of the easiest and most satisfying ways of creating a personalized repeat design. Here, one potato half is cut into a square stamp and the other half is given the same treatment with a cross shape added to make a checkerboard design.

YOU WILL NEED

MATERIALS

potato
acrylic paints: cadmium-yellow and cobalt-blue
sheet of white paper
thin blue ribbon
florist's wire (optional)

EQUIPMENT

chopping board
sharp knife or craft knife
2 plates
paper towels
scissors

1 On the chopping board, cut the potato in half with one smooth movement. Cut the sides of one half to make a plain square.

2 Cut the other potato half into a square, then cut out a cross shape by removing triangular sections around the edge and squaring off the corners of the cross.

3 Put the paints on separate plates and have some paper towels handy. Print the yellow squares first on a sheet of paper, starting in one corner and working down and across the sheet.

4 Print the blue crosses in the white squares and allow to dry thoroughly.

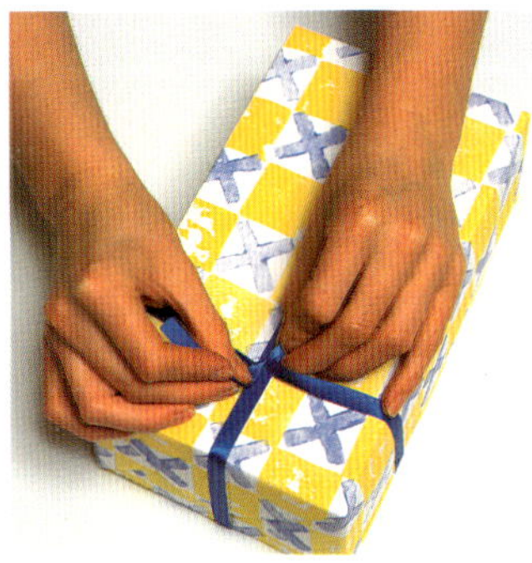

5 Wrap a gift in the paper and use a thin blue ribbon, set off-centre, as a trimming.

6 If you like, make a separate bow, securing loops of ribbon with some florist's wire.

Zodiac Cafe Curtain

Use gold fabric paints to dramatize a plain muslin (cheesecloth) curtain. Stencil the shapes at random all over the curtain, but try to plan your design so that they all appear fairly regularly. Add variety by blending the two shades of gold on some of the designs that you make.

You Will Need

Materials

tracing paper
thin card or paper
scrap fabric
fabric paints: light and dark gold
paper towels
newspaper
white muslin (cheesecloth), to fit window
masking tape
spray adhesive
matching sewing thread
curtain clips and metal rings

Equipment

pencil
craft knife
cutting mat
2 stencil brushes
iron
needle

1 Trace the templates from the back of the book, enlarging if necessary. Transfer on to 12 rectangles of thin card or paper and cut out the shapes with a craft knife. Before working on your curtain, practise your stencilling technique on some spare fabric. Don't overload your brush and wipe off any excess paint on paper towels before you begin.

2 Cover your work table with newspaper. Iron the muslin (cheesecloth), then fix one corner to the table with masking tape, keeping it flat. Coat the back of each stencil lightly with spray adhesive before positioning it on the fabric. Start with the light gold, then paint over the edges of the motif with dark gold to give depth. Allow to dry, then gently peel the card off.

3 Cover the rest of the fabric with the motifs, repositioning it on the work table as necessary and stencilling one section at a time. Fix the paint according to the manufacturer's instructions. Iron, then hem the edges and attach the curtain clips to the upper edge.

Leafy Pencil Pot

This useful pencil pot is stencilled with a simple leaf motif over a dark green background which is painted with a "dragged" effect.

You Will Need

Materials

pine slat, 8 x 45 mm/ $\frac{3}{8}$ x $1\frac{3}{4}$ in
pine slat, 8 x 70 mm/ $\frac{3}{8}$ x $2\frac{3}{4}$ in
wood glue
masking tape
sandpaper
white undercoat paint
thin card
acrylic paints: green, blue and yellow
PVA (white) glue

Equipment

ruler
fretsaw
paintbrushes
pencil
craft knife
cutting mat
paint-mixing container

1 Cut two 9 cm/$3\frac{1}{2}$ in lengths of each pine slat. Glue with wood glue to form the sides of the pot. Hold with masking tape until the glue is dry.

2 Sand all the rough edges. Measure the inside dimensions of the pot and cut a piece of wood to make the base. Glue it in place and allow to dry.

3 Paint with two coats of white undercoat, sanding lightly between coats. Cut a piece of thin card the same size as the broad side of the pot. Draw a leaf design and cut out with a craft knife.

4 Mix the paints to blue-green and yellow-green. Apply blue-green paint with a stiff brush to show the brush strokes. Stencil the leaf pattern in yellow-green. Finish with a coat of diluted white glue.

STAMPED BEDLINEN

Matching bedlinen is the last word in luxury. The white pillowcases have an all-round border of horse chestnuts and the top sheet folds back to reveal a matching pattern. Smooth cotton with straight edging is a dream to work with because the stamps can be confidently lined up with the edges and the sheeting absorbs the paint well to give a very crisp print.

1 To plan your design, stamp out several motifs on scrap paper and cut them out. Arrange these along the sheet edge or the pillowcase border to work out the position and spacing of your pattern.

YOU WILL NEED

MATERIALS

fabric paints: dark green and blue
scrap paper
sheet and pillowcase
thin card
scrap fabric

EQUIPMENT

rubber stamp
scissors

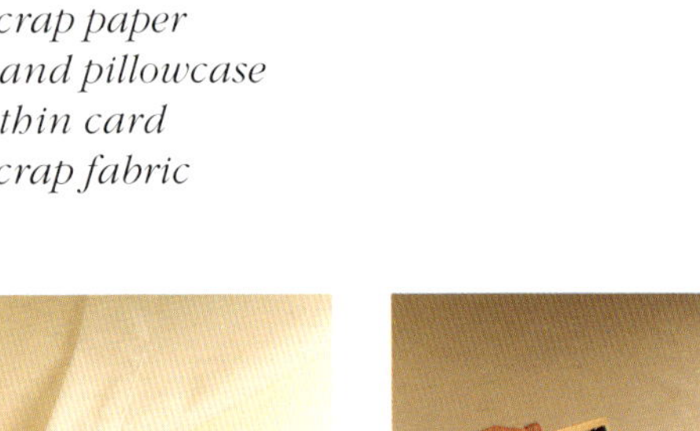

2 Place a sheet of card under the sheet or inside the pillowcase to prevent the paint from soaking through.

3 Follow the manufacturer's instructions and apply green paint to half of the stamp.

4 Apply blue paint to the other half of the stamp.

5 Test the distribution of the paint by making a print on a scrap of fabric. Re-apply and test the paint until you feel confident enough to make the first print on the bedlinen.

6 Check the arrangement of the paper-stamped motifs, then lift one at a time and stamp the fabric in its place. Press quite firmly to give the fabric time to absorb the paint.

7 Continue to re-coat and test the stamp as you print all the way around the edges to complete a matching bedlinen set. Fix the paint according to the manufacturer's instructions.

STENCILLED SEA WALL

This unusual idea for a wall decoration capitalizes on the shininess of ordinary kitchen foil. The effect is shimmering and glittering, with an underwater feel that is ideal for a bathroom wall. It can also be done directly on a wall surface.

YOU WILL NEED

MATERIALS

sheet of hardboard
emulsion (latex) paint
gloss paints: dark blue and olive-green
tracing paper
thin card
aluminium foil
clear gloss varnish
artist's oil colours: dark blue and chrome-yellow

EQUIPMENT

decorator's paintbrush
sponge or rag
pencil
scissors
dressmaker's pins
fine paintbrush

1 Paint the hardboard with an undercoat of emulsion (latex) paint. Paint the surface with dark blue gloss paint. When it is dry, sponge or rag roll the green paint in blotches all over the hardboard surface.

2 Trace the templates from the back of the book, enlarging if necessary. Cut out the templates very roughly on thin card and lay them, face-up, on one or two pieces of foil, slightly larger than the templates. Pin the layers together, then cut out the shapes and separate the layers.

3 Brush some varnish on to the hardboard and apply foil shapes to the surface. Tint some of the varnish with the artist's colours. Add detail and texture with varnish tinted with artist's colours, using a fine paintbrush. When the varnish is dry, give the whole design a further coat of tinted varnish.

Fleur-de-lys Tiles

This design is based on some original tiles from a medieval flooring. The modern version can quickly be stencilled on to plain tiles using a little imagination and some acrylic paint. Experiment with different colours and sizes to come up with an individual design for your tiles.

You Will Need

Materials

tracing paper
thin card
unglazed terracotta tiles, 13 x 13 cm/5 x 5 in
detergent
spray adhesive
cream acrylic paint
clear matt acrylic spray varnish

Equipment

pencil
craft knife
cutting mat
stencil brush

1 Trace the template from the back of the book, enlarging if necessary to fit on to a tile leaving a narrow border. Transfer it to thin card and cut out with a craft knife.

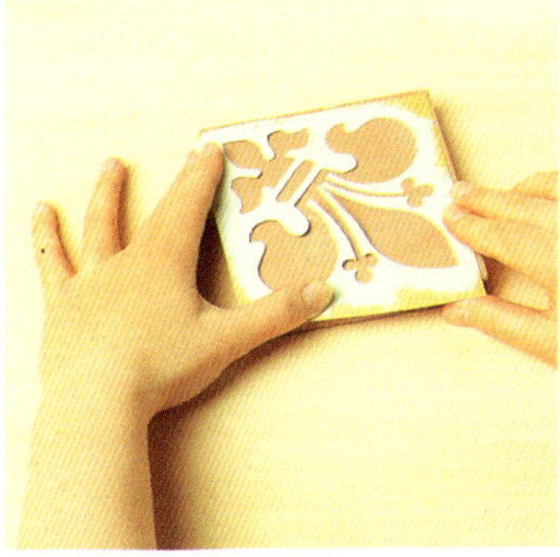

2 Wash the tiles with detergent to remove grease and dust. Allow to dry. Spray the back of the stencil lightly with adhesive and smooth in place on the first tile.

3 Paint in the design with small circular movements of the brush. Be careful not to overload the brush with paint.

4 Peel off the stencil and leave the paint to dry thoroughly. Then seal with several coats of clear matt acrylic spray varnish.

LEAFY ESPRESSO CUPS

Browsing around antique stalls, you sometimes come across coffee cups hand-painted with broad brush strokes and lots of little raised dots of paint. It is simple to decorate your own coffee service in this style.

YOU WILL NEED

MATERIALS	EQUIPMENT
white ceramic cup and saucer	*acetone or other grease-dispersing alcohol*
thin card or paper	*cotton buds*
sticky-backed plastic	*pencil*
green acrylic ceramic paint	*scissors*
pewter acrylic paint with nozzle-tipped tube	*paintbrush*
	hair dryer (optional)
	craft knife

1 Clean any grease from the surface of the china to be painted, using the acetone or alcohol and a cotton bud.

2 Draw leaves and circles freehand on to thin card or paper. Cut them out and draw around them on the backing of the sticky-backed plastic. Cut out. Peel away the backing paper and stick the pieces on the cup and saucer.

3 Paint around the shapes with the ceramic paint, applying several coats to achieve a solid colour. Leave each coat to air-dry or use a hair dryer for speed.

4 To ensure a clean edge, cut around each sticky shape with a craft knife, then peel off.

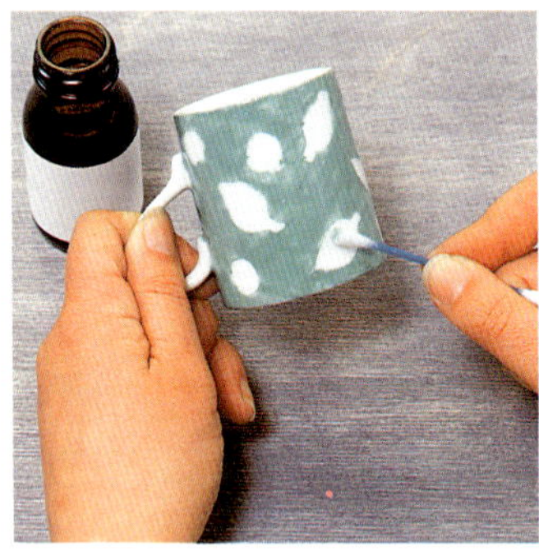

5 Clean up any smudges with a cotton bud dipped in acetone or water.

6 Using pewter paint and the nozzle-tipped paint tube, mark the outlines and details of the leaves with rows of small dots. Allow to dry for 36 hours. Fix the paints according to the manufacturer's instructions. The paint should withstand general use and gentle washing up, but not the dishwasher.

Sgraffito Eggs

The familiar scraper-board technique has a wonderful new delicacy when it is applied to the fragile surface of a real eggshell.

You Will Need

Materials

blown egg
acrylic paints: purple-brown and dark blue

Equipment

pencil
paintbrush
craft knife
white marker pencil

1 Draw a cameo outline on the front and back of the eggshell in pencil. Paint the two oval shapes in purple-brown acrylic paint, allowing one side to dry before you turn the egg over. You may need two coats. Paint the band around the egg in dark blue, again using two coats if required. Allow to dry.

2 Use the point of a craft knife blade to scratch double lines between the purple-brown and blue sections. Make a criss-cross pattern across the blue section and mark a dot in each diamond. Scratch a series of dots between the double lines of the borders.

3 Using a white marker pencil, very lightly sketch the outline of an insect in each purple-brown oval. You can copy the moth in the photograph or use a natural history print as a reference. Engrave the design following the white pencil line, adding in more intricate details.

Stencilled Picture Frame

The stylish raised leaf patterns around these frames are simple to create using ordinary white interior filler instead of paint to fill in the stencilled shapes.

You Will Need

Materials

2 wooden frames
dark green acrylic paint
fine-grade sandpaper
tracing paper
thin card
ready-mixed interior filler

Equipment

paintbrush
pencil
scissors
stencil brush

1 Paint the wooden frames dark green. When dry, gently rub them down with sandpaper to create a subtle distressed effect.

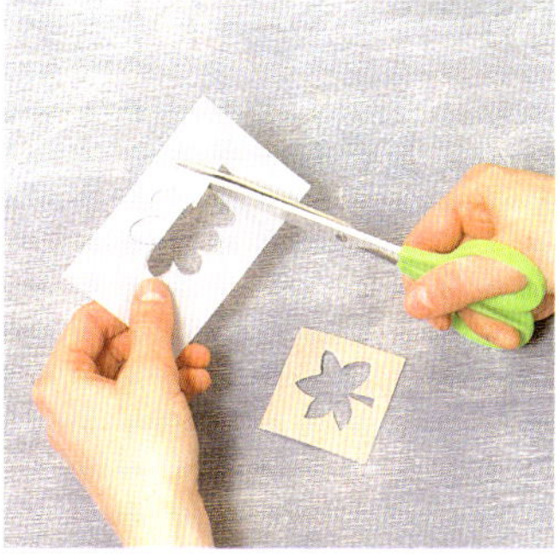

2 Trace the templates from the back of the book, enlarging to fit the frames. Transfer the designs to thin card and cut them out.

3 Position a stencil on the first frame and stipple ready-mixed filler through the stencil. Reposition the stencil and continue all around the frame. Allow to dry.

4 Repeat with a different combination of motifs on the second frame. When the filler is completely hard, gently smooth the leaves with fine-grade sandpaper.

MEXICAN CITRUS TRAY

Breakfast in bed will really wake you up if it is presented on this flamboyant tray. The bold fruit motif, painted in zingy, sunny colours, is full of the energy and simplicity of folk art.

YOU WILL NEED

MATERIALS

sandpaper
wooden tray
matt emulsion (latex) paints: dark emerald, lime-green and turquoise
tracing paper
acrylic gouache paints
matt polyurethane varnish

EQUIPMENT

medium and fine paintbrushes
hard and soft pencils

1 Sand the tray to remove any varnish. Paint the whole tray a dark emerald-green colour, then paint the inside of the tray lime-green, and the base turquoise. Allow to dry thoroughly.

2 Trace the templates from the back of the book, enlarging to fit the base and sides of the tray. Rub over the outlines on the reverse of the tracing with a soft pencil, then transfer the designs to the tray.

3 Paint the oranges, lemons and leaves on the base of the tray, and the flower motif on the sides, using acrylic gouache. When dry, add the details in white.

4 Paint a pink wavy border around the edge and the base of the tray. Paint the handle holes in bright orange. When the paint is dry, protect with several coats of varnish.

CUPID LINOCUT

Linocut images have a pleasing graphic simplicity. Here, the marvellous texture and light-enhancing qualities of gold metallic organza are contrasted with the solidity of the image. The beauty of linocuts is that the lino block can be used lots of times, so this idea can be adapted for making, for example, your own greetings cards.

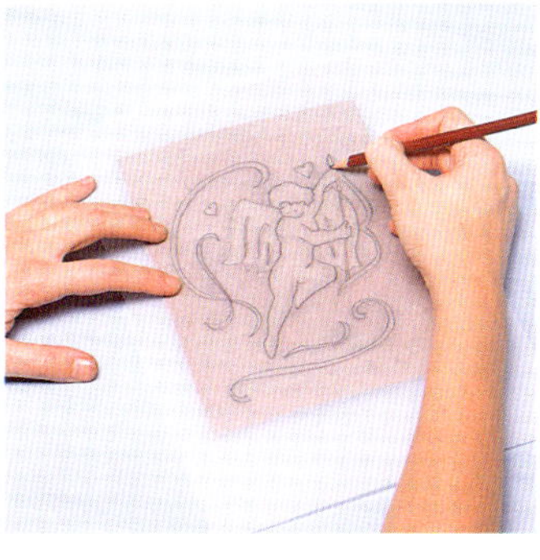

1 Trace the template from the back of the book, enlarging if necessary, and transfer to the lino block. Cut the design with the lino cutting tools: use the scoop to cut out large background areas and the nib for the fine details.

2 Squeeze the printing inks on to a plate and use the roller to mix the colours to get a deep burgundy shade. Coat the roller evenly, then roll over the surface of the linocut.

3 Tape the corners of the metallic organza to scrap paper to ensure the fabric is wrinkle free. Put the linocut over the organza and press evenly to ensure a crisp print. Use the decorative paper to create a mount, then frame.

YOU WILL NEED

MATERIALS

tracing paper
printing inks: red and blue
masking tape
gold metallic organza
scrap paper
decorative paper
picture frame

EQUIPMENT

pencil
lino block
lino cutting tools: U-shaped scoop and V-shaped nib
plate
paint roller

Medieval Cork Tiles

Transform ordinary unsealed cork tiles to look like medieval terracotta by using a variety of wood stains. They give just the right range of muted shades, and you can mix them together to add further subtlety. Use the template provided for all of your tiles or find other mythical beasts in heraldic books to create a variety of designs.

You Will Need

Materials

unsealed, unstained cork tiles, 30 x 30 cm/12 x 12 in
wood stains: pine-yellow, red and brown-mahogany
tracing paper
thin card or paper
permanent black ink
waterproof gold ink (optional)
matt polyurethane varnish

Equipment

pencil
ruler
brown crayon
fine and medium paintbrushes
scissors
dip pen

1 Mark the geometric pattern on a tile: use a brown crayon which will merge in with the design. Paint with the various wood stains. They spread on the cork, so don't overload the brush and start in the middle of each area, working outwards. A narrow gap between each colour looks very effective.

2 Scale up the animal template from the back of the book as required, transfer to thin card or paper and cut out. Position it in the centre of the tile and draw around it with permanent black ink, using a dip pen.

3 Use a fine brush to fill in the animal design in black. Highlight the design with gold ink, if you wish, then seal the tile with several coats of polyurethane varnish.

Gilded Wall Border

This simple version of stencilling produces an extremely effective and eye-catching border. Buy a cheap roll of wallpaper border paper and use the wrong side, then stick the completed design in place. This gets over the problem of stencilling on to a vertical surface.

You Will Need

Materials

tracing paper
paper glue
thin card
aerosol gloss paint
wallpaper border paper
emulsion (latex) paints: warm-blue and white
masking tape
silver acrylic paint
rub-on gold paint

Equipment

pencil
craft knife
cutting mat
scissors
paintbrush
paint-mixing container
sponges

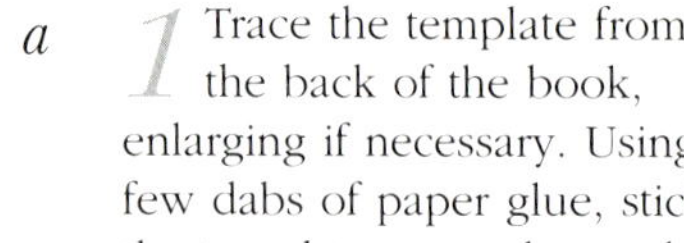

1 Trace the template from the back of the book, enlarging if necessary. Using a few dabs of paper glue, stick the template on to the card for the stencil.

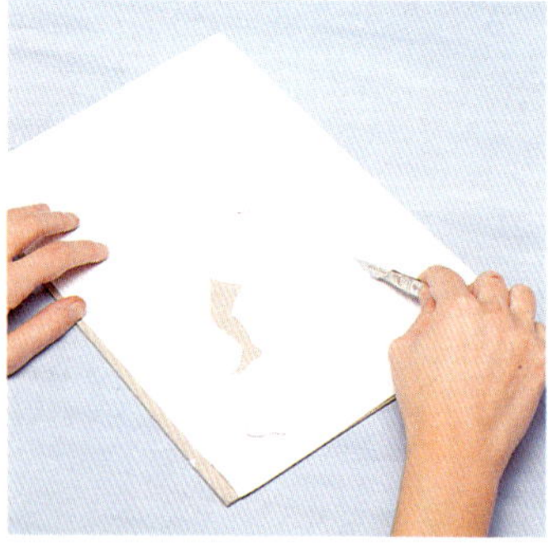

2 Cut out the stencil and remove the template.

3 Spray both sides of the stencil with gloss paint.

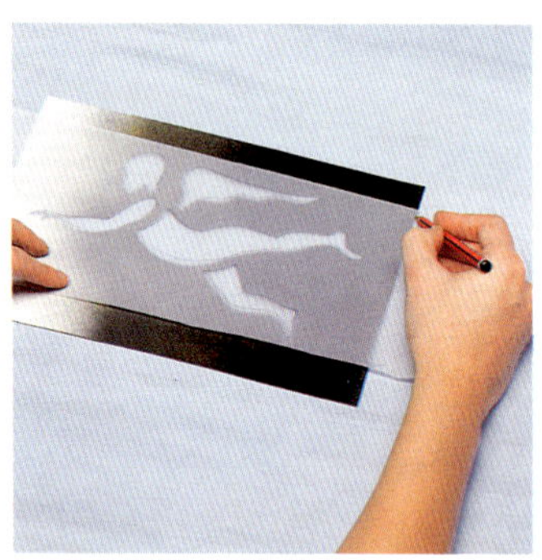

4 In order to line up the design on the border, cut a strip of tracing paper to the width of the border paper. Trace the cupid design on to it, placing it centrally. Place this tracing over the stencil, lining up the cupids. Mark the edges of the stencil at the edges of the tracing paper. Cut notches in the stencil to mark the top and bottom edges of the border. Use these to line up the stencil on the border paper.

5 Paint a background colour of warm-blue emulsion (latex) on the border paper. Place the stencil over the border, lining up the notches with the top and bottom, and fix it in place with masking tape. Dip a sponge into the silver paint and apply it sparingly over the whole stencil. Allow to dry. Repeat along the length of the border. You can use the stencil several times before it becomes clogged, then you will have to cut a new one.

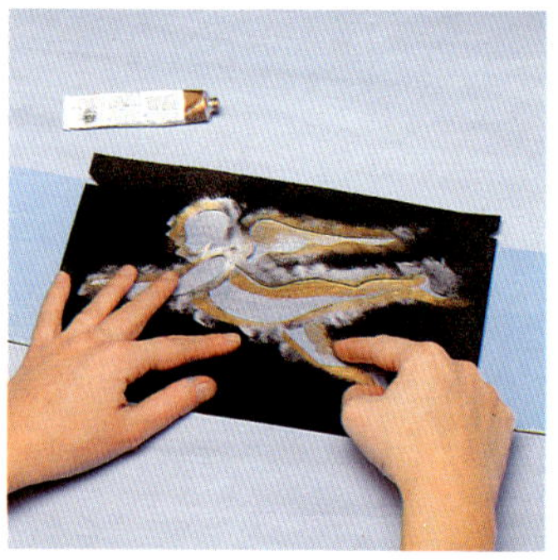

6 Use your finger to apply the gold paint to give depth to the body.

7 Remove the stencil template and sponge hair on to the cupids.

8 Apply the doves randomly between the cupids, using white emulsion (latex) paint and a second sponge.

Art Nouveau Rose Box

Inspired by the motifs of early 20th-century art nouveau, this design for a simple wooden box combines sinuous lines, swirling leaf shapes and stained-glass-style roses to dramatic effect.

You Will Need

Materials

fine-grade sandpaper
oval wooden craft box, with lid
white primer paint
tracing paper
acrylic paints: rose-pink, green, yellow, white, black and blue
clear acrylic or crackle varnish

Equipment

thick bristle and fine hair paintbrushes
hard and soft pencils
paint-mixing container

1 Sand the box and lid and give them three layers of primer. Trace the template from the back of the book, enlarging if necessary, to fit the lid of the box. Transfer it to the lid, with a soft pencil and tracing paper.

2 Paint the rose petals and the leaves as solid blocks of colour.

3 Paint the stems and thorn ring; add shade and tone to the flowers. Paint the veins on the leaves. Paint a black outline around the rose petals.

4 Colour-wash the outside rim of the lid with watered-down rose paint. Paint the box blue in the same way. Seal the surface with a coat of varnish (crackle varnish will give an antique effect).

FROSTED FLOWER VASE

This is a magical way to transform a plain glass vase into something stylish and utterly original. Check the vase all over to make sure that it is evenly frosted before you peel off the leaf shapes: it may be necessary to paint on another coat of etching cream.

YOU WILL NEED

MATERIALS	EQUIPMENT
coloured glass vase	*pencil*
tracing paper	*scissors*
sticky-backed plastic	*paintbrush*
etching cream	

1 Wash and dry the vase. Trace the templates from the back of the book, enlarging if necessary. Cut them out and draw around them on to the backing of the plastic and draw small circles freehand.

2 Cut out the shapes and peel off the backing paper. Arrange the shapes all over the vase, then smooth them down carefully to avoid any wrinkles.

3 Carefully paint the etching cream all over the cleaned vase and leave it in a warm place to dry, following the manufacturer's instructions.

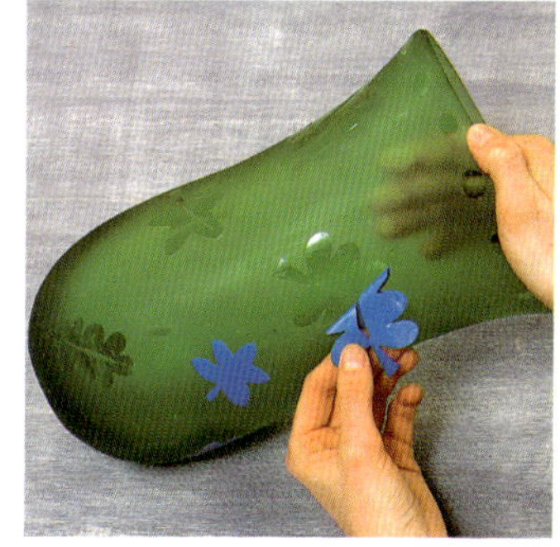

4 Wash the vase in warm water to remove the cream. If the frosting looks smooth, you can remove the shapes. If not, repeat with another coat of etching cream, then wash before removing the shapes.

Country-style Shelf

Simple in shape but conveying a universally understood message, the heart has been used in folk art for centuries. Here, the outline of a heart is drawn in four positions on a foam block, then cut out to make a stamp that resembles a four-leafed clover. The smaller heart is a traditional solid shape that fits neatly along the edges of the shelf supports.

You Will Need

Materials

tracing paper
spray adhesive
high-density foam
country-style shelf
deep-red acrylic or emulsion (latex) paint
scrap paper

Equipment

pencil
craft knife
plate
paintbrush (optional)

1 Trace the templates from the back of the book, enlarging if necessary. Lightly spray the shapes with adhesive and place them on the foam. Cut around the outline of the shapes with a craft knife.

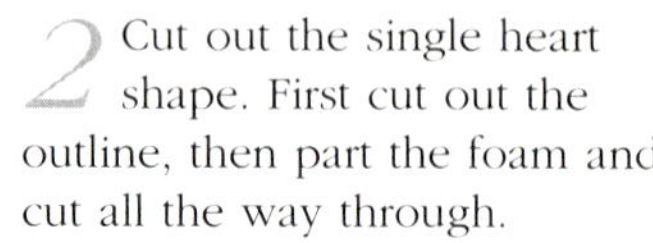

2 Cut out the single heart shape. First cut out the outline, then part the foam and cut all the way through.

3 Use the foam stamp as a measuring guide to estimate the number of prints to fit along the back of the shelf. Mark the positions with a pencil. Spread some deep-red paint on to a plate.

4 Coat the clover-leaf stamp evenly and make a test print on scrap paper to ensure that it is not overloaded with paint. (You may find it easier to apply the paint to the stamp with a paintbrush.) Using the pencil guidelines, make the first print on the shelf.

5 Continue until you have completed all of the clover-leaf shapes. Try not to get the finish too even; this is a rustic piece of furniture and an uneven effect is more suitable.

6 Finish off the shelf with a row of small hearts along the support edges, then add one heart between each of the larger motifs.

Foam-block Printing

Printing with cut-out foam blocks must be the easiest possible way to achieve the effect of hand-painted wallpaper. A special feature of this project is the paint used – a combination of wallpaper paste, PVA (white) glue and gouache colour. This is not only cheap, but it also has a wonderful translucent quality all of its own that really does produce a unique finish.

You Will Need

Materials

tracing paper
thin card
high-density foam
paper, 15 x 15 cm/6 x 6 in
wallpaper paste
PVA (white) glue
gouache paints: viridian, deep-green and off-white
clear matt varnish (optional)

Equipment

pencil
scissors
felt-tipped pen
craft knife
plumb-line
plate
paintbrush (optional)

1 Trace the templates on this page, enlarging if necessary. Transfer them to thin card and cut them out. Trace the design on to the foam, outlining it with a felt-tipped pen.

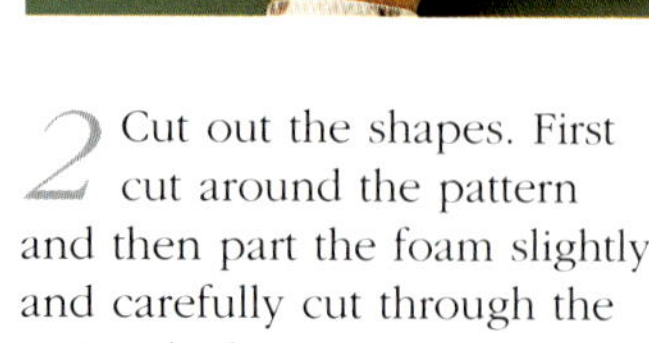

2 Cut out the shapes. First cut around the pattern and then part the foam slightly and carefully cut through the entire thickness.

3 Prepare the wall for decorating. Attach the plumb-line to the wall or ceiling in one corner of the room. Turn the paper square on the diagonal and let the plumb-line fall through the centre. Make pencil dots on the wall at each corner of the paper. Move the paper down the plumb-line, marking the corner points each time. Then move the plumb-line along sideways and continue marking dots until the wall is covered in a grid of dots.

4 Mix the wallpaper paste according to the instructions. Add PVA (white) glue, in the proportion three parts paste to one part glue. Add a squeeze of viridian and deep-green paint and blend.

5 Put some paint mixture on to a plate and dip the first sponge into it. Wipe off any excess paint and then print on the wall, using a light rolling motion. Use the dots to position the stamp.

6 Use the second sponge to complete the sprig design with leaf shapes, varying the angle slightly to add life.

7 Use the dot-shaped sponge and off-white to complete the design with berries, adding the colour to the PVA (white) mixture as before. If liked, protect the wall with a coat of varnish.

LOVE
LOVE
LOVE
LOVE

EMBROIDERY

Embroidering detail on to fabric – whether by hand or by machine – is a beautiful method of decoration, and it can be applied to a wide range of materials and objects, including clothes, linens and pictures. The wealth of threads available today means that your embroidery can be bright and vivid or muted and subtle – whatever mood you wish to evoke, there will be a thread available for you. The range of fabrics in varying colours, textures and strengths is quite astounding, and you can choose to work on a small square of fabric to create a purse, or enhance a baby's outfit with fine stitching.

Whatever project you choose to embark on, you will soon find that your embroidery skills increase with practice and experimentation. So, gather needle and thread together and enjoy one of the most rewarding of decorative crafts.

Materials and Equipment

Most of the materials used for embroidery can be purchased from craft suppliers or department stores. The range of fabrics available is immense, so consider how the texture will affect your finished piece when making your fabric choice. Cotton and silk are easy to handle, and felt, plastic and leather produce interesting results. Some key materials and pieces of equipment to help you with your embroidery are given below.

Above *Equipment required for embroidery – whether by hand or by machine – can be easily obtained from crafts suppliers. Each embroidery project in this section tells you exactly what you will need for best results.*

Bobbins are useful to have in a fair quantity so that you don't have to unwind and rewind them with each different thread colour.

Buttons and beads come in a range of shapes and sizes and a variety of materials, such as plastic, glass, wood and bone.

Dressmaker's carbon is used to transfer designs to fabric.

Embroidery hoops A wooden hand embroidery hoop can also be used for machine embroidery if the inner ring is wrapped with strips of cotton to improve tautness. Specialized **machine embroidery hoops** with spring closures are more convenient.

Fabric glue can be used instead of fusible bonding web.

Fabric paints are water-based non-toxic paints that are fixed by ironing.

Feet For most machine embroidery, a foot should be used, although a presser foot will give a cleaner satin stitch. You can work without a foot, but the thread will tend to snap more often.

Fusible bonding web is used to bond appliqué fabrics to the ground fabric temporarily during stitching. Templates can be marked out on the paper backing.

Hand embroidery threads are available in skeins and can be couched or stitched to enhance machine embroidery.

Machine embroidery threads are available in every imaginable colour and in different strengths. They are more lustrous than sewing threads.

Metallic embroidery threads are very popular and are available in many colours as well as shades of gold, silver and bronze. Be careful when stitching at high speeds on a machine, as occasionally the thread will snap.

Scissors Use dressmaker's scissors for cutting fabrics and embroidery scissors for cutting away threads and trimming.

Sewing machine The machine should have a free arm and a detachable bed for ease of movement. Take care of the machine and oil and clean it regularly to prevent stitch problems.

Stabilizers should be used to prevent the fabric from puckering and distortion. Water-soluble polythene will stabilize open-work and sheer fabrics, and is easily dissolved in cold water.

Vanishing fabric markers are available in pink and purple and will fade with exposure to air or water.

Working with Different Stitches

Satin stitch
Satin stitch is used for filling in and outlining. Ensure the fabric is held tautly in a frame to prevent puckering. Carry the thread across the area to be filled, then return it back underneath the fabric as near as possible to the point from which the needle emerged.

Slip stitch
Slip stitch is used to join together two folded edges, and for flat-hemming a turned-in edge. It should be nearly invisible. Pick up two threads of the single fabric and slip the needle through the fold for about 5 mm/$^1/_4$ in. Draw the thread through to make a tiny stitch.

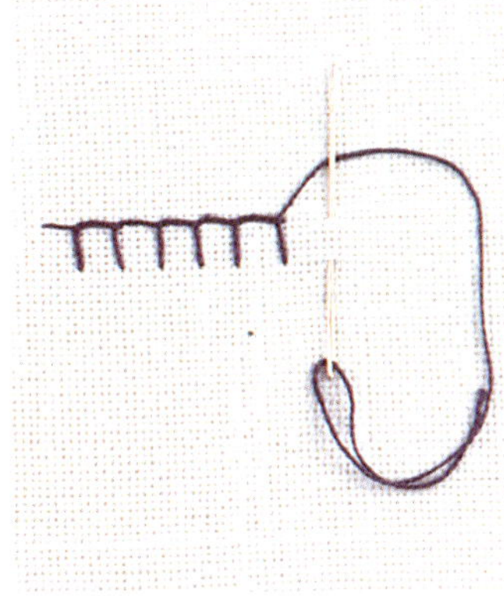

Blanket stitch
Blanket stitch can be used for finishing hems and, when the stitches are worked closely together, for buttonholes. It is used decoratively for scalloped edging. Working from left to right, bring the needle down vertically and loop the thread under its tip before pulling it through.

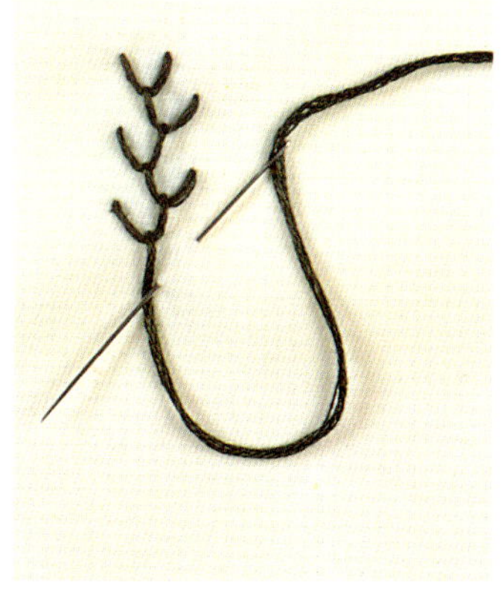

Feather stitch
Feather stitch is a looped stitch, traditionally used for smocking and decorating crazy patchwork. It can be worked in straight or curved lines. Bring the thread through the fabric and make slanting stitches, working alternately to the right and left of the line to be covered.

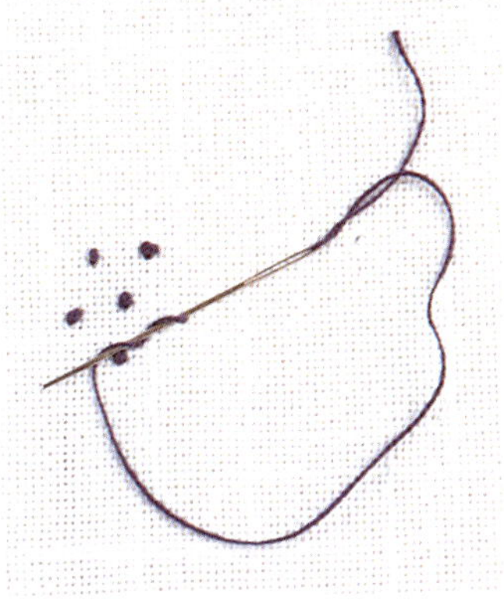

French knot
French knots are used sparingly as accents, or worked more closely together to produce a texture. The stitch should be worked with the fabric in a frame, leaving both hands free. Bring the thread through and hold down. Twist the thread around the needle a few times and tighten. Holding the thread taut, insert the needle back into the fabric with the other hand, at the point from which it emerged. Pull the needle through the thread twists to form the knot.

Tacking
This is a temporary stitch, used to hold seams together before sewing by machine. The stitches should be between 0.5–1 cm/$^1/_4$–$^3/_8$ in long and evenly spaced. Use a contrasting thread to make the stitching easy to unpick.

Right *For machine embroidery projects, keep a number of bobbins ready-wound with threads of different colours.*

EMBROIDERED INSECT DISPLAY

This pretty design is inspired by old Victorian display cases containing rows of beetles and bugs. It's ecologically sound, however, because these stylish black bugs are embroidered on calico.

YOU WILL NEED

MATERIALS

thick tracing paper
natural calico, 30 x 30 cm/12 x 12 in
embroidery threads: black, ochre, emerald and yellow
thick card, 20 x 20 cm/ 8 x 8 in
strong button thread
3 small labels
wooden frame, to fit 20 x 20 cm/8 x 8 in

EQUIPMENT

transfer pencil
iron
embroidery hoop
embroidery needle
large needle
pen

1 Using a transfer pencil, trace the template from the back of the book, enlarging if necessary, on to the calico. Fix the design according to the manufacturer's instructions.

2 Stretch the calico in an embroidery hoop and work over the design outlines using two strands of black embroidery thread in simple straight and satin stitches. Work legs and antennae in small chain stitch and pick out a few details in colour. Iron lightly from the wrong side.

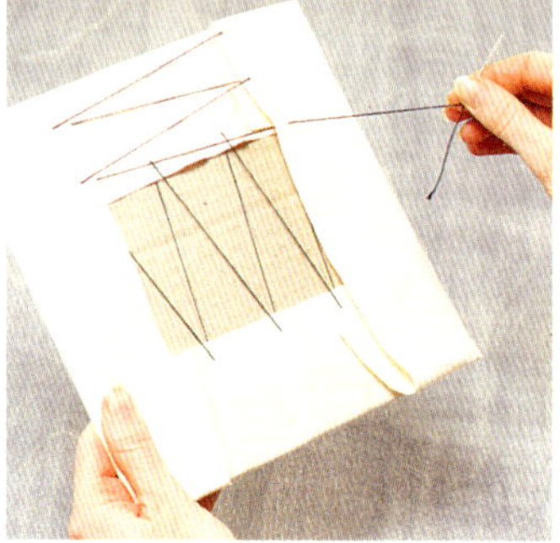

3 To mount the embroidery, place the card centrally on the back of the work and fold two opposite sides over it. Lace together with strong thread, then repeat with the other two sides. Write labels for the three orders of insects: Hymenoptera (bees and wasps), Lepidoptera (butterflies) and Coleoptera (beetles). Fix these to the fabric and insert it in the frame.

EMBROIDERED ORGANZA SCARF

Use muted, autumnal colours for this delicate, sheer scarf. The painted and embroidered leaves create an almost abstract pattern.

YOU WILL NEED

MATERIALS

laundered silk organza or chiffon
fabric paints: green and blue
machine embroidery threads: orange and red
matching sewing thread

EQUIPMENT

embroidery hoop
fine paintbrush
paint-mixing container
iron
sewing machine, with darning foot
dressmaker's scissors
needle

1 Stretch the fabric taut in an embroidery hoop. Paint the leaf shapes freehand in greens and blues, mixing the paints to achieve subtle shades. Allow to dry. Iron the silk to fix the paint, according to the manufacturer's instructions.

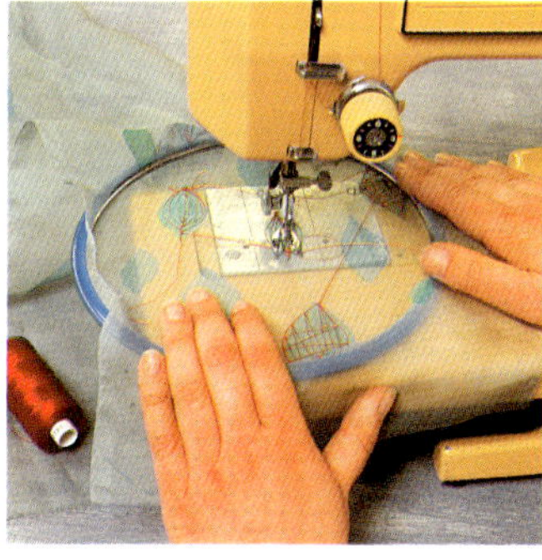

2 Select the darning or free stitch mode on the sewing machine and attach a darning foot. With the fabric in an embroidery hoop, stitch the details on the design in orange and red thread over the painted leaves.

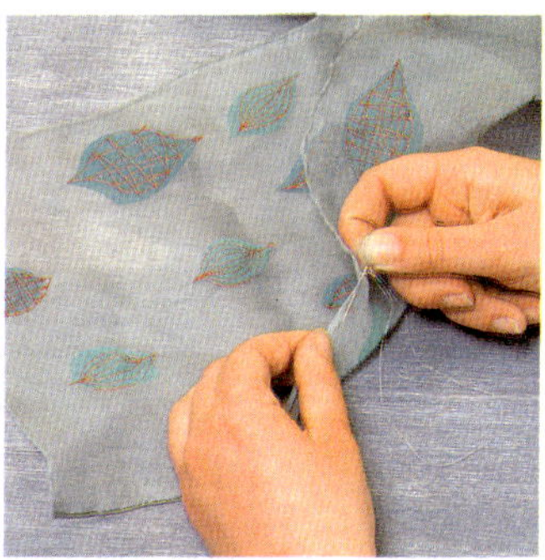

3 Trim and roll the raw edges of the scarf and slip stitch the hems in place.

LEMON SLICE NAPKINS

These lovely yellow napkins embroidered with cool lemon slices would look delightful on a table set for a summer lunch in the garden.

YOU WILL NEED

MATERIALS

tracing paper
large yellow napkin
embroidery threads: dark and pale yellow, off-white and dark green

EQUIPMENT

soft and hard pencils
dressmaker's pins
embroidery needle
iron

1 Trace the template at the back of the book, enlarging if necessary. Rub over the lemon motif on the reverse of the tracing with a soft pencil. Pin the tracing in the corner of the napkin and transfer the motif on to it.

2 Using dark yellow thread, work French knots in the centre of the lemon. Fill the segments in stem stitch using pale yellow. Fill the pith in stem stitch using off-white, and fill the skin area with dark yellow French knots.

3 Work dark green blanket stitch around the hem of the napkin. The stitches can be worked over the existing machine stitching. Work a row of dark yellow stem stitch around the edge of the lemon pith and another row outside that in green. Work a dark green running stitch around the edge of the French knots and add some small dark green stitches as shading in the segments to complete the design. Iron the embroidery on the reverse side.

FLEUR-DE-LYS SHOE BAG

Rich purple velvet and opulent gold braid suit the regal motif on this luxurious bag for your best party shoes. The appliquéd braid technique could easily be adapted to other items such as cushions and throws.

YOU WILL NEED

MATERIALS

cotton velvet fabric, 53 x 38 cm/21 x 15 in
tracing paper
thin card or paper
gold embroidery thread
gold braid
matching sewing thread
black satin ribbon, 4 cm/1½ in wide
elastic, 1 cm/½ in wide

EQUIPMENT

dressmaker's scissors
dressmaker's pins
pencil
needle
sewing machine
safety pin

1 Cut the velvet in half across the width and mark the centre of one piece with a pin. Trace the template from the back of the book on to thin card and pin it to the centre of the velvet towards the lower edge. Use gold thread to sew on the gold braid, pinning it around the template as you stitch. Work in a continuous pattern around the outline. Add the swirls.

2 Machine stitch the sides and hem, leaving a seam allowance of 1 cm/½ in. Neaten the raw edges. Fold down the top edge, leaving a generous cuff. Cover the raw edge with satin ribbon, stitching along both edges to form a casing. Fold under the ends of the ribbon and butt them together. With a safety pin, thread some elastic through the casing and stitch the ends together.

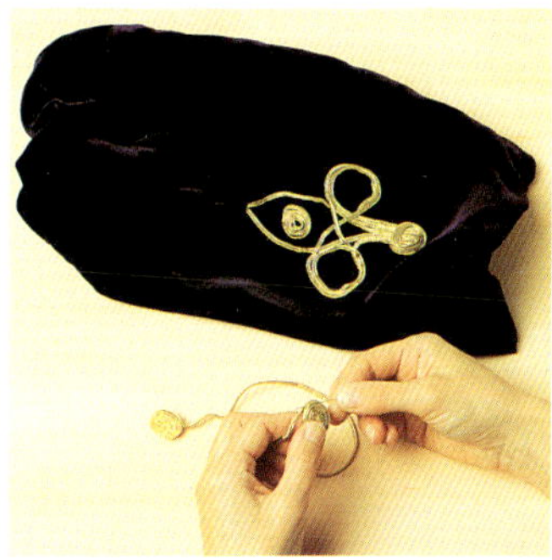

3 Complete the bag by making a tie with another length of braid, coiling and stitching the ends. Attach to one side seam and tie around the neck of the bag.

BEADED ORANGE PURSE

This luxurious purse is embroidered to look like slices of fruit with tiny beads to echo the texture.

YOU WILL NEED

MATERIALS

velvet or brocade pieces, 1 orange and 1 yellow, 15 cm/6 in
2 pieces yellow silk, 15 cm/6 in
tracing paper
embroidery threads: white, crimson, orange, yellow and lime-green
small glass beads: yellow, orange and clear
tacking (basting) thread
zip, 12 cm/4¾ in
matching sewing thread

EQUIPMENT

dressmaker's scissors
pencil
tailor's chalk
embroidery needle
dressmaker's pins
needle

1 Cut circles, 14 cm/5½ in in diameter: one each of orange and yellow velvet and two of silk. Trace the template from the back of the book, enlarging to fit the circle, and transfer it to the velvet with tailor's chalk. Sew chain stitch in white for the pith. On the orange side, sew crimson segments and orange flesh; on the lemon side, sew yellow segments and lemon and lime flesh. Use chain stitch for the segments and back stitch for flesh. Add coloured beads for the skin and clear beads for moisture. With right sides together, pin and tack (baste) the zip, leaving a 1 cm/½ in allowance.

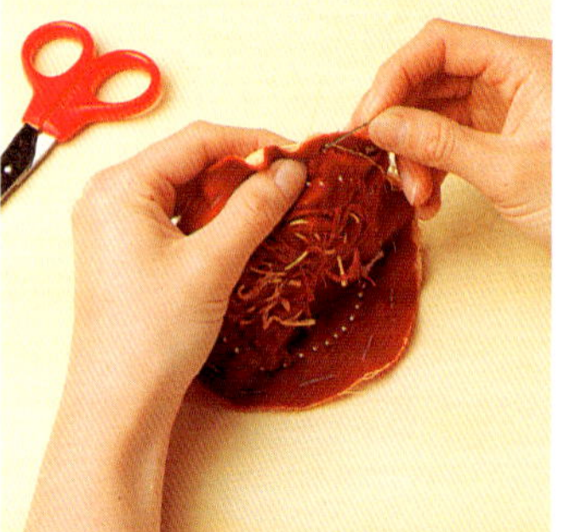

2 Stitch along the zip. Open it and complete the seam around the rest of the circle.

3 With right sides together, sew the two pieces of silk halfway round. Turn to the right side. Put the purse, inside out, inside the lining. Turn in the lining seam allowance and slip stitch it to the zip.

HEAVENLY BAG

This delicate and pretty bag is ideal for lingerie.

YOU WILL NEED

MATERIALS

2 rectangles silver metallic organza, 65 x 28 cm/ 26 x 11 in
2 circles silver metallic organza, 18 cm/ 7 in in diameter
2 rectangles gold metallic organza, 24 x 26 cm/ 7 x 11 in
contrasting metallic machine threads
tacking (basting) thread
tracing paper
ribbon

EQUIPMENT

sewing machine, with darning foot
tape measure
needle
dressmaker's scissors
fabric marker

1 Fold the rectangular pieces of fabric in half widthways. Stitch an 8 cm/3 in seam from the folded edge on both side edges. Turn the rectangles right sides out. To make the ribbon casing, stitch two parallel lines 8 and 10 cm/3 and 4 in from the folded edge. Make a grid of tacking (basting) lines to attach a gold rectangle to a silver rectangle, matching the bottom edges.

2 Using a fabric marker, trace the template from the back of the book, enlarging if necessary, and transfer it to the gold side of the two silver and gold pieces. On the sewing machine, set the dial to the darning or free embroidery mode. Work the circles in straight stitch, with contrasting thread in the top and bobbin.

3 Cut away the gold organza inside the stitched line. Work the remaining signs in contrasting colours. Cut away and discard the organza again. Top stitch 1.5 cm/⅝ in from the top edge and pull away the weft threads, to produce a gold fringe. Remove the tacking (basting). Lay the two embroidered sides right sides together.

4 Stitch the sides to make a tube-shaped outer, embroidered bag, with a lining formed by the folded half. Stitch one silver circle to the bottom of the outside tube, and the other to the bottom of the lining. Turn right sides out. Tuck the lining inside the bag and slip stitch the gap. Thread a ribbon through the casing.

SPARKLING IVY GARLAND

Make this beautiful jewelled crown of leaves for a midsummer night's party, or perhaps for a summer wedding.

YOU WILL NEED

MATERIALS

water-soluble fabric
paper or thin card
fine green wool or green embroidery thread
metallic threads: silver and blended gold and silver
sewing threads: dark and light green
paper towels
fine silver or brass wire: 0.6 mm for circlet, 0.4 or 0.2 mm for leaves
selection of beads

EQUIPMENT

embroidery hoop
fabric marker
large-eyed needle
sewing machine, with size 11 needle
dressmaker's scissors

1 Stretch the water-soluble fabric on to the embroidery hoop. Using a fabric marker, trace the template from the back of the book, enlarging if necessary, on to the fabric. For the first style of leaf, hand stitch the central veins in fine green wool or embroidery thread. Use a running stitch and a thicker thread for the larger leaves.

2 For the second style of leaf, work the veins and outlines on the machine with a straight stitch, using silver metallic thread in the bobbin and dark green sewing thread in the needle. Fill in between the veins with the lighter green. For the first style of leaf, fill in with blended gold and silver thread in the bobbin and silver thread in the needle.

3 Sew randomly across the machined lines within each section of leaf to make the tiny veins. (This also holds the embroidery together.)

4 Work a zigzag stitch up the central veins and around the outer edge of each leaf to stiffen it.

5 Cut the leaves off the hoop and dissolve the fabric of each one in turn in water. Pat dry on paper towels. While still damp, fold each leaf in half and press with your fingers to make a crease along the central vein. Open out and allow to dry.

6 Continue to embroider more leaves in both styles to make enough for the whole garland. Sew each leaf on to fine wire.

7 Twist a piece of thicker wire into a band to fit your head. Twist on more wire to make loops for attaching the leaves. Make the loops higher at the front of the garland.

8 Wind the wired leaves on to the loops on the band, using the larger leaves at the front. Add beads threaded with more wire. Bend and arrange the leaves into shape.

TUDOR ROSE BUTTON

These buttons take up the theme of the Tudor Rose, a famous heraldic union of the red rose of Lancaster and the white rose of York.

YOU WILL NEED

MATERIALS

water-soluble fabric
machine embroidery threads: green, red and white
fine metallic thread
a few small pearl beads
self-cover buttons, 22 mm/¾ in
piece of metallic fabric
piece of sheer organza
PVA (white) glue

EQUIPMENT

embroidery hoop
fine magic marker
embroidery needle
sewing machine
dressmaker's scissors
fine paintbrush

1 Stretch the water-soluble fabric on to the embroidery hoop. Trace the template from the back of the book on to the fabric using a fine magic marker. Hand or machine embroider the leaf detail in green, using straight stitch and sewing back and forth to link the stitches. Cut off the trailing green threads and hand or machine embroider in red or white over the flower, making sure that you interlock the stitches. To make the mesh, thread the machine with metallic thread and sew straight rows, first one way then the other, to make a net. Remove the embroidery from the hoop.

2 Cut around the flowers and mesh and sew them together, adding a few beads, before you dissolve the water-soluble fabric.

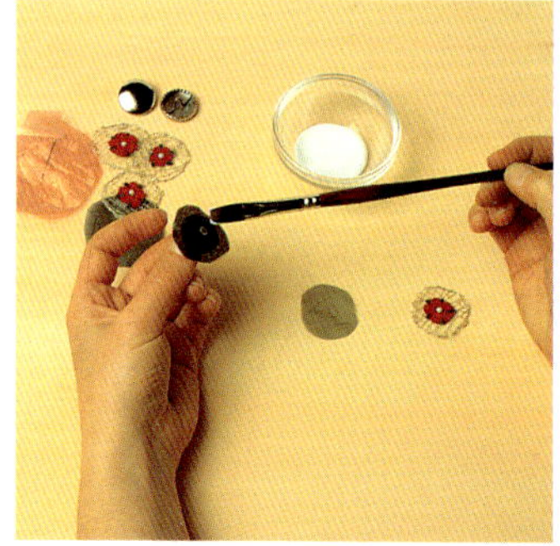

3 Follow the manufacturer's instructions to cover the buttons. Cut circles of metallic and sheer fabrics and dab a little glue in the centre of each button before covering with the layers of fabric.

UNDERWATER PICTURE

The effect of the layers of delicate blue and green chiffon is marvellously evocative of an undersea scene. This tranquil picture would be ideal in a bedroom, where its calm, reflective quality is bound to induce plenty of sweet dreams.

YOU WILL NEED

MATERIALS

shot organza in shades of green and blue
white paper
metallic organza
shot velvets
shot silk
shot organza
pearlized lamé
metallic embroidery threads

EQUIPMENT

dressmaker's scissors
dressmaker's pins
embroidery hoop
sewing machine, with embroidery foot

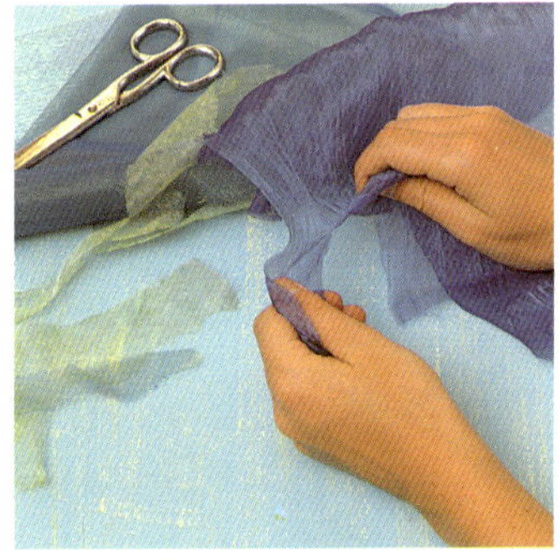

1 Use one sheet of organza as the base of the sea. Tear strips of organza to form the sea background.

2 Assemble all the strips, pin them together, and fit them into the embroidery hoop. Pin them in place.

3 Make shell, fish and starfish paper templates. Cut out shells from the metallic organza, fish from the velvets and silk, and starfish from the shot organza and lamé. Pin and machine stitch to the sea base, using metallic threads.

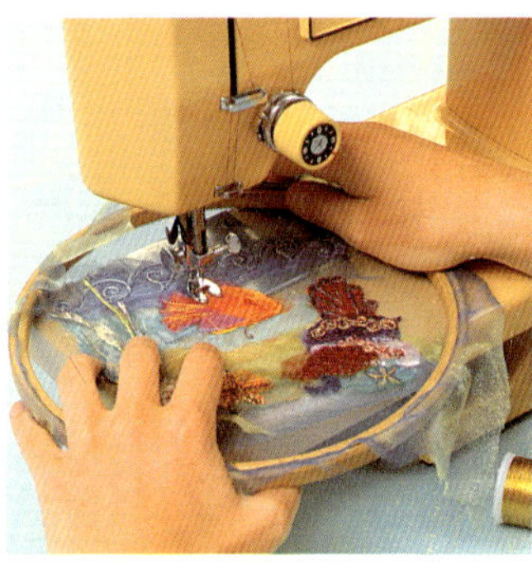

4 Build up the design with texture and colour. Remove the embroidery from the hoop and stretch it back into shape, ready for framing.

UNICORN PENNANT

This richly embroidered pennant uses the unicorn as its motif. Cool colours are used to great effect to reflect his elusive nature.

YOU WILL NEED

MATERIALS

4 toning cotton fabrics, 15 x 21.5 cm/6 x 8½ in
matching sewing thread
tracing paper
fusible bonding web
unbleached calico, 25 x 25 cm/10 x 10 in
gold machine embroidery thread
1.5 m/1½ yd wire-edged fleur-de-lys ribbon
tacking (basting) thread
cotton backing fabric, 28 x 40 cm/11 x 16 in
wooden pole, 36 cm/14 in
dark blue craft paint

EQUIPMENT

sewing machine
iron
pencil
dressmaker's scissors
needle
dressmaker's pins
paintbrush

1 Join the fabric rectangles in pairs along the long edges. Iron the seams open, then join the two pairs to form a large rectangle. Iron the seams open.

2 Trace the template from the back of the book, enlarging it to 23 cm/9 in across. Transfer it, in reverse, to the backing paper of the fusible bonding web. Iron it on to the calico, then cut it out along the outline. Peel off the backing paper and iron it on to the centre of the patchwork. Draw on the features.

3 Using a narrow satin stitch and gold thread, sew around the outside edge of the motif and over the various details of the design.

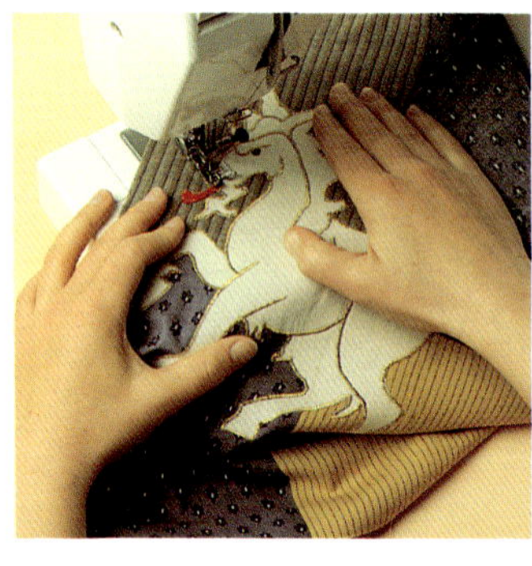

4 Embroider the eye, tongue and nostril by hand or with a machine.

5 Cut three 15 cm/6 in lengths of ribbon, that match the design, and remove the wire from the edges. Fold each piece in half, then pin and tack (baste) in place on the upper edge of the banner so that the loops are facing downwards.

6 With right sides facing, pin the backing fabric to the banner and sew around the edge leaving a 1 cm/½ in seam allowance. Leave a 10 cm/4 in gap at the lower edge for turning. Trim the corners and turn. Iron.

7 Paint the pole and allow to dry, then thread the banner on to the pole.

8 Tie each end of the remaining ribbon to the pole in a bow. Secure with a few stitches and pull the wired edges of the loops into shape.

WILD ROSE CHIFFON SCARF

Shimmering silk chiffon or organza and glittering silver metallic paint combine here to make a ravishing scarf that would completely transform a plain outfit. You do not have to wear this, though; it is a technique that could equally well be used to make beautiful fabric wall hangings.

YOU WILL NEED

MATERIALS

silk chiffon or organza, 30 x 50 cm/12 x 20 in
tracing paper
silver metallic fabric paint
metallic paint with nozzle-tipped dispenser

EQUIPMENT

iron
wooden frame
drawing pins
pencil
paintbrush
fabric marker
needle

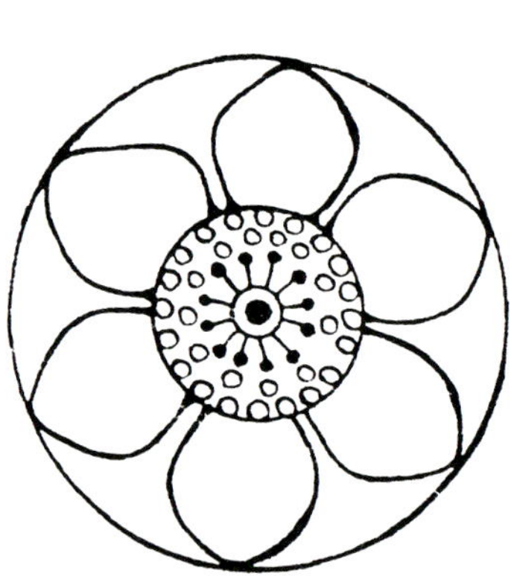

1 Wash, dry and iron the silk. Fold it in half and iron twice. Fold diagonally and iron. Unfold and stretch the fabric taut on the frame using drawing pins. Trace the template on this page, enlarging if necessary, on to the back of the silk at the centre. Trace eight more motifs around it, using the pressed folds as a guide.

2 Turn the frame over and go over the outlines of the design with silver paint on the front of the fabric. Allow to dry. Unpin the scarf and fix the paint according to the manufacturer's instructions. Stretch the fabric again.

3 Using the nozzle-tipped tube, make dots of metallic paint around the outer edges of each rose and fill in the details. Mark lines of dots 5 cm/2 in from the edges of the scarf, with the marker. To fray the edges, work one side at a time. Use a needle to separate and remove threads from the raw edges, then pull away up to the dotted edges.

HEAVENLY HAT

This richly coloured hat is made from a circle and a rectangle. Measure your head and add a 5 cm/2 in seam and shrinkage allowance. The height of the hat shown is 12 cm/4¾ in plus a 2.5 cm/1 in seam allowance. Cut a circle for the top, according to the size required, and add on a seam allowance of 2.5 cm/1 in.

YOU WILL NEED

MATERIALS

3 colours of dupion silk
heavy iron-on interfacing
velvet, 10 x 10 cm/4 x 4 in
paper
contrasting cotton threads
contrasting metallic machine embroidery threads
metallic fabric paints

EQUIPMENT

dressmaker's scissors
tape measure
iron
pencil
dressmaker's pins
sewing machine, with darning foot
paintbrush

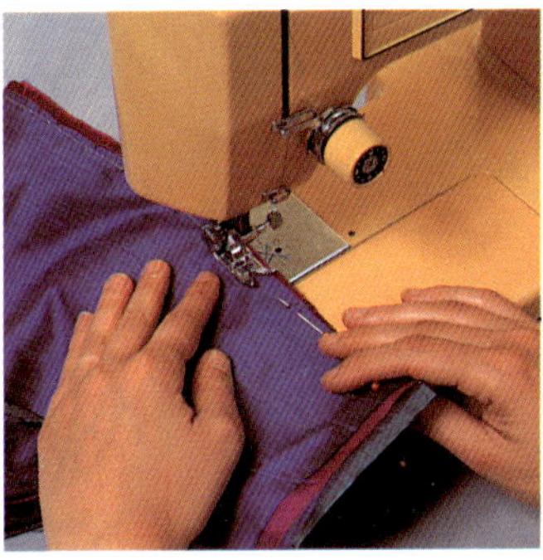

1 Cut three rectangles of silk and one of interfacing to the correct size. Iron the interfacing on to the back of the bottom layer of silk. Stitch around the edge of the rectangles, leaving a gap in one long seam. Insert the square of velvet slightly larger than the moon template through the gap, on top of the top layer of silk.

2 Draw and cut out the sun and moon shapes and pin on to the silk. With the machine in embroidery mode, stitch on top of the moon template, then stitch the features. Stitch the stars and outline stitching in the same way, using different coloured threads. Go over all the stitching twice, then tear away the paper.

3 Next, cut out the fabric layers to reveal your desired colours. Random whip stitch in a loop fashion inside the moon, with metallic thread. Paint areas of the hat with metallic fabric paints. Stitch the crown and top of the hat together and clip into the seam allowances.

DRAGONFLIES

These beautiful iridescent creatures look almost ready to fly away! If you've never tried free machine embroidery, look in your sewing machine manual for detailed instructions.

YOU WILL NEED

MATERIALS

water-soluble fabric
tracing paper
opalescent cellophane (or cellophane sweet wrappers)
small pieces of sheer synthetic organza: brown and green
fine metallic thread
thicker metallic thread
paper towels
piece of card
spray varnish
glitter pipecleaners
fine wire and a few glass beads, for the butterflies

EQUIPMENT

embroidery hoop
fine magic marker
dressmaker's pins
sewing machine, with fine needle
dressmaker's scissors
needle

1 Stretch the fabric on to the hoop. Trace the template from the back of the book on to the fabric with the magic marker. Sandwich the cellophane between the sheer fabrics and pin under the hoop. Machine around the wing details in straight stitch with fine thread.

2 Remove the hoop from the machine and trim away the spare fabric and cellophane with scissors.

3 With fine metallic thread in the needle and the thicker metallic thread on the bobbin, machine all round the outlines of the insects in ordinary straight stitch.

4 Put the fine thread on the bobbin and fill in between the outlines, joining all of the design. To stiffen the edges, go over the outlines in zigzag.

5 Hold the work to the light to check that the outlines are linked. Remove from the hoop and dissolve the fabric in water. Dry on paper towels.

6 Pin the insects out flat on a piece of card and spray with varnish. Allow to dry.

7 Cut a piece of glitter pipecleaner longer than the dragonfly body and sew it to the underside of the body part as far as the head. Trim it.

8 Bend the rest of the embroidery under the head and upper body to cover the pipecleaner. Stitch in place. Finally, fold the wings together and secure with a few stitches near the body so that the wings are raised.

9 Thread some small glass beads on to fine gold wire and twist into two antennae for the butterfly. Thread these on to the head, and then complete it as for the dragonfly.

Contemporary Tablemat

Here, a very traditional and popular motif is depicted in bright and bold modern colours.

You Will Need

Materials

light grey Zweigart Annable evenweave fabric, 38 x 56 cm/ 15 x 22 in
matching and black sewing thread
tacking (basting) thread
tracing paper
Anchor "Marlitt" shades 836, 815, 801 and 1032

Equipment

tape measure
dressmaker's scissors
dressmaker's pins
sewing machine
iron
needle
pencil

1 Cut two fabric rectangles, 28 x 38 cm/11 x 15 in. Pin them together and stitch around the edges, 1.5 cm/⅝ in from the edge, with matching thread and leaving a gap on one side. Mitre the corners, turn right side out and iron. Top stitch 1 cm/½ in from the edge. Tack (baste) guides around the edge of the mat, 2.5 cm/1 in and 4 cm/1½ in from the edge. Machine zigzag stitch over the top of the guidelines, using black thread. Use the presser foot as a guide to stitch the crossways lines. Stitch in the thread ends on the reverse side.

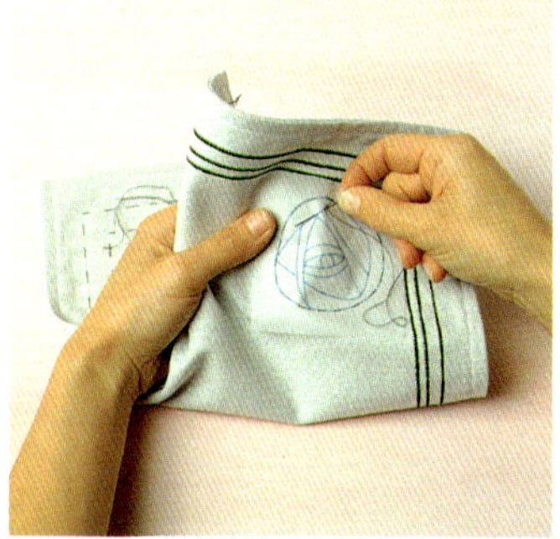

2 Trace the template from the back of the book, enlarging if necessary. Pin in position. Tack (baste) around the lines, then tear the tracing paper away. Machine zigzag along the lines and sew in the ends.

3 Fill in the coloured areas of the border in satin stitch, using two strands of Marlitt. Ease the satin stitches on the rose to fit round the curves, and fill in the centre to complete.

EMBROIDERED DRESS

Seashore motifs make for a pleasing decoration on this denim dress. Shown here as a repeat pattern, the shell and starfish shapes are appliquéd, then decorated with embroidery; the embroidered detail helps to unify the design as a whole.

YOU WILL NEED

MATERIALS

ironed white cotton
lining paper or newspaper
selection of fabric paints
tracing paper
dress
fabric glue
embroidery threads

EQUIPMENT

paintbrush
paint-mixing container
iron
pencil
embroidery scissors
selection of needles
towel

1 Lay the cotton on a larger sheet of paper and paint separate pieces of fabric in different colours. Allow to dry for 24 hours, then fix them, according to the manufacturer's instructions. Draw starfish and shell shapes on tracing paper.

2 Transfer the shapes several times on to the painted fabric. Cut them out, leaving a 5 mm/¼ in border outside the outlines. Lay the shapes on the hem of the dress and work out a pleasing pattern. Glue the shapes down sparingly.

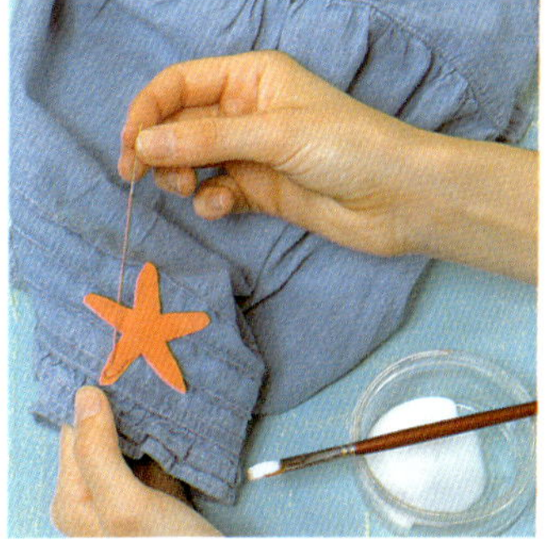

3 Embroider a running stitch, or a continuous double running stitch, around the template outlines.

4 Embroider details to represent sand, stones, etc. Tidy loose threads and iron on the wrong side, over a towel.

BABY SUIT

This ribbonwork decoration for a ready-made romper or sunsuit is easy to achieve and it looks really delightful. This type of ribbonwork is simple, because you can follow the existing oversewn garment seams, which act as sewing lines. Choose a plain, not patterned, suit, without any motifs.

YOU WILL NEED

MATERIALS

chocolate-brown ribbon, 6 m/6 yd
romper or sunsuit
tracing paper
rust ribbon, 3 m/3 yd
sewing threads: orange and chocolate-brown
salmon or peach ribbon, 3 m/3 yd

EQUIPMENT

needle
pencil
fabric marker
dressmaker's scissors

1 Use running stitch to attach chocolate-brown ribbon to the seams of the suit. Turn under, and finish the ends.

2 Trace the template from the back of the book, enlarging if necessary. Transfer to the suit four times. As an alternative, draw your own motifs with a pencil or marker.

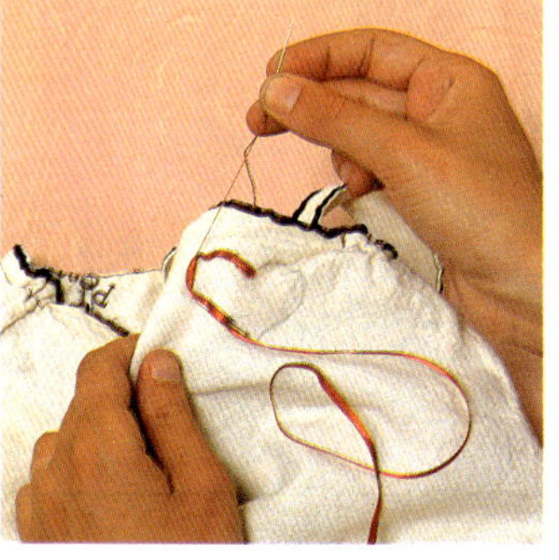

3 Turn under the end of the rust ribbon. Working anti-clockwise from the top of the heart, sew in place with running stitch in orange thread.

4 Repeat the process with the salmon or peach ribbon, using chocolate-brown or orange thread.

Midnight Sky Picture

Glittering metallic threads against shimmering dark blue shot silk create a real feeling of the night sky in this picture, which combines appliqué and machine embroidery techniques.

You Will Need

Materials

thin card
pearlized chiffon and lamé
dark blue shot silk, 23 x 23 cm/9 x 9 in
embroidery threads: metallic silver, gold and blue
wadding (batting)
thick card
all-purpose glue

Equipment

pencil
scissors
fabric marker
embroidery hoop
ruler
dressmaker's pins
sewing machine, with darning foot

1 Draw the moon and stars freehand on to thin card and cut out to use as templates. Draw round the templates on the pearlized fabrics, using the fabric marker, and cut them out.

2 Stretch the silk in an embroidery hoop. Mark out a 10 cm/4 in square in the centre, using the fabric marker. Position the pearlized shapes and pin them in place.

3 Using metallic thread and with the machine on the darning or free embroidery mode, define the shapes with machine embroidery. Continue building up colours and layers. Take the piece out of the hoop. Cut 10 cm/4 in squares of wadding (batting) and thick card. Lay the embroidery face down and place the wadding (batting) and card on top. Glue the edges of the card and then stretch the silk over and press it down firmly. Add a few stitches to hold the silk.

VELVET SCARF

This sinuous velvet scarf is encrusted down its full length with the "sigils", or abstract symbols, of the twelve signs of the zodiac. The shiny metallic decorations contrast deliciously with the silky smooth fabric. Choose some darkly glowing colours to wear on a starry evening. Before sewing the seams, make sure that the pile of each piece of velvet is running in the right direction.

YOU WILL NEED

MATERIALS

velvet in main colour, 1.5 m x 64 cm/60 x 26 in
velvet in toning colour, 36 x 64 cm/14 x 26 in
matching sewing thread
tracing paper
metallic organza
matching embroidery thread

EQUIPMENT

dressmaker's scissors
tape measure
sewing machine
pencil
tailor's chalk
embroidery hoop
needle

1 Cut two lengths of velvet to 1.5 m x 32 cm/ 60 x 13 in in the main colour, and four pieces 18 x 32 cm/7 x 13 in in the toning velvet. With right sides together and a 1 cm/½ in seam allowance, machine stitch one toning panel to each end of each scarf length.

2 Mark out the positions for the astrological signs along the side of the scarf length, placing them 2 cm/¾ in from the seam line and at 13 cm/5 in intervals. Trace the templates from the back of the book, enlarging if necessary. Copy on to the velvet using tailor's chalk.

3 Place the velvet in a hoop. Cut 2 cm/¾ in strips of metallic organza. Stitch one end of the organza to the marked line, twist the strip tightly and stitch in place. Work all the designs in the same way. With right sides together, join the two scarf lengths, leaving a small opening. Turn to the right side and slip stitch the opening.

SILVER MOTH SCARF

Ethereal silver moths flutter delicately over one side of this lovely silk scarf, their glitter reflected in the pleated organza on the other side. Your sewing machine manual will provide details of how to do free machine embroidery.

YOU WILL NEED

MATERIALS

tracing paper
fusible bonding web
small amounts of contrasting silk, velvet and organza
silk satin, 142 x 30 cm/56 x 12 in
matching fine machine embroidery thread
pleated metallic organza, 142 x 30 cm/56 x 12 in
matching sewing thread

EQUIPMENT

pencil
iron
dressmaker's scissors
embroidery hoop
sewing machine
dressmaker's pins
needle

1 Trace the templates from the back of the book, enlarging if necessary. Lay the bonding web over the templates and trace the moths. Iron the bonding to the wrong side of the silk. Trace the same number of body shapes on the bonding and iron to the wrong side of the velvet. Cut out the shapes.

2 Remove the backing paper and iron the shapes to the right side of the silk satin. Place the satin in a hoop. Cut some pieces of organza slightly larger than the moths and machine stitch them to the satin along the wing outlines. Trim the organza close to the line of stitching round each motif.

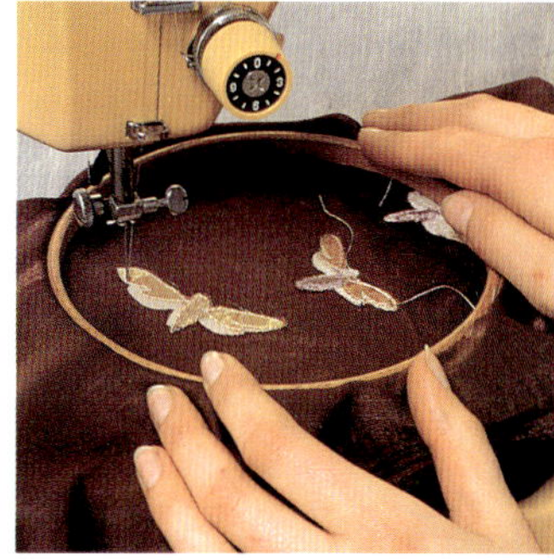

3 Work two or three lines of stitching around each moth to conceal the raw edges. Pin the pleated organza to the satin with right sides together, and stitch all around the edge, leaving a gap of 10 cm/4 in on one side. Turn the scarf to the right side and slip stitch the gap.

Fishy Ornaments

These charming fish are quickly made and would be a rewarding project for children. The symbol of Pisces represents coming and going, past and future, so hang them to swim in different directions!

You Will Need

Materials

scrap paper
thin card or paper
scraps of woollen fabric
mother-of-pearl buttons
embroidery cotton in contrasting colours
scraps of polyester wadding (batting), 5 mm/¼ in thick

Equipment

pencil
dressmaker's pins
dressmaker's scissors
needle

1 Draw a fish motif on to scrap paper and transfer it on to thin card or paper to make a template. Pin it to two layers of the fabric and cut out the fish. (No seam allowance is required for these shapes.)

2 Separate the pieces and sew on the buttons to make eyes. Embroider each side of the fish, using three strands of embroidery cotton, in cross stitch, stem stitch and feather stitch as shown in the picture.

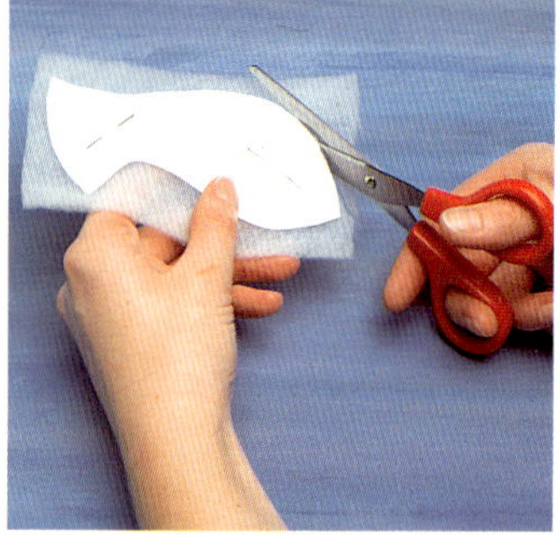

3 Cut a piece of wadding (batting) using the template, then trim it so that it is slightly smaller all round than the fish.

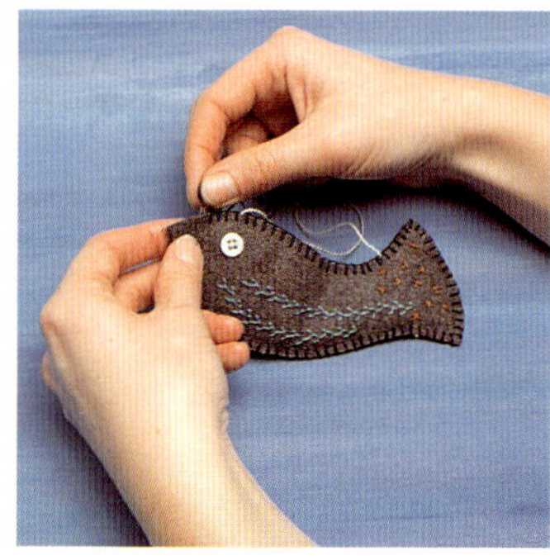

4 Sandwich the wadding (batting) between the two sides and attach a length of thread for the hanger. Blanket stitch round the edge to join the sides together.

BRIDAL HEART

Pink satin and lace are the essence of femininity; this delicate bridal favour would be the perfect loving touch for the wedding day of a daughter, sister or friend. The decoration of sequins, pearls and motifs can be as simple or elaborate as you like, and you can be sure that no two of these will ever be the same.

YOU WILL NEED

MATERIALS

tracing paper
pink satin fabric, 40 x 20 cm/16 x 8 in
lace fabric or mat, 20 x 20 cm/8 x 8 in
contrasting tacking (basting) thread
ready-made silk flowers (optional)
matching sewing thread
flat sequins
seed pearls
polyester wadding (batting)
narrow lace edging, 60 cm/24 in
short lengths of matching satin ribbon

EQUIPMENT

pencil
dressmaker's scissors
dressmaker's pins
very fine needle
sewing machine (optional)

1 Trace the heart template from the back of the book, enlarging if necessary. Cut out two hearts from pink satin. Place one under the lace fabric or mat, and move it about to find the most attractive pattern area. Pin and then tack (baste) through both layers. Cut the lace, carefully following the outline of the satin heart.

2 From the remaining lace, cut flowers and motifs. Sew to the centre of the lace heart. (Or use silk flowers.) Add sequins and pearls. Pin the hearts together, right sides facing. Stitch 1 cm/½ in in from the edges, leaving a 5 cm/2 in gap. Trim seams and clip curves. Turn right side out. Fill the heart with wadding (batting) and slip stitch the gap.

3 Run a gathering thread along the straight edge of the lace edging and pin one end to the top of the heart. Adjusting the gathers evenly, continue to pin the lace around the outside edge and then slip stitch it firmly in place with small, invisible stitches. Remove the gathering thread. Finish with a hanging loop, small ribbon bows and additional beads and sequins.

DECORATIVE PINCUSHION

An essential item on Victorian dressing tables, pincushions are still as useful as they are decorative. There is no more appropriate way to personalize them than with the pins themselves. The symbols used here are Capricorn and Taurus.

YOU WILL NEED

MATERIALS

plain velvet,
28 x 14 cm/11 x 5½ in
brass-headed pins,
1 cm/½ in long
matching sewing thread
polyester wadding (batting)
fine white tissue paper

EQUIPMENT

dressmaker's scissors
tailor's chalk
sewing machine
needle
pencil
tracing paper
dressmaker's pins

1 Cut the velvet into two 14 cm/5½ in squares and pin them together with right sides facing. Mark a 1 cm/½ in seam allowance with tailor's chalk. Machine around all four sides, leaving a 5 cm/2 in gap in the centre of one side.

2 Trim the seam allowance at the corners of the cushion and turn it to the right side, easing out the corners with the points of the scissors. Stuff very firmly with polyester wadding (batting). Sew up the opening neatly by hand along the seam.

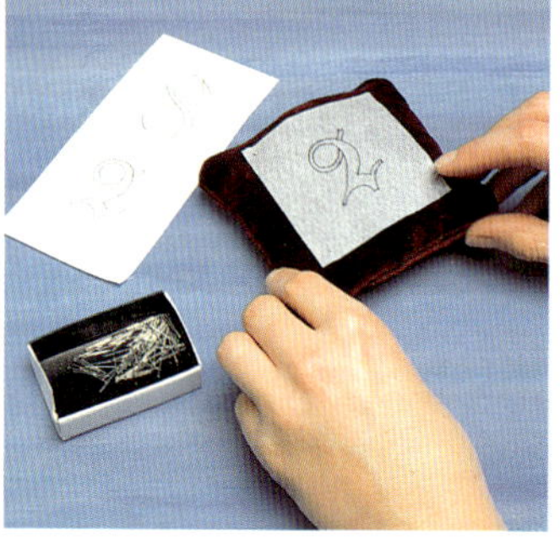

3 Trace the signs you want from the templates in the back of the book, enlarging if necessary, and transfer them to fine white tissue paper. Centre and pin a motif on the pincushion.

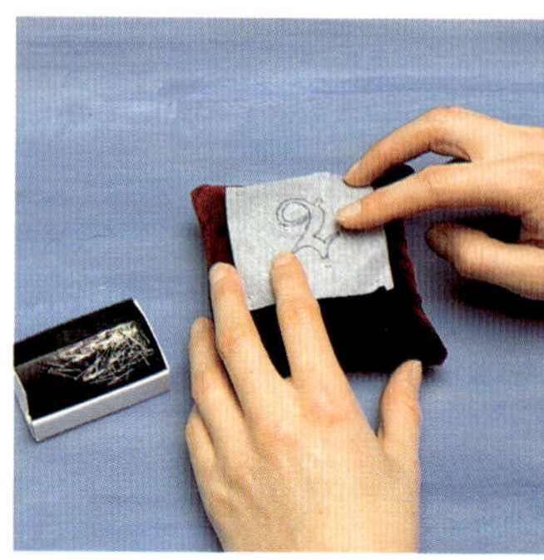

4 Work the motif with the brass-headed pins. When complete, tear away the tissue, gently pulling any bits from between the pins.

Cupid Camisole

This beautiful camisole will make you feel like a million dollars. You will need a commercial paper pattern for a camisole, which you can then embellish with machine embroidery. You can embroider over the tissue paper pattern first and then tear away the paper, leaving an outline to be filled in with colour.

You Will Need

Materials

satin fabric, 1 m x 90 cm/ 1 x 1 yd
tissue paper
machine embroidery threads: cream, white, gold and grey

Equipment

commercial camisole pattern
dressmaker's scissors
dressmaker's pins
embroidery hoop
sewing machine, with darning foot

1 Cut out the pattern from the satin, with 1 cm/½ in extra all around to allow for any shrinkage during embroidery. Make a tissue paper duplicate of the front pattern piece. Trace the template from the back of the book, enlarging if necessary, and trace it on to the tissue paper duplicate, rotating it each time and avoiding the darts.

2 Use the tissue paper duplicate for embroidering by pinning it to the satin. Place the satin in the embroidery hoop. Set the machine to darning mode and attach the darning foot. With cream thread, stitch along the outline of the design.

3 Remove the tissue paper and fill in the design. Use white thread for the face, body and hearts, gold for the hair and features and grey for the wings and cloud. Make up the camisole according to the pattern instructions.

NEEDLEPOINT BEETLE

This delightful beetle on its subtly coloured background is easy to work in tent stitch. Measure the frame you have chosen and work enough of the background to ensure that no bare canvas will be visible when the picture is framed.

YOU WILL NEED

MATERIALS

needlepoint canvas, 25 x 25 cm/10 x 10 in with 24 holes per 5 cm/ 12 holes per 1 in
picture frame
masking tape
tapestry wools: as listed in key at the back of the book

EQUIPMENT

waterproof magic marker
dressmaker's scissors
tapestry needle
iron
damp cloth
dressmaker's pins (optional)

1 To prepare the canvas, mark a vertical line down the centre and a horizontal line across the centre using a magic marker. Mark the edges of the aperture in the frame you intend to use, positioning it centrally over the marked lines.

2 Bind the edges of the canvas with masking tape to keep it straight and prevent the yarn catching as you sew.

TENT STITCH Begin with a knot on the right side of the canvas, bringing the needle up again about 2.5 cm/1 in away. Work the first few stitches over this thread to secure it; the knot can then be cut away neatly. To work tent stitch, insert the needle one row up and one row to the right, bringing it back up through the hole to the left of your starting point. All the stitches must slant in the same direction – at the end of a row, turn the canvas upside down in order to work the next row.

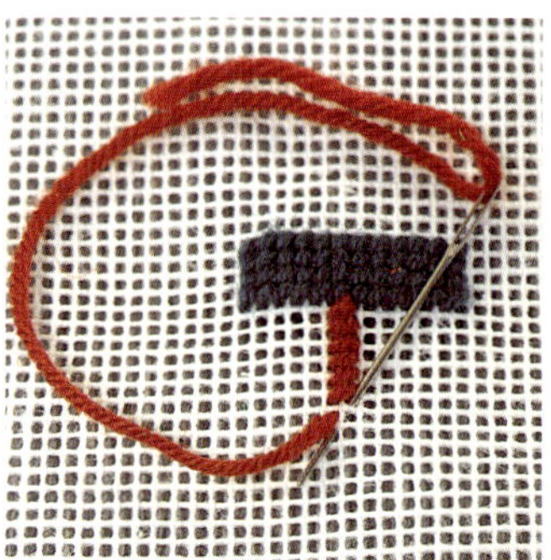

VERTICAL TENT STITCH Tent stitch is worked horizontally, but it can be worked vertically where necessary. Always keep the stitches on the reverse side longer and more sloping than those on the front to avoid distorting the fabric. Try to keep an even tension and do not pull too tightly.

3 Cut a 45 cm/18 in length of tapestry wool and work the design from the chart at the back of the book in tent stitch. Start from the centre and work outwards to help keep the piece from distorting as you sew. When the design is completed and the background is large enough to fill the frame, remove the masking tape.

4 Use a hot iron and a damp cloth to steam the work gently, pulling it into shape as you go. If the canvas is very distorted, pin it into shape on the ironing board before steaming it. Dry the canvas thoroughly and quickly.

5 Cut away the excess canvas and mount your picture into the frame.

Sweet Hearts

The heart is the ultimate symbol of devotion, so heart-shaped gifts have a special significance, whether they are given to friends and family, or exchanged by lovers. These padded hearts are made from leftovers of old lace fabric, embellished with tiny beads and gauze ribbons. The golden versions are filled with pot-pourri and edged with metallic lace, giving an antique richness.

1 Cut out two hearts from the backing fabric and one from lace, leaving a 1 cm/½ in seam allowance all around.

You Will Need

Materials

silk backing fabric
small pieces of lace fabric
matching sewing thread
polyester wadding (batting)
rocaille embroidery beads
lace, 50 x 2.5 cm/20 x 1 in
gauze ribbon, 1 m x 4 cm/ 1 yd x 1½ in

Equipment

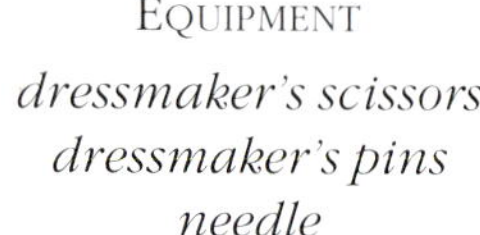

dressmaker's scissors
dressmaker's pins
needle

2 Pin the hearts together, sandwiching the lace heart between the two layers of silk. Sew together along one straight edge, leaving a 4 cm/1½ in gap for turning through.

3 Turn the heart the right way out and stuff it firmly, ensuring that the wadding (batting) fills out the point of the heart. Slip stitch the sides, making sure that the fabric lies flat and has no wrinkles.

4 Sew the beads on to the lace, picking out and highlighting the various designs within the pattern of lace itself.

5 Gather the length of lace to fit around the outside edge of the heart, then stitch it in place.

6 Cut a 30 cm/12 in length of gauze ribbon and sew it to the top of the heart to form a hanging loop. Make a bow from the rest of the ribbon and sew it to the base of the loop.

To My True Love.

Applique, Patchwork and Cross Stitch

Appliqué and patchwork are crafts requiring only a modicum of skills that nevertheless produce individual and stunning results. The techniques can be used to give an extra sparkle to a whole range of items such as cards, bags, towels and mats as well as bed linen and clothes. The materials needed are all readily available, and most needleworkers will probably already have most of the equipment required. Once you have mastered the techniques, you will be able to experiment fully to create your own designs and projects on fabrics of your choice.

There are few constraints with these needlework techniques, as even the most unassuming scraps of fabric and old clothes can be rejuvenated given a little imagination and some basic know-how. In addition there is a selection of cross-stitch projects for enthusiasts of this most popular of needlecrafts!

BASIC TECHNIQUES

The materials and equipment required for appliqué, patchwork and cross stitch are more or less the same as those for hand and machine embroidery.

ABOVE *Appliqué and patchwork projects make full use of any fabric remnants.*

Using fusible bonding web

1 Fusible bonding web is useful for stabilizing appliqué pieces, as it binds on to the fabric when pressed with an iron. You can then cut around the shape to be appliquéd, with the bonding web in place to act as a stiffener.

2 Fusible bonding web has a backing paper that can be peeled off. The pieces can then be pressed in place on the ground fabric.

Basic cross stitches

Cross stitch can either be worked as a single stitch or in a row that is completed in two journeys. Irrespective of which method is used, the top stitch should always face in the same direction. If working a border or a detailed piece of cross stitch, it is helpful to put a pin in the work showing the direction that the top stitch should face.

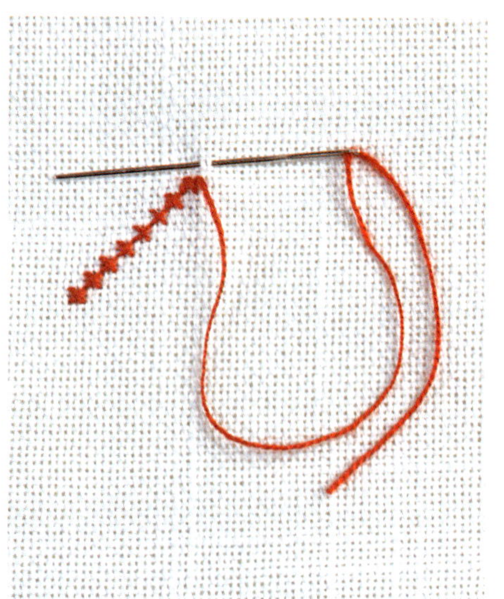

Single cross stitch

This produces a slightly raised cross and should be used for individual stitches and small details. It is also ideal when stitching with tapestry wool.

Row of cross stitches

First work a row of cross stitches either diagonally or in a straight line. Complete the cross stitches by stitching the other half on the way back.

Basic Techniques

Simple appliqué

Embroidered appliqué pieces

Draw the shape on the fabric with a fabric marker and embroider the pattern over the edges of the outline.

Straight stitch appliqué

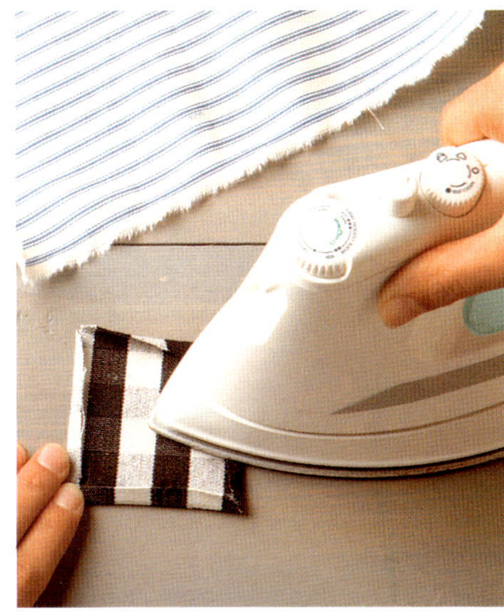

1 Cut out the shape, making sure to leave a 1 cm/½ in allowance all round. Press the allowance to the wrong side, snipping away corners and curves.

2 Pin the piece to the fabric and work a straight stitch all round.

Zigzag or satin stitch appliqué

Pin the appliqué piece to the ground fabric and stitch around the outline. Trim away the excess fabric close to the stitched line. Work a zigzag stitch around the outline, covering raw edges. This can be followed by a second line of satin stitch.

Shadow appliqué

1 Work the appliqué pieces using one of the methods described before, then pin and tack a piece of sheer fabric over the design.

2 Use matching thread to stitch over the sheer fabric, close to the stitches on the appliquéd pieces.

Oak Leaf Potholder

Many quilt patterns are inspired by natural images. This oak-leaf pattern is based on a block from an appliqué quilt made in 1850.

You Will Need

Materials

thin card or paper
fusible bonding web
green felt, 15 x 15 cm/6 x 6 in
checked cotton fabric, 22 x 30 cm/9 x 12 in
2 polyester wadding (batting) squares, 22 cm/9 in
thick cotton backing fabric, 18 x 18 cm/7 x 7 in
tacking (basting) thread
matching sewing thread
small eyelet screw
wooden toggle

Equipment

pencil
tape measure
fabric marker
iron
dressmaker's scissors
dressmaker's pins
needle

1 Trace the template from the back of the book, enlarging it to 14 cm/5½ in across. Transfer the outline to the bonding web with a fabric marker and iron it on to the green felt. Cut out the shape.

2 Cut a 22 cm/9 in square from the checked cotton fabric. Peel off the backing paper from the felt square and iron it centrally on to the cotton fabric square. Iron under a hem of 1 cm /½ in.

3 Pin the polyester wadding (batting) squares between the backing fabric and the decorated square. Pin, tack (baste) and slip stitch the turned edge over the backing square to conceal the raw edges.

4 For the hanger, sew together the long sides of the remaining checked cotton fabric. Screw the eyelet into the toggle and thread the hanger through. Fold it in half and sew it in place.

Heraldic Tablemat

Medieval retainers used to wear circular badges with a distinctive family motif on their clothes to identify them with their feudal overlord: such emblems were much simpler designs than armorial bearings and were often animals or flowers. For this project, you could create your own heraldic design.

You Will Need

Materials

PVC (vinyl) coated cotton fabric: plain blue, plain red and co-ordinating print
PVA (white) glue
tracing paper
thin card or paper
baize or felt, for backing
quilting thread

Equipment

pair of compasses
pencil
scissors
paintbrush
sheet of plastic
sewing machine, with leather needle

1 Decide on the diameter of your mat, then draw and cut out a rim of plain blue fabric. Glue this to the background print fabric, to secure it while you sew.

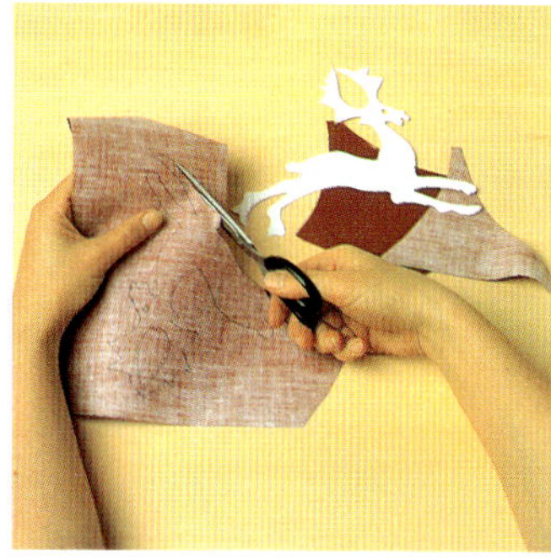

2 Trace an animal template from the back of the book, enlarging if necessary, and transfer it to thin card or paper. Cut it out and draw around it on the reverse of the plain red fabric. Cut it out.

3 Glue the animal in the centre of the mat, and glue a piece of baize or felt to the back. Cover with a sheet of plastic and leave under a weight until it is dry.

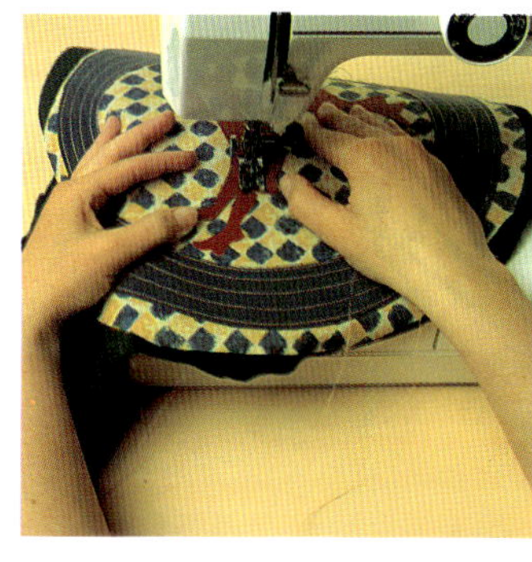

4 Using quilting thread, machine stitch around the edges of the motif and in rows around the border. Use a long, straight stitch. Trim the edge of the mat and wipe off any glue.

Matisse Outfit

The artist Henri Matisse spent his later years creating dynamic and exciting paper collages, characterized by bold colours and strong graphic shapes. They were the inspiration behind this collection of clothes, which shows just how easy it is to customize a ready-made garment and so transform it into something really individual.

You Will Need

Materials

tracing paper
plain white T-shirt
fusible bonding web
scraps of plain cotton fabric in bright colours
matching sewing threads
plain white long-sleeved shirt
coloured buttons
denim jacket

Equipment

pencil
fabric marker
dressmaker's scissors
iron
sewing machine
needle

1 Trace the template from the back of the book, enlarging it to fit your T-shirt, and transfer each element of the design, in reverse, on to fusible bonding web with a fabric marker. Cut out roughly.

2 Choose three colours for the background shapes and iron one rectangle on to each. Cut out along the outline, peel off the backing paper and iron in place. Stitch around the outside edge with a narrow zigzag stitch in matching thread.

3 Cut out the branched and single leaf shapes in the same way and iron them on to the T-shirt.

4 Sew each shape in place with zigzag stitch, working accurately around the curves. Iron lightly.

5 Finish off on the reverse of the work, knotting the ends of the threads together and clipping close to the surface.

6 Customize a plain white shirt by removing the buttons and pocket. Wash and iron. Sew appliqué motifs to each side of the front, as you did for the T-shirt.

7 Replace the white buttons with brightly coloured ones, chosen to match the appliquéd design.

8 Decorate the back of the denim jacket in the same way; again, use coloured buttons to add the final detail.

APPLIQUED SUNFLOWER CARD

A home-made card is much nicer than a bought one and this cheery sunflower design would be perfect for someone with a high-summer birthday.

YOU WILL NEED

MATERIALS

tracing paper
yellow and brown fabric scraps
fabric glue
background fabric
embroidery thread
green paper scraps
blank card and envelope
paper glue

EQUIPMENT

pencil
fabric marker
dressmaker's scissors
needle

1 Trace the template from the back of the book, enlarging if necessary. Using the fabric marker, transfer the outline to the yellow fabric first and cut it out. Then cut out the smaller centres from brown fabric.

2 Stick the yellow piece on to the background fabric and the brown one on top. Then stick the third piece on top. Sew from the edge of the inner ring, using a running stitch on the centre piece.

3 On the dark brown ring, sew from the outer to the inner edge in one large stitch, like a very loose, random satin stitch, to give a textured effect. Continue all the way round.

4 On the centre piece, sew running stitches at random, to give the effect of seeds. Sew on green paper leaves. Check for any loose threads on the back and tie them in. Trim the fabric to the correct size for the aperture of the card. Stick the appliqué in position cleanly.

Star Patchwork Sachet

Patchwork stars made out of diamond shapes appear on many early American quilts; this one is based on the eight-point Lone Star motif. Lining the patches with backing paper is the traditional English way of making patchwork. It keeps the shapes sharp and accurate when joining the points of the star.

You Will Need

Materials

tracing paper
thin card
mustard-yellow cotton fabric, 12.5 x 20 cm/5 x 8 in
green and white check cotton fabric, 12.5 x 20 cm/5 x 8 in
dark orange cotton fabric, 20 x 40 cm/8 x 16 in
backing paper
tacking (basting) thread
matching sewing thread
dried herbs or pot-pourri
1 small pearl button

Equipment

pencil
scissors
dressmaker's scissors
ruler
needle
iron
dressmaker's pins

1 Trace the templates from the back of the book, enlarging if necessary. Cut eight diamonds, four squares and four triangles from thin card. Add a 5 mm/¼ in allowance and cut out four yellow and four check diamonds, four orange squares and four orange triangles. Lay the backing paper in the centre of each shape, turn the seam over the paper, folding at the points, and tack (baste) in place.

2 Stitch a yellow and a check diamond together along one edge, then sew an orange square into the right angle. Make four of these units, then join together to form a star. Sew the orange triangles into the remaining spaces to complete the square. Iron lightly and remove all the tacking (basting) threads.

3 Cut a 19 cm/7½ in square from the remaining orange fabric and iron a 5 mm/¼ in seam allowance all round. With wrong sides together, pin this square to the patchwork and overstitch around the outside edge leaving a 7.5 cm/3 in gap on one side. Fill with herbs or pot-pourri and sew up the opening. Sew the button to the centre of the star.

APPLIQUE THROW

This appliqué throw recycles an old blanket as its background fabric and is pleasingly quick to put together, using fusible bonding web. Old buttons and bold woollen embroidery stitches add detail and colour.

YOU WILL NEED

MATERIALS

cream blanket
matching and contrasting crewel wool
tracing paper
thin card or paper
four pieces of flannel fabric, 25 x 50 cm/10 x 20 in
green, rust and brown felt, 30 x 30 cm/12 x 12 in
fusible bonding web, 1.5 m/1½ yd
assorted shirt buttons (optional)
65 larger brown buttons (optional)

EQUIPMENT

dressmaker's scissors
tape measure
tapestry needle
pencil
fabric marker
iron
pressing cloth

1 Cut a rectangle measuring 1 x 1.3 m/40 x 50 in from the blanket. Fold a 1 cm/½ in hem around the outside edge and sew with a large blanket stitch worked in cream wool.

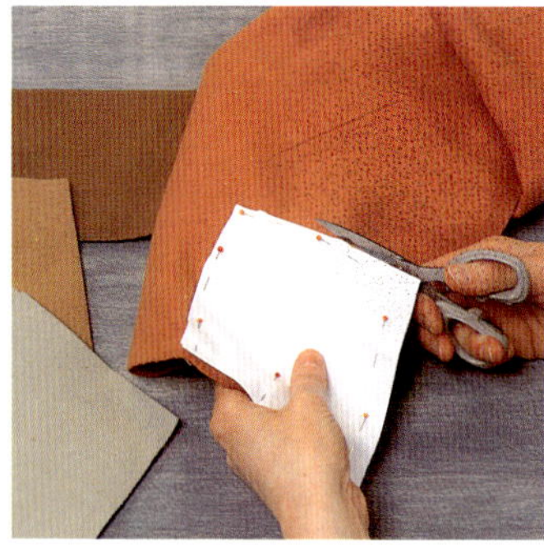

2 Trace the template for the diamond from the back of the book, carefully enlarging it to 20 cm/8 in high. Use this as a guide for cutting 25 diamonds of different colours from the flannel fabric.

3 Enlarge the leaf templates to fit within the diamonds. For each motif, choose a felt colour that tones with the background fabric. Trace the various leaf outlines, in reverse, on to fusible bonding web with a fabric marker. Cut out roughly and iron on to the felt, then cut out neatly. Peel off the backing paper and iron a leaf to the centre of each diamond.

4 Sew the leaves down using a single strand of crewel wool and a running stitch or blanket stitch – follow the picture as a guide. Some of the leaves have an extra appliquéd motif or a cut-out shape; you can make your own variations on these ideas.

5 Use straight stitch to embroider a vein pattern on some leaves and sew on the extra motifs using a cross or straight stitch.

6 Sew on tiny shirt buttons as a finishing touch, or add embroidered stars. (If the throw is for a small child, do not use buttons.) Each leaf can be different, or you could make several in the same colours.

7 Iron fusible bonding web on to the back of each diamond. Peel off the backing paper and arrange them in five rows of five, leaving an even border all around. Iron in place using a pressing cloth.

8 If desired, sew a large button over each diamond intersection, using wool in a contrasting colour.

Rose Applique Bag

This attractive shopping bag recycles old table linen, fabric remnants and buttons. Look for unworn areas of old tablecloths or damask napkins: even the smallest scraps can combine effectively with other kinds of material.

You Will Need

Materials

rose-print furnishing fabric remnant
fusible bonding web
tracing paper
striped or checked table napkins, cloths or remnants
calico, 60 x 83 cm/ 24 x 33 in
matching sewing threads
6 old buttons

Equipment

dressmaker's scissors
iron
pencil
sewing machine
ruler
fabric marker
safety pin
needle

1 Pick out five interesting rose motifs and eight single leaf motifs from the fabric and cut them out roughly.

2 Iron the wrong side of the roses and leaves to the bonding web. Cut around the edges, simplifying the outlines to make them easier to sew.

3 Trace the template from the back of the book, enlarging if necessary, and trace six flower shapes on to the paper side of more bonding web. Cut them out roughly and iron them on to the striped or checked fabrics. Cut around the outlines. Make ten leaves in the same way and one large blue and white jug.

4 Cut a 50 x 83 cm/20 x 33 in calico rectangle and fold it in half widthways. Peel the backing paper from the jug and iron in place on the centre front. Using matching thread and a narrow satin stitch, sew in place. Remove the backing paper from the leaves and flowers and arrange them around the jug. Iron in place.

5 Sew the shapes in place with satin stitch, using matching thread and working over the outside edges of the fabric. Finish off all the threads on the wrong side.

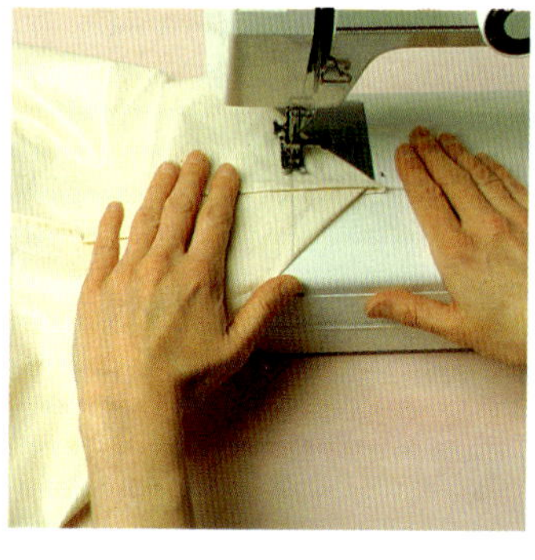

6 Join the bottom and side edges with French seams, for strength. Turn inside out and flatten one corner, to make a right-angled point at the end of the bottom seam. Measure 5 cm/2 in down from the end and mark a line across the corner. Sew across this line. Repeat for the other corner, to make a flat base for the bag.

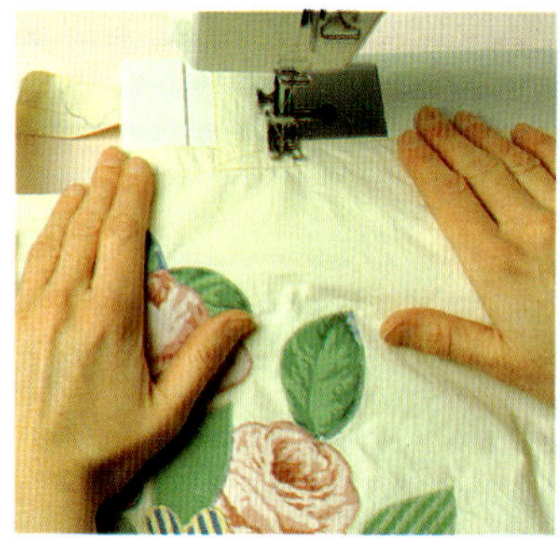

7 Turn under, press and stitch a double hem of 2.5 cm/1 in around the top of the bag. Cut the remaining calico into two equal strips and fold each in half lengthways. Join 1 cm/½ in from the outside edge and, using a safety pin, turn inside out. Top stitch both sides and sew one handle to each side of the bag.

8 Sew a button to the centre of each plain flower, as a finishing touch.

Fleur-de-lys Tieback

Make this smart tieback with a beautifully stylized lily to add restrained elegance to a plain or striped curtain.

You Will Need

Materials

tracing paper
white cotton poplin, 20 x 90 cm/ 8 x 36 in
navy cotton poplin, 30 x 90 cm/ 12 x 36 in
navy-white striped poplin, 50 x 90 cm/20 x 36 in
polyester wadding (batting),
thin card or paper
fusible bonding web, 20 x 90 cm/ 8 x 36 in
tacking (basting) thread
matching sewing thread
two white "D" rings

Equipment

pencil
dressmaker's scissors
dressmaker's pins
fabric marker
iron
needle
sewing machine

1 Trace the tieback template from the back of the book, enlarging it to fit the width needed for your curtain. Cut out the shape in each of the fabrics and the wadding (batting). Mark the positions of the motifs on the white fabric.

2 Trace the fleur-de-lys motif and cut it out on card or paper. Draw around it seven times on the backing paper of the bonding web and iron on to the remaining navy fabric. Cut out the shapes carefully.

3 Iron the motifs on to the white fabric. Layer the wadding (batting) between the striped and navy fabrics, lay the white fabric on top and tack (baste). Quilt around the motifs. Cut two 6 cm/2¼ in bias strips from the striped fabric. Pin one piece along the top edge and stitch, leaving a 1.5 cm/⅝ in allowance. Fold the binding to the back, turn in the raw edge, pin and hem. Stitch the second strip along the bottom edge. Loop each end of the binding through a "D" ring, turn in the raw edge neatly and stitch.

Orange Sampler

The fruit basket, piled high with oranges and lemons, was a popular cross-stitch motif in the nineteenth century. You can use the colours suggested here, or experiment with your own shades of embroidery threads to make a more personalized design.

You Will Need

Materials

tacking (basting) thread
white cross stitch fabric, 15 x 20 cm/6 x 8 in
stranded embroidery threads: orange, light orange, yellow, ochre, dark olive, light olive and chocolate-brown
mount board
plain wooden frame, with 9 x 14 cm/3½ x 5½ in opening

Equipment

needle
tapestry needle
embroidery scissors
iron
craft knife
cutting mat

1 Using tacking (basting) thread, mark guidelines vertically and horizontally across the centre of the fabric. Follow the chart at the back of the book; the sampler is worked with three strands of embroidery thread throughout, and one square of the chart represents one cross stitch. Using orange thread, work the centre orange of the bottom row of fruit.

2 Stitch the other oranges, then work the leaves around them and the basket. Use the guidelines to establish the position of the other motifs and count the squares between them carefully. When the design is complete, unpick the tacking (basting) threads and iron lightly from the back of the work.

3 Cut a piece of mount board to fit the finished piece, using the lining paper from the frame as a guide. Place the board centrally on the back of the work and lace the two long sides together using long stitches. Repeat the process with the two short sides, then insert in the frame.

CRADLE QUILT

With its contrasting patchwork squares and heart motifs reminiscent of American folk art, this embroidered quilt will look really special in a cradle or crib.

YOU WILL NEED

MATERIALS

blue cotton chambray, 140 x 90 cm/54 x 36 in
white cotton fabric, 15 x 60 cm/6 x 24 in
graph paper, 20 x 20 cm/8 x 8 in
tracing paper
dressmaker's carbon paper
stranded embroidery threads: white, red and blue
fusible bonding web, 25 x 37 cm/10 x 15 in
5 scraps of checked or striped cotton shirting
matching sewing thread
iron-on wadding (batting), 60 x 60 cm/24 x 24 in
tacking (basting) thread
strips of chambray, 5 x 65 cm/2 x 26 in

EQUIPMENT

iron
dressmaker's scissors
pen or hard pencil
dressmaker's pins
sewing machine
needle

1 Iron the fabric. Using the graph paper as a template, cut four squares of blue chambray and five of white cotton. Make sure that you cut all the squares exactly in line with the grain of the fabric.

2 Trace the heart template from the back of the book, enlarging if necessary. Using dressmaker's carbon paper, transfer it on to the centre of one blue square, using a pen or hard pencil and pressing firmly to achieve a strong line.

3 Using three strands of white thread, work over the lines in a small, regular running stitch. Work a red whipstitch over the inner and outer heart outlines. Work a blue whipstitch over the parallel lines inside the heart. Repeat the process with the three remaining blue squares.

4 Trace just the outline of the heart template on to the paper side of the bonding web. Cut out roughly around the edge and then iron the heart on to a piece of shirting, following the manufacturer's instructions. Make sure that the centre line matches the stripes or checks. Cut out carefully around the outline. Repeat with the remaining fabric scraps.

5 Remove the backing paper and iron the heart on to the centre of a white square. With three strands of embroidery thread, work a row of feather stitching around the outside of the heart, to conceal the raw edges. Repeat with the remaining four pieces of shirting and white squares.

6 Lay the nine squares in three rows of three, with alternating colours. Machine stitch along each row, with right sides facing, and allowances of 1 cm/½ in. Iron with the allowances lying on the blue squares. Pin the rows together, matching the joins. Sew along the long edges with 1 cm/½ in allowances. Clip the seams where the squares meet. Iron the seams towards blue squares.

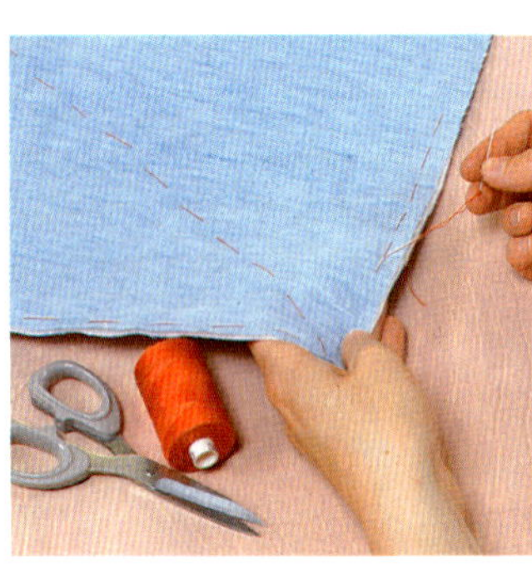

7 Cut a square of iron-on wadding (batting) the same size as the completed quilt. Secure it to the back of the quilt, following the manufacturer's instructions. Cut a square of chambray the same size for the backing. Tack (baste) it to the back of the wadding (batting).

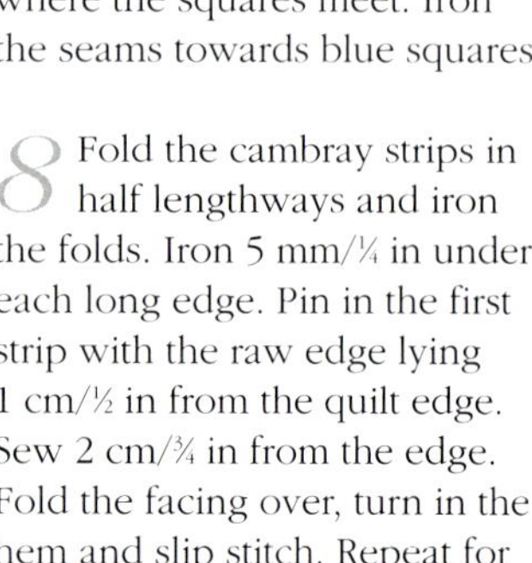

8 Fold the cambray strips in half lengthways and iron the folds. Iron 5 mm/¼ in under each long edge. Pin in the first strip with the raw edge lying 1 cm/½ in from the quilt edge. Sew 2 cm/¾ in from the edge. Fold the facing over, turn in the hem and slip stitch. Repeat for each side. Neaten each corner and remove the tacking (basting).

Seashell Beach Bag

Crisp cream and navy give this smart beach bag a nautical feel. The charm of the project lies in combining colours to give a three-dimensional feel.

You Will Need

Materials

cream cotton drill or denim, 55 x 75 cm/21½ x 30 in
tracing paper
stencil card
spray adhesive
2 lengths blue cotton drill or denim, 15 x 38 cm/6 x 15 in
dry fabric stencil paints: dark yellow, dark red and navy blue
sewing threads: white, dark orange and blue
cream cord, 2 m/2 yd
masking tape

Equipment

dressmaker's scissors
craft knife
cutting mat
3 stencil brushes
iron
sewing machine
dressmaker's pins
ruler or tape measure

1 Cut the cream cotton drill in two lengthways. Trace the template from the back of the book, enlarging if necessary. Transfer it to stencil card and cut out. Spray the back lightly with adhesive and stencil five shells on to each piece of fabric, using two or three colours. When thoroughly dry, fix the paint according to the manufacturer's instructions.

2 With right sides together, sew a blue strip to the top edge of each cream piece, leaving a 1 cm/½ in seam allowance. Press the seam upwards. Pin rectangles right sides together and stitch around the main bag. Press under the seam allowances on the open sides of the blue fabric and top stitch in orange. Fold in half lengthways. Machine stitch parallel to the top stitch.

3 Cut the cord in half and bind the ends with masking tape. Thread both pieces through the bag. Remove the tape and bind the ends with blue thread, 5 cm/2 in from the ends. Fringe and comb the cord to make tassels. Trim neatly.

Star-spangled Scarf

A lavish scattering of gold appliqué and beads on dark velvet creates a luxurious scarf for winter evenings.

You Will Need

Materials

burgundy velvet, 23 x 63 cm/9 x 25 in
gold velvet, 23 x 63 cm/9 x 25 in
tracing paper
fusible bonding web, 23 x 30 cm/ 9 x 12 in
gold machine embroidery thread
translucent gold rocaille beads
matching sewing thread
black velvet, 32 x 122 cm/12½ x 48 in
black glazed cotton, 56 x 89 cm/22 x 34½ in

Equipment

dressmaker's scissors
pencil
iron
pressing cloth
sewing machine
needle
dressmaker's pins

1 Cut the burgundy velvet into two rectangles 23 x 32 cm/9 x 12½ in. From the gold velvet cut two 4 x 32 cm/ 1½ x 12½ in strips and two 6 x 32 cm/2½ x 12½ in strips.

Trace the templates from the back of the book, enlarging if necessary. Draw and cut out each star twice on the fusible bonding. Iron on to the wrong side of the remaining gold velvet. Cut out each star neatly along the outline. Peel off the backing paper and arrange eight stars on each burgundy rectangle. Iron in place using a pressing cloth. Using gold thread, machine around the edge of each appliqué star and work a spiral over the centres of the three largest shapes. Sew a thick sprinkling of beads to the background with double thread.

2 Join one wide and one narrow gold velvet strip to the long sides of each burgundy panel, using a 1 cm/½ in seam allowance. Attach a panel to each end of the black velvet, joining the narrow gold strip to the main scarf. Iron all seams open lightly, using a cloth. Cut the lining fabric in half lengthways and join to form one long strip. Press the seam open, then pin the cotton lining to the scarf along the long edges with right sides facing. Stitch, leaving a 12.5 cm/5 in opening in the centre of one seam. Remove the pins and adjust the ends so that an equal amount of velvet lies on each side of the lining. Pin, then stitch across the ends. Clip the corners and turn the scarf to the right side. Press lightly and slip stitch the opening.

Star-spangled Banner

Make a bold statement with this cheerful wall hanging, based on an American bed quilt from 1876.

You Will Need

Materials

tracing paper
fusible bonding web, 76 x 142 cm/30 x 56 in
white cotton fabric, 30 x 40 cm/12 x 16 in
blue cotton fabric, 76 x 40 cm/30 x 16 in
matching sewing thread
dark red cotton fabric, 76 x 38 cm/30 x 15 in
medium weight wadding (batting), 66 x 66 cm/26 x 26 in
6 curtain rings, 2.5 cm/1 in
curtain pole with decorative finials, 86 cm/34 in
acrylic paints: dark red and cream
red cord, 130 cm/50 in

Equipment

pencil
dressmaker's scissors
iron
dressmaker's pins
sewing machine
needle
tacking (basting) thread or safety pins
paintbrush

1 Trace the star template from the back of the book, enlarging if necessary. Transfer it to fusible bonding nine times and cut out. Iron them on to white fabric, then cut out and peel off the backing paper. Cut nine 14 cm/5½ in blue cotton squares and fuse a star to the centre of each.

2 Neaten the edges of the stars by stitching over them with a narrow satin stitch in white thread. Cut out four red and four white rectangles, each 7.5 x 14 cm/3 x 5½ in. Press all seams flat and join the red and white pieces in pairs along the longer sides.

3 Lay the squares alternating with the blue star squares as a border around the central star. Pin and sew together in three rows of three, then join the rows to form a square. Cut out four red and four white rectangles, each 7.5 x 40 cm/3 x 15½ in, and join in pairs along the longer sides.

4 With right sides together, stitch a blue square to each end of two of the rectangles. Stitch the remaining pieces to opposite sides of the central panel, with the white sides on the inner edge, then stitch the longer strips to the other two sides.

5 Cut 66 cm/26 in squares of wadding (batting) and blue cotton and tack (baste) to the patchwork with tacking (basting) thread or safety pins. Machine or hand quilt along the seam lines, then stitch all round the outside, 3 mm/⅛ in from the edge. Trim.

6 From the remaining blue cotton, cut four strips, each 3 x 66 cm/1¼ x 26 in for the binding. Iron in half lengthways, then press under 5 mm/¼ in along one edge. Pin each strip along one side of the quilted square, raw edges even, and stitch. Turn the folded edge to the back and slip stitch in place. Neaten the corners.

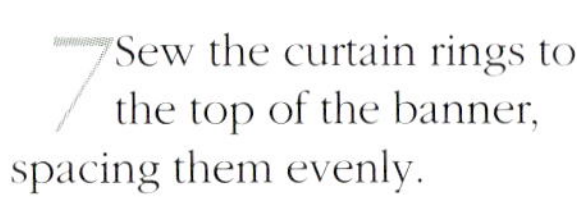

7 Sew the curtain rings to the top of the banner, spacing them evenly.

8 Remove the finials from the curtain pole and paint dark red, using a dry brush for a dragged effect. Paint cream stripes or details on the turned ends. Thread the pole through the rings and replace the finials. Attach the cord to one end of the pole and wrap it round, securing with matching cotton. Do the same with the other end, then make a loop in the centre.

Spice-scented Pot Stand

The lovely homespun look of this pot stand is achieved by tinting all the fabrics with tea. Placing a hot pot on the mat releases a rich, spicy scent of cloves.

You Will Need

Materials

calico, 18 x 18 cm/7 x 7 in
red gingham, 22 x 44 cm/9 x 18 in
blue ticking, 6 x 22 cm/2½ x 9 in
small blue check cotton, 6 x 22 cm/2½ x 9 in
tea bags
tracing paper
stencil card
masking tape
yellow-ochre stencil crayon
paper towels
stranded embroidery threads: yellow-ochre and beige
4 buttons
matching sewing thread
whole cloves

Equipment

bowl
iron
pencil
craft knife
cutting mat
metal ruler
masking tape
stencil brush
dressmaker's pins
needle
sewing machine

1 Wash all the fabrics to remove any dressing. Brew some strong tea and soak the fabrics until you are satisfied with the colour. It is best to do this in stages, re-dipping if you need to make them darker. Allow to dry and press well.

2 Trace the star template from the back of the book, enlarging if necessary. Transfer it to stencil card. Cut out the star using a craft knife and a ruler.

3 Tape the stencil in the centre of the calico. Work around the card with the stencil crayon, scribbling the paint near the edges of the shape, avoiding getting any on the fabric. Work the stencil brush into the crayon and gently ease the paint from the stencil on to the fabric with a light scrubbing action. Add more paint if necessary. Do not try to get an even coverage as this adds to the "antique" effect.

4 Iron the calico on the wrong side between sheets of paper towels to fix the motif and blot excess paint. Fold under the edges of the calico fabric until it measures 11.5 x 12 cm/4½ x 4¾ in. Press.

5 Pin the calico in the centre of one gingham square. With your fingers, gently fray one long edge of the ticking and check strips and pin them to opposite sides of the gingham, with the frayed edges pointing inwards.

6 Using three strands of yellow thread, stitch the strips to the gingham with a running stitch near the frayed edges. Using beige thread and running stitch, attach the calico square and sew a button in each corner. With wrong sides together, machine stitch the second gingham square to the decorated square, leaving an opening in one side.

7 Turn the holder to the right side and fill it with cloves. Do not overfill or the pot will be unsteady when resting on the mat. Neatly sew up the opening by hand.

Oranges Tea Towel

Appliquéd shapes and machine embroidery make a hard-wearing decoration for bright tea towels. Choose a strong base shade to match your own kitchen colour scheme, or use these motifs on a set of towels in different colours.

You Will Need

Materials	Equipment
tracing paper	*pencil*
thin card or paper	*scissors*
fusible bonding web	*iron*
scraps of yellow, orange and green cotton fabric	*tailor's chalk*
tea towel	*embroidery hoop*
black machine embroidery thread	*sewing machine, with darning foot*
	needle

1 Trace the template from the back of the book, enlarging if necessary. Transfer it to thin card or paper and cut out the orange and lemon motifs. Draw around each motif several times on the paper backing of fusible bonding web. Cut out roughly. Iron the web on to the wrong side of the fabric scraps and cut neatly around the outlines.

2 Arrange the shapes along the bottom of both ends of the tea towel until you are happy with your design. Remove the paper backing from the fusible bonding web and iron the motifs on to the towel.

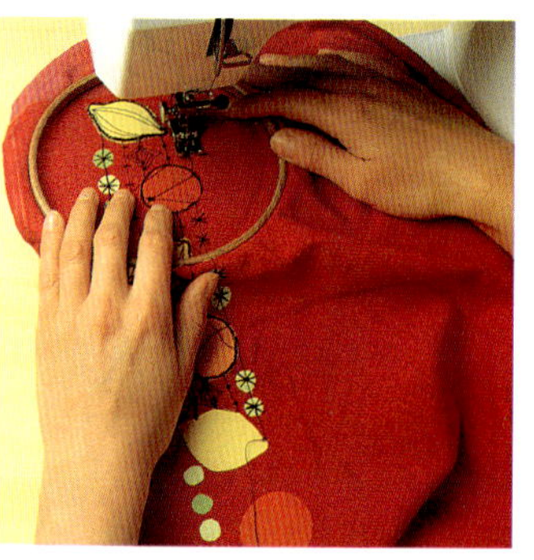

3 Use tailor's chalk to join up the motifs with a series of parallel lines. Put the work in an embroidery hoop. Select the darning or free embroidery mode on the sewing machine and work several lines of black stitching around each fruit. Work down the chalk lines with a series of small embroidered motifs. Hand sew French knots on the oranges.

Shaker Towel

Cross-stitched hearts and initials conjure up the art of the Shakers, for whom the heart was a well-loved decorative image. Hearts denoted not the traditions of romantic love, but the spiritual devotion of the movement's followers, summed up in the saying "Hands to work, hearts to God."

You Will Need

Materials

homespun cotton gingham, 20 x 90 cm/8 x 36 in
cotton seersucker towel
tacking (basting) thread
stranded embroidery threads: dark and light crimson and dark turquoise
matching sewing thread

Equipment

dressmaker's scissors
tape measure
needle
embroidery hoop
iron
dressmaker's pins
sewing machine (optional)

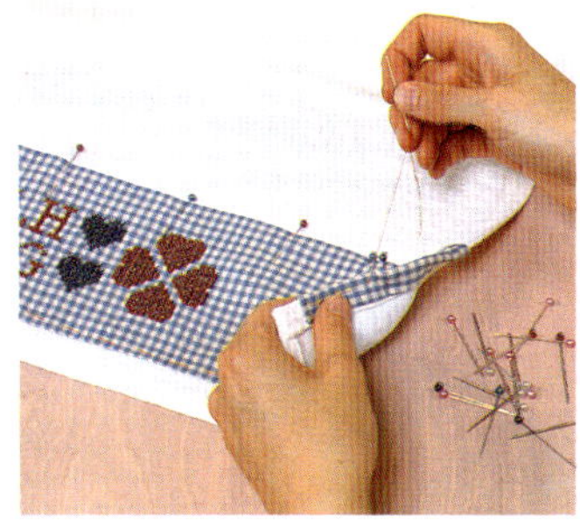

1 Wash the gingham and towel. Cut the gingham 5 cm/2 in wider than the towel. Mark the centre with two intersecting lines of tacking (basting) thread. Stretch the fabric in a hoop. Using the charts at the back of the book, embroider four initials in three strands of dark crimson thread. Work the second diagonal in the same direction each time.

2 Again, following the charts, embroider the four dark turquoise hearts in cross stitch on each side of the monogram. Then work the light crimson hearts. These are given extra definition with an outline of running stitch, worked in dark crimson thread. Press the embroidery lightly.

3 Trim the long edges so that there is 3.5 cm/1½ in of fabric on each side of the embroidery and press under 1 cm/½ in along each side. Fold the towel in half to find the centre point and pin the gingham along the bottom edge. Turn the sides of the gingham to the back of the towel and tack (baste) in place. Then stitch with matching thread.

Needlepoint Mat

In the 1950s, leaves were a great inspiration to designers, who turned them into almost abstract shapes. The muted colours of this needlepoint are also expressive of the period.

You Will Need

Materials

tacking (basting) thread
needlepoint canvas square
tapestry wools: 3 shades of cream, 2 shades of green, yellow, gold and black
card
black velvet, for backing
PVA (white) glue

Equipment

needle
fabric marker
tapestry needle
scissors
metal ruler
craft knife
cutting mat

1 Tack (baste) vertically and horizontally across the canvas to mark the centre. Mark the design on to the canvas, following the chart at the back of the book; each square represents a stitch. Work the pattern in half cross stitch.

2 When the half cross stitch is complete, use black wool to embroider the details. Work the straight lines in back stitch and use French knots for the dots.

3 Measure the needlepoint and cut out a piece of card to the same size. Cut out a piece of velvet to this size plus a 2 cm/¾ in turning allowance all round. Spread glue on the card and stick it centrally on to the back of the velvet. Clip the corners, fold over the turning allowance and glue in place. Trim the canvas and clip the corners; turn the allowance to the wrong side. Spread glue on the wrong side of the card and press the needlepoint in place.

APPLIQUE STAR CARD

A beautiful birthday card to treasure, in which the traditional craft of tin-punching is combined with appliqué and embroidery.

YOU WILL NEED

MATERIALS

light blue check cotton, 16 x 12 cm/6 x 4¾ in
medium blue check cotton, 10 x 12 cm/4 x 4¾ in
blue stranded embroidery thread
dark blue check cotton, 4 x 16 cm/1½ x 6 in
tacking (basting) thread
silver embroidery thread
plain, unridged tin can, 14 x 24 cm/5½ x 9½ in
tracing paper
small piece of wood
all-purpose glue
silver card, folded in half

EQUIPMENT

dressmaker's scissors
dressmaker's pins
needle
can opener
tin snips
pencil
hammer
bradawl or large nail

1 Cut the light blue fabric into four 4 cm/1½ in strips. Fold under the raw edge along the long side of each strip and pin it to the medium blue fabric. Using blue embroidery thread, sew small running stitches close to the fold line on both edges.

2 Cut out four 4 cm/1½ in squares of dark blue fabric. Turn under the edges of each square and pin in each corner of the panel. Turn under the remaining edges and tack (baste). Sew small running stitches in silver thread around the edges of the corner squares and embroider a simple star in the centre.

3 Remove the top and bottom of the tin can, cut down the back seam with tin snips and flatten. Trace the template from the back of the book, enlarging if necessary. Cut three tin stars and hammer the points flat. Lay the stars right side up on the wood and punch a star shape using the hammer and bradawl. Embroider three stars in silver thread. Glue the panel to the front of the card. Glue the tin stars in position.

Applique Notebook

Stitch a delicate appliquéd cover for a special diary, address book or birthday book. This design is appropriate for a gardening or cookery notebook.

You Will Need

Materials

scraps of plain cream, green check and orange patterned cotton fabrics
hardback notebook
tracing paper
fusible bonding web
stranded embroidery threads: green, orange and cream
green cotton fabric
tacking (basting) thread
matching sewing thread
orange, yellow and green buttons

Equipment

dressmaker's scissors
pencil
iron
embroidery needle
needle
sewing machine

1 Cut a rectangle of cream fabric slightly smaller than the front of your notebook. Trace the template from the back of the book, enlarging it to fit the notebook. Trace the shapes on to the backing paper of the fusible bonding web and cut out roughly. Iron the pieces on to their respective fabrics, then cut out.

2 Peel off the backing paper and iron on to the cream fabric. Chain stitch around the leaves in green. Work the urn handles in orange, and chain stitch around it. Cut the green fabric for the cover: the width is four times that of the book and the depth 2.5 cm/1 in more. Press under a 2.5cm/1 in fold at each short edge.

3 Fold in half, wrong sides together, and wrap around the book. Tuck the loose fabric under the front cover and stitch the embroidered panel on the centre front. Fold all the flaps underneath the book covers and loosely tack (baste) the raw edges together at top and bottom. Slip the cover off and machine stitch along the tacked lines. Turn the cover right side out and press. Sew the buttons on to the tree.

Hand Towel and Washcloth

Transform a plain white hand towel and washcloth into an individual gift set, by adding appliquéd pansies in velvet and cotton prints.

You Will Need

Materials

tracing paper
velvet, 20 x 15 cm/8 x 6 in
medium-weight iron-on interfacing
3 different cotton floral print fabrics
tacking (basting) thread
matching embroidery thread
white cotton tea towel and washcloth
machine embroidery threads: matching and white

Equipment

pencil
iron
fabric marker
dressmaker's scissors
dressmaker's pins
needle
sewing machine

1 Trace the templates from the back of the book, enlarging if necessary. Back the velvet with interfacing. Transfer the pansy to the interfacing and cut out three large and one small petal shape from the backed velvet. Cut one large flower shape from each of the three floral prints and one small flower from one of them.

2 Pin and tack (baste) the shapes to the flowers. With matching thread and satin stitch, stitch around the edge of the inner petals. Embroider details on to the flowers. Fill in the centre of each pansy with satin stitch and sew the petal markings with two lines of stem or back stitch. Iron the interfacing on to the back of each flower.

3 Tack (baste) flowers on the towel and cloth. Using matching thread on top and a white spool, appliqué in place.

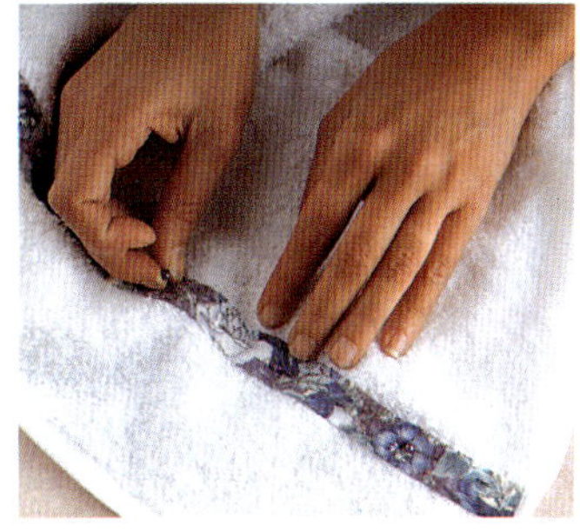

4 Cover the towel borders with strips of floral fabric. Cut a piece 4 cm/1½ in wide to fit from the edge to the pansies with an allowance of 1 cm/½ in at each end. Press, pin and tack (baste) in place. Zigzag to finish.

Appliquéd Sheet and Pillowcase

This bold design gives bedlinen a unique appeal. The shapes can be cut from either patterned or checked fabrics, according to your personal taste.

You Will Need

Materials	Equipment
tracing paper	*pencil*
graph paper	*dressmaker's scissors*
fusible bonding web	*tape measure*
coloured or patterned fabrics	*iron*
sheet and pillowcase	*dressmaker's pins*
matching machine embroidery thread	*sewing machine*

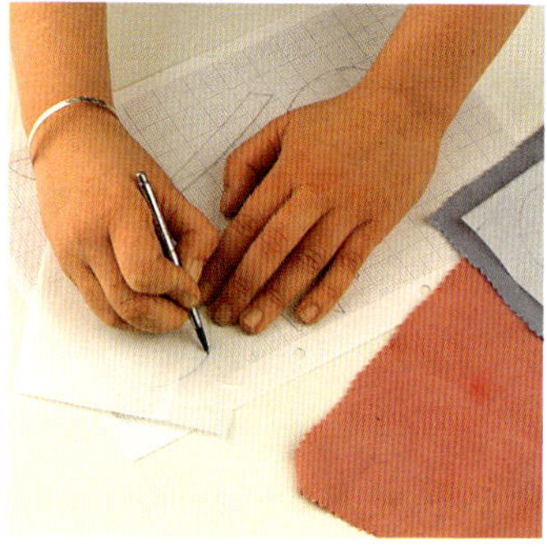

1 Trace selected fabric patterns (or use the template from this book), enlarging as necessary for your design. Cut a piece of bonding web 25 x 25 cm/ 10 x 10 in. Lay it over the designs, and, with paper side facing, trace along the outlines.

2 Cut four or five pieces of the fabric to squares, each about 20 x 20 cm/8 x 8 in. Iron the bonding web on to the wrong side of the fabric and cut the shapes out.

3 Peel away the backing paper and arrange the cut-outs on the sheet and pillowcase, parallel to the fabric edge. Pin in place, then iron over the pieces, removing the pins as you go.

4 Work a zigzag machine stitch all around the fused edges to complete the design.

Child's T-shirt

An ordinary T-shirt is transformed, with appliquéd fabric scraps, machine embroidery and beads, into something really special. There's no reason why the same idea couldn't be used for an adult-size T-shirt.

You Will Need

Materials

tracing paper
unbleached cotton T-shirt
fusible bonding web, 30 x 30 cm/12 x 12 in
yellow, orange and brown cotton fabric scraps
machine embroidery threads: light orange and brown
small orange beads

Equipment

pencil
dressmaker's scissors
iron
pressing cloth
sewing machine

1 Trace the template from the back of the book, enlarging it to fit the T-shirt. Number the petals consecutively 1–12. Trace the even-numbered petals on to the paper side of the bonding and cut out. Iron the bonding to the yellow cotton. Repeat with the other petals in orange, and with brown for the centre.

2 Cut out all the shapes around the outlines and remove the backing paper. Place the petals in a circle on the front of the T-shirt, using the template as a guide. Iron them in place, using a cool iron and a pressing cloth.

3 Thread the sewing machine with orange thread and set it to a closely spaced medium-size zigzag. Stitch around the edges of all the petals to conceal the raw edges. Iron the flower centre in position and sew around its circumference with brown thread. Using brown thread, sew the beads on to the flower centre, making sure they are evenly scattered.

Initial Cushion

Adapt this design by using the initials of a special person or a couple as the centrepiece. It would make an ideal wedding gift, and a larger version could even include the couple's full names and the date and location of their wedding.

You Will Need

Materials
stranded embroidery threads
cream cross stitch fabric, 15 x 15 cm, 8 holes per cm/ 6 x 6 in, 18 holes per in
cream silk backing fabric
thread
polyester wadding (batting)
cream cotton lace, 1 m x 6 cm/1 yd x 2½ in
4 mother-of-pearl buttons

Equipment
needle
dressmaker's scissors
dressmaker's pins
tape measure

1 Following the chart at the back of the book, or using an alphabet of your own, embroider the initials on to the cross stitch fabric. Work in cross stitch, using two strands of thread. Make sure that the four letters are squared up.

2 Cut the backing fabric to the same size as the front piece of the cushion. Pin with right sides together. Allowing a seam of 1 cm/½ in, stitch together, leaving a 5 cm/2 in gap at one edge. Trim the seam allowance and clip the corners. Turn inside out and stuff firmly. Slip stitch the opening.

3 Join the ends of the lace together and run a neat gathering thread along the straight edge. Gather the thread to fit around the outside of the cushion and pin it in place, allowing for extra fullness at the corners. Oversew the lace on to the cushion with matching thread, using small, neat stitches. Finish off by sewing a button to each corner.

COUNTRY-STYLE PILLOWCASE

Customize some plain bedlinen and give it a country appeal with this charming heart design. Emphasize the hearts and raise the design with a halo of multi-coloured running stitches.

YOU WILL NEED

MATERIALS

iron-on interfacing, 25 x 25 cm/10 x 10 in
brightly coloured fabric scraps
tacking (basting) thread
pillowcase
matching and contrasting threads

EQUIPMENT

pencil or fabric marker
dressmaker's scissors
iron
needle
dressmaker's pins
crewel needle

1 Draw 17 hearts on to the interfacing and cut them out. Iron the interfacing to the fabric scraps and cut out the shapes, leaving a 5 mm/¼ in seam allowance.

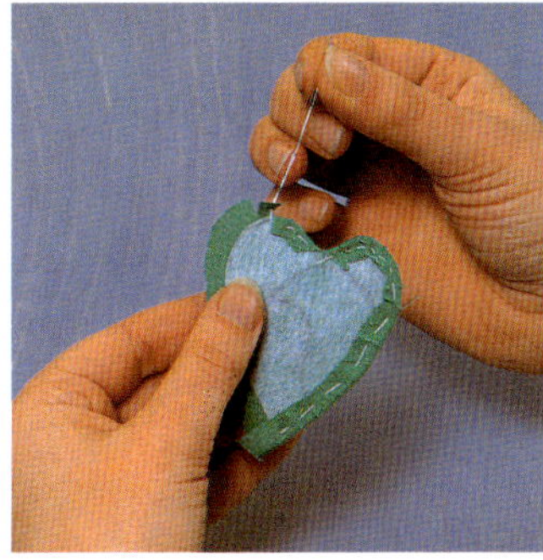

2 Clip the seam allowance around the curves, fold over and tack (baste) in place.

3 Arrange the hearts randomly over the pillowcase. Pin, tack (baste) and then slip stitch them in place. Using an assortment of coloured threads in one strand, work lines of tiny stitches around each heart in halos. Iron to finish the design.

MODELLING AND SALT DOUGH

Modelling is a craft particularly suitable for children of any age, as it is soft, safe and a lot of fun to do. The modelling projects in this section use polymer clay, self-hardening clay and salt dough. Working with salt dough has the added attraction that children can take an active part in preparing and baking the dough, as well as shaping it as they wish. When buying commercial modelling materials for use by children, look particularly for non-toxic varieties.

Children and adults alike will find plenty of inspiration within these next pages. There are projects to suit all abilities, ranging from simple and effective motifs that can be stamped on to clay or salt dough using pastry cutters, to more technically challenging three-dimensional creations.

Materials and Equipment

Modelling with self-hardening clay or salt dough requires very little in the way of materials and equipment, and you will probably already have the basic items at home. You should work on a clean, smooth, flat surface, and take care to keep sharp implements, glues, paints and varnish well out of the reach of children. Polymer clay (see picture) is a highly adaptable modelling medium that comes in a dazzling array of colours.

Right *Salt dough is economical to make and easy to use - yet produces wonderfully decorative results. Here you can see a selection of special pastry cutters from the wide range now available.*

Tinting dough and clay

Food colouring is ideal for use on salt dough, and it is available in liquid and paste form. The paste is easier to use and more than one colour can be added to the dough to produce the shade required. Self-hardening clay can be bought from craft suppliers in a variety of colours, or you can colour it with paints and varnishes. Salt dough, too, can be decorated with paints and varnishes.

Left *Polymer clay is a versatile, easy-to-handle medium that can be used to make objects as diverse as picture frames and jewellery. Once shaped, it can be baked hard at low temperature in a domestic oven.*

SALT DOUGH RECIPE

Salt dough recipe

Simply follow the method below, adjusting the quantities to make the amount of salt dough you need. The quantities given here are sufficient to make a bowl with a diameter of about 23 cm/9 in.

The addition of 15 ml/1 tbsp vegetable oil to the recipe adds suppleness, while 10 ml/1 tbsp wallpaper paste gives the dough elasticity.

INGREDIENTS

230 g/8 oz/2 cups plain flour
200 g/7 oz/1 cup salt
250 ml/8 fl oz/1 cup water

Raw dough

Once the dough has been kneaded, it is pliable and easily manipulated, suitable for even intricate details.

Remember that salt dough is susceptible to steam and damp, so always keep your creations in a dry atmosphere to prevent deterioration.

1 Mix together the flour, salt and half the water in a mixing bowl. Knead the mixture, gradually adding more water until the dough has a smooth, firm consistency. Be careful not to add too much water or the dough will sag and become sticky.

2 Remove the dough from the bowl and continue to knead for 10 minutes. The dough can be modelled immediately, but is best left to rest for 30 minutes in an airtight container. Bake the salt dough in an oven at 120°C/ 250°F/Gas 1/2 until the dough is completely hardened all over.

Working with salt dough and clay

Dough and clay can be rolled out flat with a rolling pin. Work directly on baking parchment if you are using salt dough, otherwise work on a clean, flat surface. A small, craft knife or clay modelling tool is indispensable for cutting dough and clay and indenting details. A cocktail stick, knitting needle or thick sewing needle is also useful, and can be used to pierce holes for hanging or decorating models. Make any holes about 3 mm/1/8 in wider than needed to allow for any distortion during painting and varnishing.

Various bowls, plates and dishes make suitable moulds for modelling (if the dough is to be baked, then the mould must be heat-resistant). Also, there is an exciting range of beautiful pastry moulds, biscuit cutters and icing cutters that can all be used to great effect.

LEFT *Rolling out salt dough on baking parchment.*

Wheatsheaf

The wonderful golden colour of baked salt dough lends itself beautifully to the theme of a sheaf of wheat. This makes an ideal decoration for a kitchen wall, but keep it away from steam.

You Will Need

Materials

tracing paper
salt dough (see Salt Dough Recipe)
baking parchment
polyurethane satin varnish

Equipment

pencil
rolling pin
craft knife
clay modelling tool (optional)
baking tray
paintbrush

1 Trace the template from the back of the book, enlarging if necessary. Roll out the dough flat on baking parchment to a thickness of 1 cm/½ in. Use the template to cut the wheatsheaf shape. To make the stalks, roll out thin spaghetti-like strands of dough to a length of about 12 cm/5 in and build them up into a bundle as shown. Moisten the strands with a little water to prevent them from drying out.

2 To make the tie for the bundle, roll four strands of dough to a length of 12 cm/5 in. Join the ends together with a little water and gently separate out the strands. Lay the first strand over the second, and the third over the fourth. Then lay what is now the third strand back over the second strand. Repeat these two steps until the plait (braid) is complete. Pinch the bottom ends together, using a little water to moisten and stick in place.

3 Moisten one side of the plait (braid) and place it over the stalks at the narrowest point. Tuck the ends of the plait (braid) neatly under to conceal them. Reserve sufficient salt dough to make the "ears" of the wheatsheaf.

4 Roll sausages from the salt dough, measuring 3 x 1 cm/ 1¼ x ⅜ in. Taper the rolls at one end and flatten them slightly. Use a knife or modelling tool to mark separate grains, curving the edges of each one. Moisten and apply the ears of wheat in overlapping layers. Place the wheatsheaf, on the baking parchment, on a tray and bake at 120°C/250°F/ Gas ½, for 10 hours. Allow to cool. Apply five layers of the satin varnish.

Gingerbread Hearts

The designs of these Germanic hearts are based on edible gingerbread and fondant cakes. They are formed from a salt dough base with painted motifs applied in contrasting and complementary patterns.

You Will Need

Materials	Equipment
tracing paper	*pencil*
paper or thin card	*scissors*
salt dough (see Salt Dough Recipe)	*rolling pin*
baking parchment	*craft knife*
metal eyelet loop	*aspic cutters*
acrylic gesso or matt emulsion (latex) paint	*baking tray*
acrylic or craft paints	*paintbrushes*
polyurethane matt varnish	
paper ribbon	

1 Trace the gingerbread heart template from the back of the book, enlarging if necessary. Transfer it to paper or thin card and cut out. Roll an orange-size ball of salt dough out flat on baking parchment to 1 cm/½ in thick. Place the template on the dough and cut around the edge. Pat the raw edges to round them. Roll some more dough to 5 mm/¼ in thick and cut out shapes with aspic cutters. Moisten the border of the main heart shape and apply the small shapes. Fix the eyelet loop to the top of the heart. Place the model, on the baking parchment, on a tray and bake at 120°C/250°F/Gas ½, for nine hours. Allow to cool.

2 Paint on an undercoat of acrylic gesso or matt emulsion (latex) and allow to dry. Pick out the applied decoration with bright acrylic or craft paints, using a fine paintbrush to avoid getting paint on the base heart. When dry, apply five layers of matt varnish, allowing each coat to dry between layers. Cut a 40 cm/16 in length of paper ribbon, thread it through the eyelet and tie in a reef knot about 10 cm/4 in from the heart. Unravel the ribbon and cut out a chevron shape from each end.

HANGING SHAPES

Abstract astrological symbols are combined to create an original mobile, decorated with glass panels and beads that will catch the light as the pieces swing in the breeze.

YOU WILL NEED

MATERIALS

tracing paper
thin card or paper
1.5 kg/3 lb modelling clay
5 glass circles, 5 mm/¼ in thick, 5 cm/2 in in diameter
1 glass circle, 5 mm/¼ in thick, 3 cm/1¼ in in diameter
0.8 mm copper wire
glass beads in a mixture of colours and sizes
sandpaper
10 cm/4 in thin wire, 2 m/2 yd
2 mm galvanized wire

EQUIPMENT

pencil
scissors
rolling pin
clay modelling tools
polythene bag
wire-cutters
jewellery pliers
needle

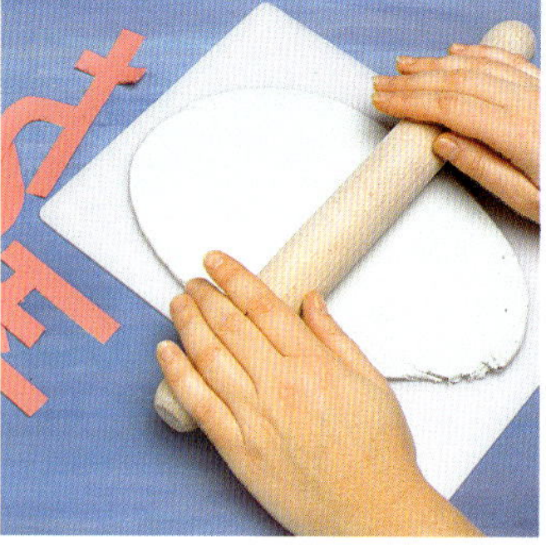

1 Trace the templates from the back of the book, enlarging if necessary. Transfer to thin card or paper and cut out. Roll out the modelling clay to a flat sheet 5 mm/¼ in thick.

2 Place one shape on to the clay sheet and cut around it with a modelling tool. Return any excess clay to a polythene bag to keep moist. With wet fingers, smooth all the surfaces and edges of the shape.

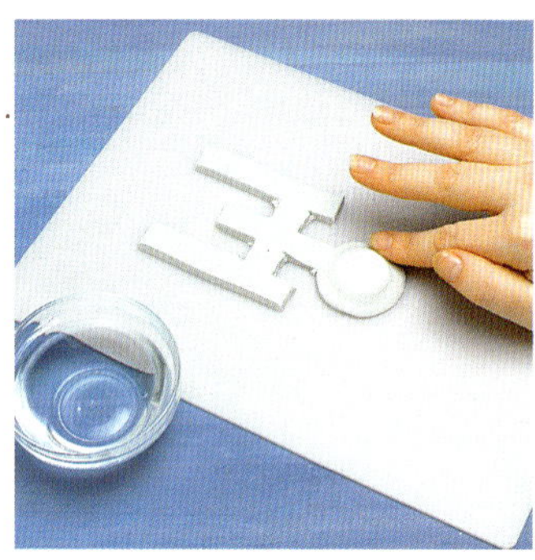

3 Lift up the circular part of the clay shape and hold it gently while positioning a circle of glass centrally underneath. (Use the damp mark left by the clay on the work surface as a guide.) Press the clay around the glass circle with wet fingers.

4 Cut out a circle of clay to reveal the glass, leaving a 3 mm/⅛ in border.

5 Cut the copper wire in half and twist it into two small spirals using pliers. Press gently into the surface of the clay.

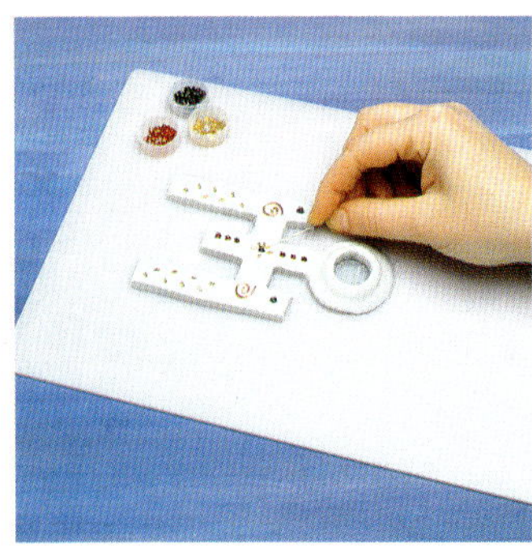

6 Use a needle to help you lift and position the coloured glass beads and press them into the clay.

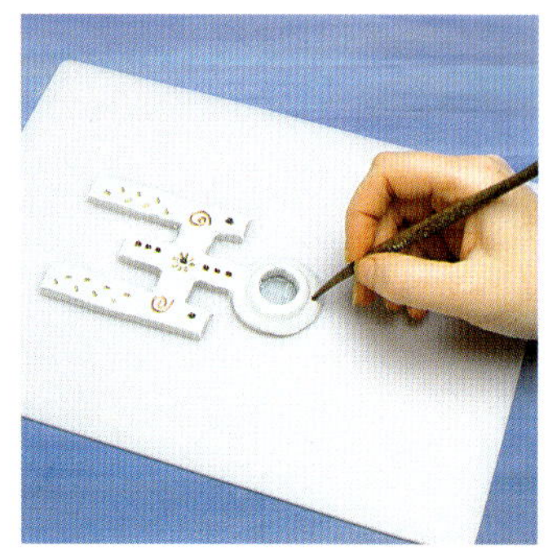

7 Pierce a small hole in the top and bottom of the piece and allow to dry thoroughly. Repeat the process with the other shapes.

8 Once the pieces have fully dried and hardened, sand down all the edges.

9 Use thin wire to join all the shapes together and then hang them from a galvanized wire hanger.

Spider Buttons

Brighten up a child's coat (or your own!) with these friendly spiders. Use the metal buttons that are sold for covering in fabric and match the size to your buttonholes. Snap the fronts on to the button backs before you start to decorate them. You can coat the baked buttons with a gloss varnish, if you wish.

You Will Need

Materials

polymer clay: bright green, black and white
set of metal buttons
clear gloss varnish (optional)

Equipment

rolling pin
craft knife
cutting mat
paintbrush (optional)

1 Roll the green clay out thinly and cut a circle large enough to cover the button. Mould the clay over the button.

2 Using black clay, roll very thin strands for the legs and press them on to the button. Roll a finer strand for the spider's thread.

3 Roll a pea-size ball of black clay and press it into the centre of the button for the spider's body.

4 Roll two small balls of white clay and press in position to make the eyes. Make the pupils from tiny black balls. Bake in a low oven, following the manufacturer's instructions.

STAR FRAME

A plain frame can be transformed by decorating it with brightly painted cut-out shapes. The result is guaranteed to cheer up any wall.

YOU WILL NEED

MATERIALS

tracing paper
salt dough (see Salt Dough Recipe)
baking parchment
fine-grade sandpaper
acrylic gesso
emulsion (latex) paints
PVA (white) glue
wooden frame
polyurethane satin varnish

EQUIPMENT

pencil
rolling pin
craft knife
baking tray
paintbrushes

1 Trace the template from the back of the book, enlarging if necessary. Roll out the dough and cut out the star shapes. Place the stars, on baking parchment, on a tray and bake at 120°C/250°F/Gas ½, for five hours. Allow to cool.

2 Sand all of the baked stars with fine-grade sandpaper.

3 Paint each star with gesso and allow to dry. Decorate the stars with a coat of emulsion (latex) paint as a base colour. Allow to dry thoroughly.

4 Paint patterns in other colours on the stars. Glue the stars to the frame. Finish with a coat of satin varnish.

Engraved Mirror Frame

The zodiac stands for the wheeling of the seasons as the sun appears to circle the earth, and astrologers draw it as a circle, with each of the twelve sections presided over by its familiar sign. Here, the ancient calendar is the inspiration for a stunning engraved frame. Secure the hook firmly to the back of the frame to support the weight of the mirror.

You Will Need

Materials

pencil
thin card or paper
1 kg/2¼ lb modelling clay
3 mm/⅛ in thick circular mirror, cut to 15 cm/6 in in diameter
acrylic paints: deep turquoise, white, lemon-yellow and purple
matt varnish
hook
epoxy resin glue

Equipment

plate
rolling pin
clay modelling tools
paint-mixing container
paintbrushes

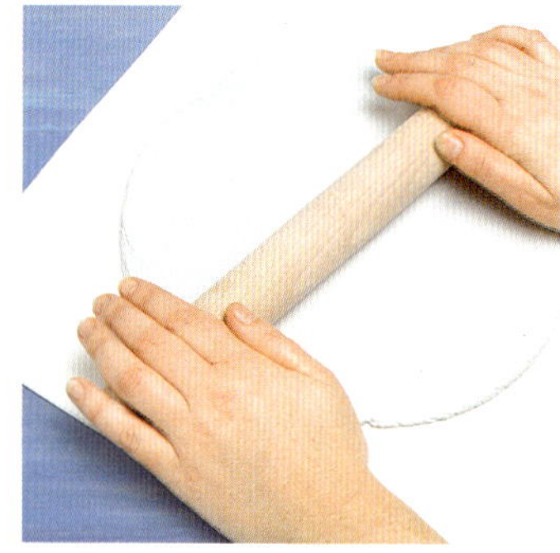

1 Draw around a plate on to thin card or paper to make a template. Roll out the clay to a large flat sheet 5 mm/¼ in thick. Cut two circles of clay.

2 Place the mirror on one of the circles and cut around it. Fit the mirror between the two frames, stretching the clay over the edge of the mirror.

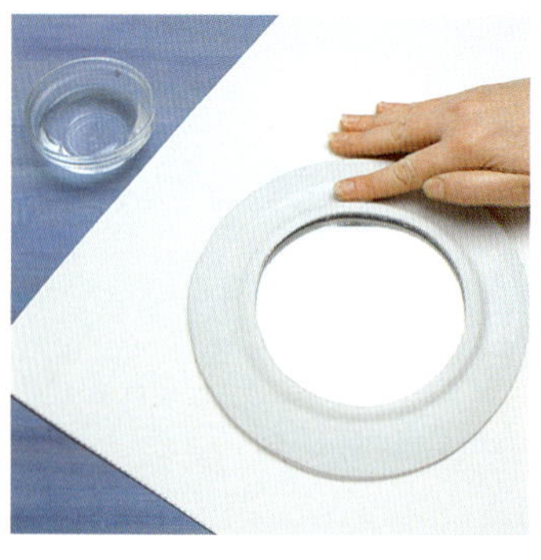

3 Bond the frame by pressing down through both layers with wet fingers at intervals around the outer edge, then smooth the inner and outer edges to leave a neat finish.

4 Trim the inner edge of the frame to leave an overlap of 5 mm/¼ in around the mirror. Neaten with a modelling tool.

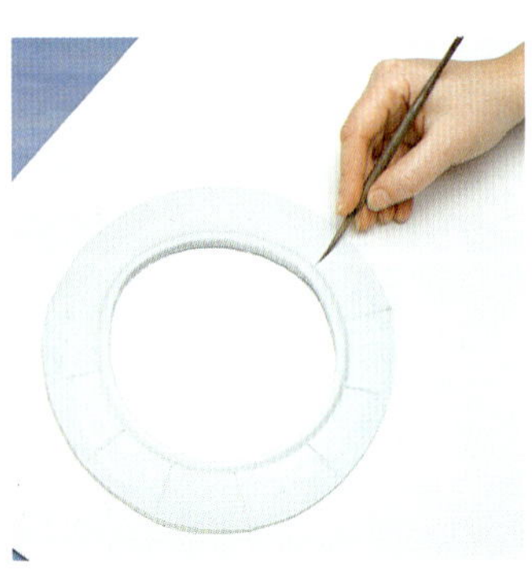

5 Wet and smooth the surface, then divide it into 12 equal sections by engraving straight lines with a wet modelling tool, working from the raised inner border to the edge of the frame.

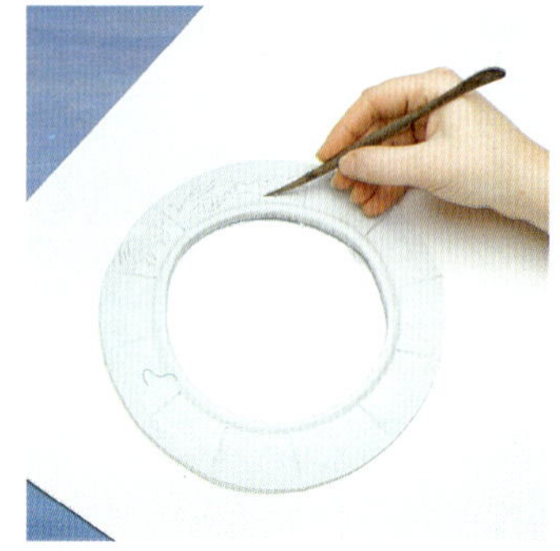

6 Engrave an astrological sign in each section of the frame, following the correct order as shown in the photograph. Allow to harden.

7 Mix turquoise, white and lemon paint, adding water to get a creamy consistency, and paint the frame in two thin coats, allowing the brush strokes to show through. Allow the first coat to dry before applying the second.

8 Mix purple and white paint, this time to a thicker texture, and apply with a wide dry brush so that the engraved figures and raised inner edge remain green. When dry, coat with a layer of clear varnish and attach the hook to the back with epoxy resin glue.

MODELLED MIRROR

A magical frame that uses up little odds and ends you have lying about the house. Use old buttons, beads, shells and even keys.

YOU WILL NEED

MATERIALS

copper wire
strong glue
odds and ends to decorate, such as shells, glass and plastic nuggets
modelling clay
card template, outer diameter 18 cm/7 in, inner diameter 20 cm/4½ in
mirror, 9 cm/3½ in in diameter
2 pieces of aluminium tubing, 1 cm/½ in in diameter, 20 cm/8 in long
small plastic drinks bottle
plaster of Paris
acrylic paints

EQUIPMENT

wire-cutters
round-nosed pliers
rolling pin
acetate sheet
clay modelling tool
craft knife
paintbrushes

1 Cut the wire into lengths and curl into shapes. Glue odds and ends on one end of each wire. Bend the other ends to make a hook.

2 Roll out pieces of clay on the acetate sheet. Use the template to cut two circles, 18 cm/7 in in diameter. Cut a 11.5 cm/4½ in circle from one centre.

3 Place the mirror in the middle of the circle and arrange the wires around the edge, with the decorated ends outwards. Push the hooked ends into the clay. Put one aluminium tube in the position which you want to become the bottom of the mirror frame.

4 Place the clay ring on top and smooth off the overlap around the mirror and the tube with your finger and a little water. Smooth off the sides with the modelling tool. Decorate the front of the frame with small circles of clay. Allow to dry for several days.

5 Cut the bottle in half and make four 5 cm/2 in cuts around the top half of the bottle. Make a hole in the lid. Mix enough plaster of Paris to half-fill the bottle base and pour it in. Push the top of the bottle part-way into the base and push the second aluminium tube through the hole in the bottle lid down into the plaster.

6 When dry, remove the plastic from the plaster. Remove the tube and fit the real tube and mirror into the plaster base. Paint the base, stand and frame with acrylic paints.

Antique Wall Tile

The subtle look of this charming tile is achieved very simply by staining it with tea; wiping the design with colour accentuates the relief and you can repeat it as many times as you like until you get the shade you desire.

You Will Need

Materials	Equipment
tracing paper	*pencil*
450 g/1 lb modelling clay	*rolling pin*
tea bag	*clay modelling tools*
matt varnish	*paintbrush*

1 Trace the template from the back of the book, enlarging if necessary. Roll out the clay to a flat sheet 1 cm/½ in thick.

2 Place the tracing on top of the clay and mark all the lines using a modelling tool.

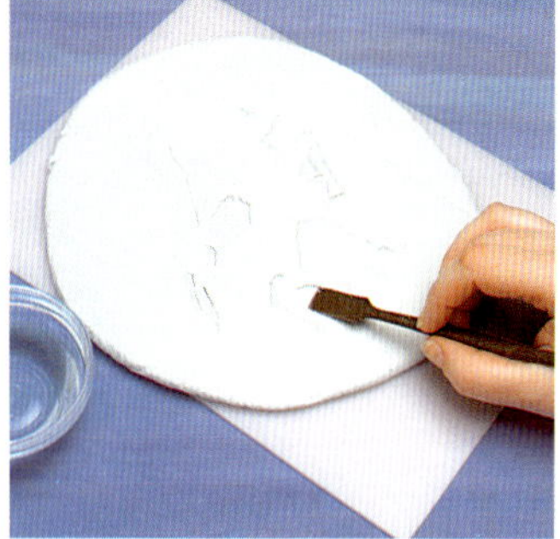

3 Wet the clay surface thoroughly to make it easier to manipulate. Indent the lines of the design, moulding the figure's body to raise it above the background area.

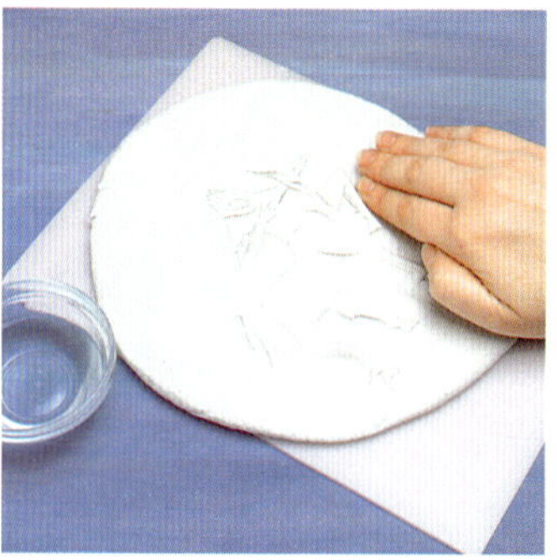

4 Smooth the surface with wet fingers as you work to keep the clay moist.

5 Cut out the tile shape and engrave a double border around the edge to frame the central motif.

6 Stipple the background with the point of a wet modelling tool to create texture. Then leave the tile to harden completely before staining.

7 Brew a strong cup of tea with a tea bag and use it to stain the clay, wiping over the design with the tea bag. When you are satisfied with the colour, allow to dry, then protect the tile with a coat of matt varnish.

Display Case

This purpose-made unit suits the scale of shells and echoes their sinewy curves in its shape. It is the perfect way of displaying beautiful shells, as the aquamarine colour sets off the tints of the shells and is a reminder of the water that is their natural setting. The gold decoration, like sunlight on water, is the perfect finishing touch.

You Will Need

Materials

tracing paper
thin card or paper
modelling clay
acrylic paints: turquoise, white and lemon-yellow
gold powder
clear matt varnish
selection of seashells
epoxy resin glue

Equipment

pencil
rolling pin
polythene sheet (optional)
clay modelling tools
paint-mixing container
small flat-bristled and fine paintbrushes

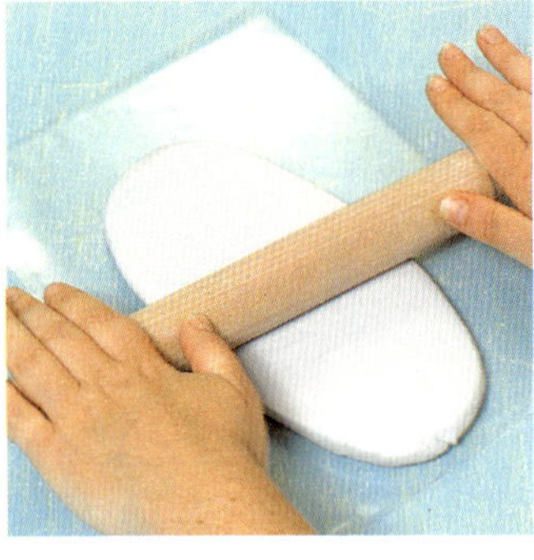

1 Trace the template from the back of the book, enlarging if necessary, and transfer to thin card or paper. Roll out the clay in an approximation of the swirl shape, to 8 mm/⅓ in thick. You may find it helpful to work on a sheet of polythene.

2 Lay the template on the clay and, with a wet modelling tool, cut out the shape for the back of the unit.

3 Roll out long clay snakes and cut them into rectangles about 2.5 cm/1 in wide, with perfectly straight edges, to make the side walls. Attach the walls to the back, moulding, smoothing the join with a wet modelling tool. Make a hole for hanging in the middle "wave" at the top.

4 Roll out and cut shorter rectangles, for the shelves, and attach them to the back and the walls. Use a small piece of clay, smoothed over the joins, to strengthen them. Allow to dry for several days.

5 Mix the acrylic paints to make a sea-green colour. To achieve a slight verdigris effect, do not mix the colours too thoroughly. Paint the inside and outside of the display unit and allow to dry.

6 Mix the gold powder with varnish, varying the amount of varnish depending on the consistency you wish to achieve. Paint the edges of the display case and the waves gold, using a fine paintbrush.

7 Working from the top down, arrange the shells in the compartments and glue them in position.

SALT DOUGH BASKET

Make this delightful wall decoration from simple ingredients you are bound to have in your kitchen already. Salt dough is quite durable once it is varnished, but remember not to hang it anywhere damp or steamy as this may make it crumble slightly.

YOU WILL NEED

MATERIALS

salt dough (see Salt Dough Recipe)
paper bowl
paperclip
aluminium foil
4 cloves
baking parchment
acrylic paints: green, white, yellow, orange, burnt sienna and black
polyurethane satin varnish

EQUIPMENT

rolling pin
craft knife
fork
scissors
cheese grater
heart-shaped pastry cutter
baking tray
paintbrushes

1 Roll out some salt dough to a thickness of 5 mm/¼ in. Cut out a large oval and a half oval. Mark a basket pattern on the dough with a fork.

2 Cut the paper bowl in half and trim to fit the large oval. Place the half dough oval on top of the bowl, moisten the edges and stick to the large oval. Cut 2 cm/¾ in slits along the rim for the ribbon.

3 Use a thinly rolled piece of dough to attach a paperclip to the top of the basket on the reverse side.

4 Roll out two long thin sausages of dough to fit down the side of the basket. Twist them together, moisten the surfaces and stick them to the edge. Make another twist for the other side. Trim and join invisibly at the top and overlap in a "knot" at the bottom of the basket. Make a smaller twisted length for the handle at the top.

5 Roll four walnut-size balls of aluminium foil. Mould some dough over the foil and make two lemon shapes and two oranges. Roll the fruit over a fine grater to simulate the texture of the skin, and insert a clove at the top. Arrange the fruit inside the basket.

6 Roll out some more dough thinly. Cut small rectangles to fit between the slits to look like ribbon. Cut out four heart shapes, then cut them in half and trim to make leaves. Mark the veins with the point of the knife and shape them. Moisten and arrange around the fruit. Place the basket, on baking parchment, on a tray and bake at 120°C/250°F/Gas ½, for eight hours, or until the basket is hardened. Allow to cool.

7 Paint the fruit with acrylic paints. Thin the green paint slightly and paint the leaves. Brush off some of the paint with a stiff, dry brush to add highlights. Paint the ribbon white, then allow to dry thoroughly. Paint in a gingham pattern with yellow, orange and green stripes.

8 Paint the basket with a thin wash of burnt sienna mixed with a little black paint. Brush off the excess with a dry brush. Paint the completed basket with at least two coats of polyurethane satin varnish.

Folk Angel

This plaque-style angel is a perfect model to create from salt dough. On flat pieces of dough, the baking process takes place evenly through the sheet of dough, thus avoiding any hardening inconsistencies.

You Will Need

Materials	Equipment
tracing paper	*pencil*
salt dough (see Salt Dough Recipe)	*scissors*
baking parchment	*rolling pin*
watercolour paints	*craft knife*
polyurethane matt varnish	*dressmaker's pin*
coloured string or fine ribbon	*wire-cutters*
	paperclip
	baking tray
	paintbrushes

1 Trace the template from the back of the book, enlarging if necessary, and cut out. Roll out the salt dough on baking parchment to 1 cm/½ in thick. Place the template on the dough and cut out the shape. Remove the template and pat the cut edges with a moistened finger to neaten them. Replace the template and transfer the details of the design by pricking along the lines with a pin, working on one layer at a time. Lightly moisten the pricked line, then draw along it with the tip of the knife, leaning the blade towards you then away from you to make an inverted division. Prick and indent all the lines.

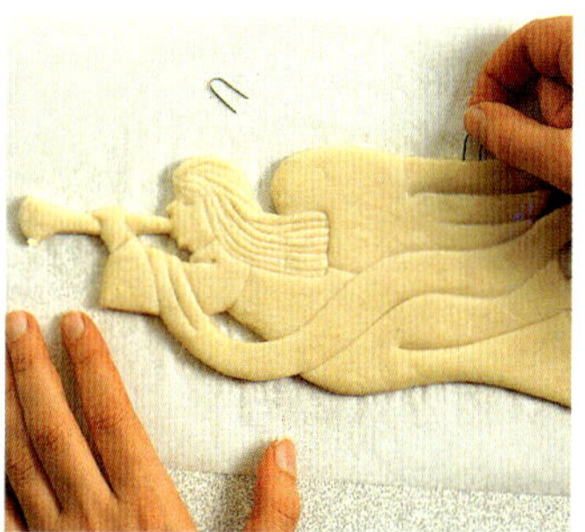

2 Cut a paperclip in half and insert the two outer halves into the edges at the crosses, leaving the loops visible. Bake at 120°C/250°F/Gas ½, for ten hours. Allow to cool.

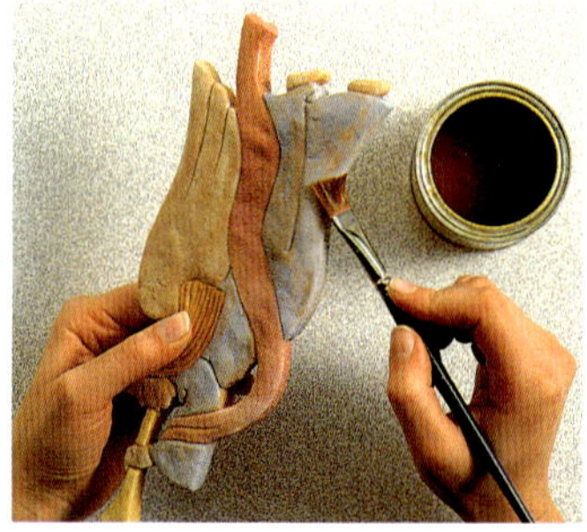

3 Apply the paint thinly to the model, lightening the colours with white. Leave the flesh areas unpainted, but highlight the cheek in pink. Allow to dry. Apply five coats of varnish. Hang up the angel.

Shaker Hand

The unpainted salt dough of this open, friendly hand gives it an amazingly lifelike appearance. The bordered heart motif is typical of the influential Shaker style founded in 18th-century America.

You Will Need

Materials

salt dough (see Salt Dough Recipe)
baking parchment
eyelet loop
polyurethane matt varnish

Equipment

rolling pin
knitting needle
craft knife
heart-shaped cutter (optional)
clay modelling tool
baking tray
paintbrush

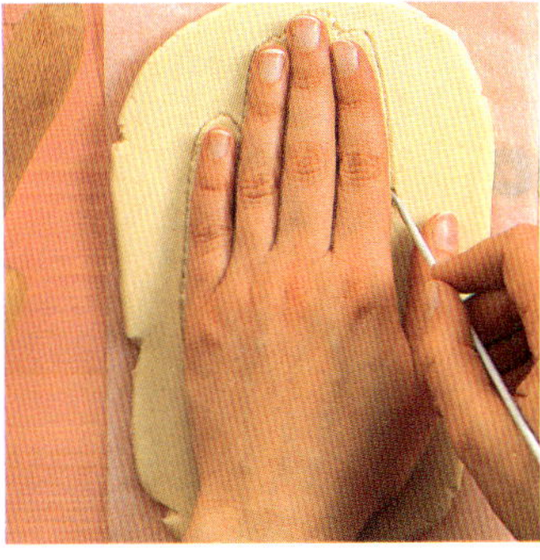

1 Roll out the salt dough on to baking parchment to a thickness of 1.5 cm/⅝ in. Lay your hand flat on to the dough with your fingers together. Use a knitting needle to trace around the edge and mark your fingers, then cut out the outline with a craft knife. Pat the cut edges with a moistened finger to round them.

2 Cut out a heart shape from the palm, either cutting freehand or using a pastry cutter. Turn the hand over and insert an eyelet loop for hanging it up. Bake at 120°C/250°F/Gas ½, for ten hours. Allow to dry, then apply five coats of varnish.

Salt and Pepper Pots

A request to pass the salt will be the starting signal for these eager mobile ladybirds to wheel their way down the table to you. They're based on toy trucks with a friction drive, and are sure to be a big hit at family mealtimes.

You Will Need

Materials

pair of matching toy trucks
stiff card
matching salt and pepper pots
polymer clay: black, red and white
coloured paperclips
epoxy resin glue
clear gloss varnish
enamel paints: red and black

Equipment

screwdriver
pencil
scissors
rolling pin
craft knife
pliers
paintbrushes

1 Undo the fixing screws and remove the body from each toy truck.

2 Mark out two matching templates on card which will fit over the truck chassis and around the bases of the salt and pepper pots, leaving a rim of about 5 mm/¼ in. Cut them out.

3 Roll a piece of black clay thinly to cover the template. Cut to shape. Stand the salt cellar in position on the base and mould a sausage of clay around it.

4 Press a ball of clay on to the front of the template and mould it into shape for the head of the ladybird. Make two holes for the feelers with the end of a paperclip. Remove the pot and template carefully. Make a matching base for the pepper pot in the same way.

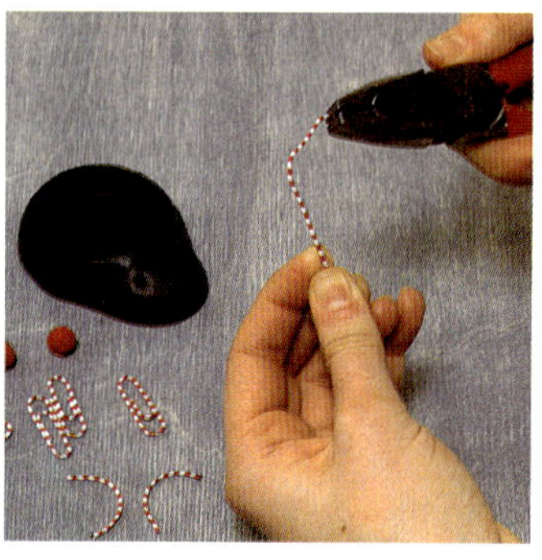

5 Straighten out the paperclips and trim to length to make the feelers. Roll out four small balls of red clay and make a hole in each one with a paperclip. Mould two pairs of eyes from white and black clay.

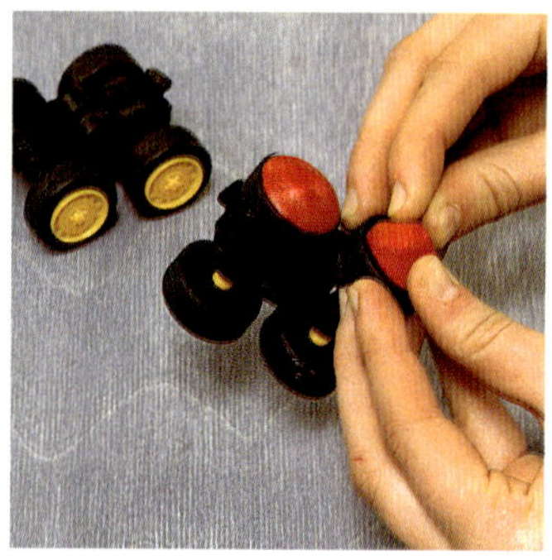

6 Roll a ball of red clay for each truck wheel and press it on, moulding it into a dome shape. Remove carefully.

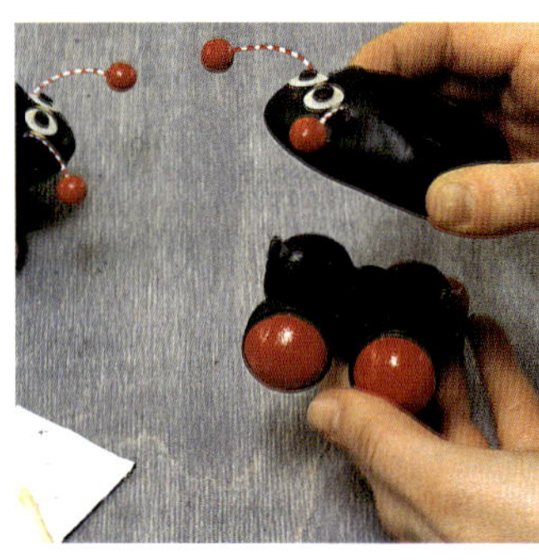

7 Bake the clay elements in a low oven, following the manufacturer's instructions. Fix everything in place with epoxy resin glue, avoiding the drive mechanism in the truck chassis. Varnish the wheel hubs and allow to dry.

8 Paint the salt and pepper pots in bright red. Allow to dry, then add ladybird spots in black. Allow to dry.

WINGED HEART

This salt dough wall decoration is a charming way to tell someone absent that you are thinking of them – with a heart that has, literally, taken wing.

YOU WILL NEED

MATERIALS

salt dough (see Salt Dough Recipe)
baking parchment
aluminium foil
2 screw eyes
acrylic paints: red, white, black, green, blue and gold
clear varnish
length of cord

EQUIPMENT

pencil
scissors
rolling pin
craft knife
clay modelling tools
sponge
paint-mixing container
small and fine paintbrushes

1 Follow the instructions to make the salt dough (see Salt Dough Recipe). Trace the template from the back of the book, enlarging if necessary, on to baking parchment and cut it out.

2 Roll about two-thirds of the dough on to a sheet of baking parchment so that it is about 5 mm/¼ in thick. Put the template on the dough and cut around it with a craft knife. Make a thin roll of dough to fit each side of the background. Moisten the edges and put the rolls in place. Smooth the joints with a modelling tool and finish by moulding a small dough heart for each corner.

3 Using the template as a guide, mould a solid heart shape from foil. Roll out some dough to 5 mm/¼ in thick and place it over the foil heart. Trim the edges and place the heart in the centre of the background. Smooth with a damp sponge. Roll out some more dough to 5 mm/¼ in thick. Cut out the wing templates from the baking parchment and place them on the dough. Cut around the edges with a modelling tool and make the feather divisions. Moisten the backs and then put them on to the background and smooth the edges.

4 Bake the clay heart at 120°C/250°F/Gas ½, for two hours and then remove it and carefully insert the screw eyes on the back, one at each side. Return to the oven for at least six hours, or until it is completely hard. Allow to cool. Paint the heart red, the wings white and background black.

Following the template and picture, decorate the heart with a painted daisy chain and add feathery markings to the wings. Highlight with gold paint and then finish with at least two coats of varnish, to protect the dough. When dry, thread the cord through the screw eyes, so you can hang it on the wall.

Love Bug

A most lovable insect, with a heart-shaped body – this is perfect for giving a friend as a token of your affection.

You Will Need

Materials

copper wire
tracing paper
thin copper sheet
modelling clay
red acrylic paint
clear varnish
gold powder

Equipment

round-nosed pliers
pencil
tin snips
rolling pin
acetate sheet
clay modelling tools
small paintbrushes

1 Curl the wire. Trace the templates from the back of the book, enlarging if necessary. Trace two wings on to the copper sheet and cut out with tin snips. Roll out the clay on the sheet. Cut out a heart with a wet modelling tool and model the face.

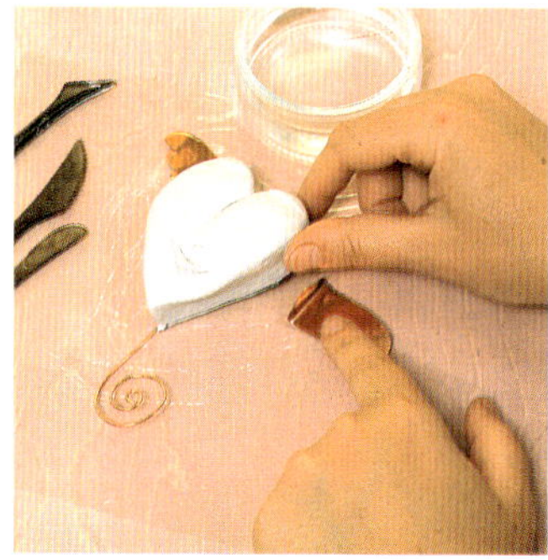

2 Stick the wings and wire curl into the clay and allow to dry for several days.

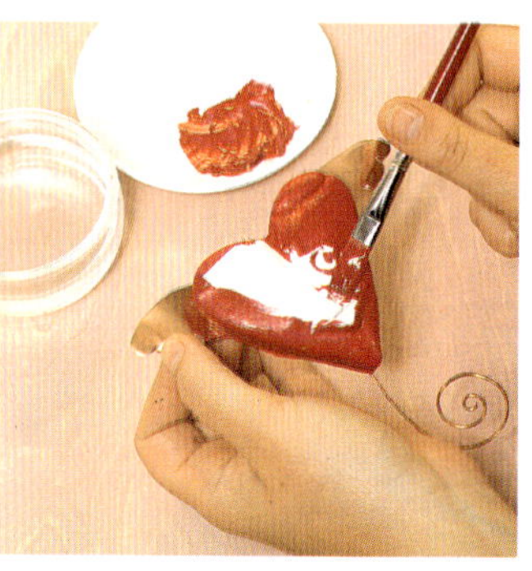

3 Paint the love bug red and allow to dry. Then give it a coat of varnish.

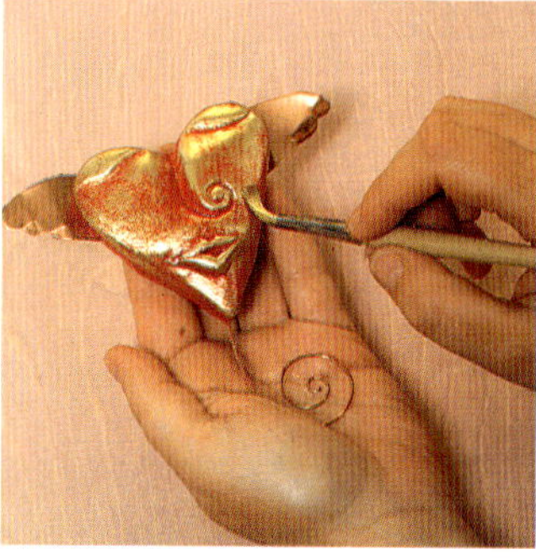

4 With a dry brush, apply gold powder mixed with a little varnish, to finish.

Wall Decoration

Salt dough is a great medium for making architectural-style reliefs. This charming "bronze" wall plaque can easily be incorporated into an interior scheme – or simply used for decoration.

You Will Need

Materials

baking parchment
salt dough (see Salt Dough Recipe)
paperclip
white acrylic primer
acrylic paints: verdigris and bronze

Equipment

pencil
clay modelling tools
flat pliers
scissors
medium and fine paintbrushes
small sponge

1 Trace the template from the back of the book, enlarging if necessary, on to baking parchment. For the outer wings, make ten thin rolls of salt dough. Moisten the edges and press them gently together on the template. Use a flat-edged modelling tool to make some "feathers".

2 Shape the inner wing to fit the parchment outline. Moisten the back of the wing and press it gently in place. Make the face and hair in the same way, shaping the pieces separately and pressing them in place. Cut the paperclip in half with the pliers. Press one piece into the top of the cupid's head for hanging.

3 Bake the decoration at 120°C/250°F/Gas ½, for at least eight hours. Trim the baking parchment and allow to cool. Leaving to dry between each stage, paint with white acrylic primer, then with the verdigris paint. To complete, burnish the raised details with bronze paint.

Cornucopia

A wealth of dusky painted fruit seems to burst from the natural dough base. This harvest cornucopia follows the traditional salt dough theme of natural objects used to decorate the home.

You Will Need

Materials	Equipment
tracing paper	*pencil*
salt dough (see Salt Dough Recipe)	*scissors*
baking parchment	*rolling pin*
2 cloves	*craft knife*
eyelet loop	*dressmaker's pin*
watercolour inks	*clay modelling tools*
polyurethane matt varnish	*knitting needle*
	baking tray
	paintbrushes

1 Trace the template from the back of the book, enlarging if necessary. Roll the dough out on baking parchment to a thickness of 8 mm/5⁄16 in. Place the template on the dough and cut around it. Prick out the design with a pin.

2 Shape a pear, plum and apple from dough, following the template. Moisten with water and press into place. Shape the leaves, with veins, moisten them with water and press into position.

3 Mould grapes, blackberries, cherries, nuts, redcurrants and strawberries. Use a knitting needle to add detail. Moisten each shape and press in place. Make stalks as shown and insert a clove into the bases of the apple and pear.

4 Attach four leaves to the underside of the cornucopia. Press an eyelet loop into the back and bake at 120°C/250°F/Gas ½, for 20 hours. Cool, then paint. When dry, apply five coats of varnish.

Checkered Heart

This heart takes its inspiration from traditional Scandinavian folk art. Although seeming to be separate pieces, the salt dough "squares" are actually formed by deep indentations.

You Will Need

Materials

tracing paper
salt dough (see Salt Dough Recipe)
baking parchment
gold paperclips
acrylic gesso or matt emulsion (latex) paint
cherry-red acrylic or craft paint
polyurethane matt varnish
coloured raffia

Equipment

pencil
rolling pin
dressmaker's pin
craft knife
wire-cutters
baking tray
paintbrushes

1 Trace the template from the back of the book, enlarging if necessary, and cut out. Roll the dough out on baking parchment to 1 cm/½ in thick. Cover with the template and mark the squares with a pin.

2 Neaten the cut edge by patting it with a moistened finger to round and smooth it. Indent lines on the heart, following the pricked marks, leaning the knife first towards you and then away.

3 Cut a paperclip in half and insert it into the top of the heart. Make two or three more hearts in the same way. Bake on the parchment paper on a tray at 120°C/250°F/ Gas ½, for nine hours.

4 Paint with acrylic gesso or emulsion (latex), then paint in cherry-red, leaving alternate squares plain. Allow to dry. Apply five coats of varnish. Thread some raffia through each loop and tie in a bow.

Gingerbread Cupids

What better token of your affection than a gift of these gilded cherubs? They taste as delicious as they look, and they make excellent decorations.

You Will Need

Materials

350 g/12 oz/3 cups plain white flour
15 ml/1 tbsp ground ginger
7.5 ml/½ tbsp ground cinnamon
2.5 ml/½ tsp grated nutmeg
75 g/3 oz/6 tbsp butter, cut into small pieces
50 g/2 oz/4 tbsp soft brown sugar
225 g/8 oz/1 cup black treacle
baking parchment
powdered food colouring: silver and gold

Equipment

mixing bowl
wooden spoon
rolling pin
pencil
scissors
craft knife
baking tray
saucer
spoon
fine paintbrush

To make the dough

Sieve the flour and spices into a mixing bowl. Add the butter and rub it in with your fingers, until the mixture looks like fine breadcrumbs. Stir in the sugar. Make a well in the centre and pour in the treacle. Mix well and beat until the mixture comes away from the sides of the bowl. Knead until smooth.

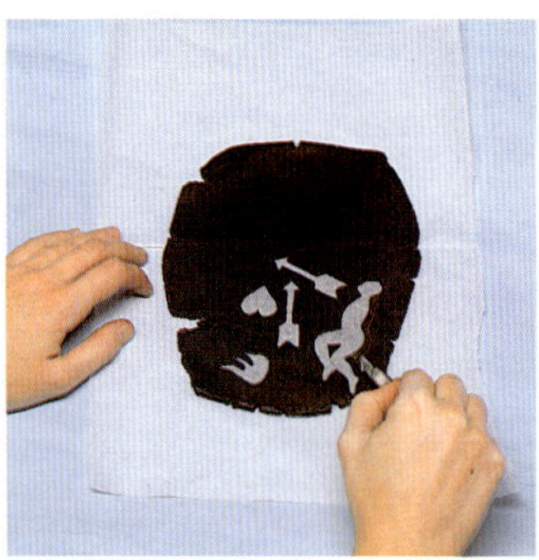

1 Place the dough between two sheets of parchment and roll out very thinly. Trace the templates from the back of the book on to baking parchment, cut out and place on the dough, then cut out. Join the sections and mark on details. Place on baking parchment on a baking tray. Bake at 180°C/350°F/Gas 4 for 10–15 minutes. Leave to cool.

2 Mix each food colouring with water, to make a paste. The easiest way is to tip some on to a saucer, add a drop of water and grind into a paste with the bowl of a spoon. Paint the wings and the centre of the arrows silver.

3 Paint the body, the hearts and the flights of the arrows with gold paste. Allow to dry thoroughly.

Cookie Hearts

Delicious to eat – or you can double-bake them to use as decorations.

You Will Need

Materials	Equipment
dough (see Gingerbread Cupids)	*rolling pin*
baking parchment	*selection of heart-shaped cookie cutters*
white royal icing	*baking tray*
garden twine	*piping bag, with fine icing nozzle*
homespun cotton	*bradawl or skewer*
checked fabric	*scissors*
clear glue or glue gun	
cotton gingham fabric	
buttons	
ribbons	
picture-hanging hook	
card (optional)	

1 Make the dough as for Gingerbread Cupids. Roll out the dough thinly and evenly on a floured board. Cut out the shapes and place on baking parchment on a baking tray. Bake at 180°C/350°F/Gas 4 for 10–15 minutes. Make a hole for hanging while warm, then allow to cool completely.

2 For edible cookies, decorate them with white royal icing, using a piping bag and a fine icing nozzle.

3 If the cookies are not to be eaten, put them back in a low oven for a couple of hours to dry them out. String some together with garden twine. Make bows for tying from checked fabric for some; cut out heart motifs and glue them on others. Do the same with the gingham. Decorate the ties with buttons and ribbons. Use the bradawl to decorate the cookies with a pattern of holes (or do this with a skewer before baking). If the cookie breaks, repair the damage with glue. To make a cookie for hanging on the wall, glue a picture-hanging hook on the back. Large cookies need careful handling and you can glue pieces of card on to the backs, to reinforce them.

Metal Embedded Bowl

These rustic bowls have the appearance of weather-worn stone. The heat-resistant qualities of metal provide an exciting source of decorative materials to use with salt dough – here, coins, bronze decorations, jewellery, wire and copper motifs are all embedded in the dough.

You Will Need

Materials

cooking fat or vegetable oil
salt dough (see Salt Dough Recipe)
baking parchment
fine copper sheet
metal for embedding, such as jewellery accessories, coins and bonsai wire
paper
watercolour paints
metallic craft paints
polyurethane satin varnish
PVA (white) glue
jewellery stones

Equipment

2 ovenproof bowls
rolling pin
craft knife
old pair of scissors
baking tray
pair of compasses
pencil
ruler
paintbrushes
paint-mixing container
natural sponge

1 Smear the upturned bowls with cooking fat or oil. Roll two pieces of dough on baking parchment to 1 cm/½ in thick. Lift each piece of dough over a bowl and smooth it down. Cut the edges level. To make spirals, cut rough circles from a sheet of copper, then cut into spirals. Press your chosen metal pieces into the dough. Bake at 120°C/250°F/Gas ½, for nine hours, removing the bowls once the dough has dried completely.

2 To make a flat lid, draw a circle on paper, 2 cm/¾ in larger than the dough bowl. Cut out the circle to use as a template. Roll some more dough out to 1 cm/½ in thick and cut a circle with the template. Roll a ball of dough, moisten it and press to the centre. Smooth the edges and join it to the lid. Coil two lengths of bonsai wire and bend the ends downwards to form two halves of a heart for the handle.

3 Insert the metal handle ends into the centre of the lid. Transfer the lid, on the parchment paper, to a tray and bake as before for five hours, until it is almost hardened. Measure across the dough bowl between the inner edges. Draw a circle on paper with a diameter 1 cm/½ in less than that of the measurement. Cut out and use as a template to cut a circle from dough.

4 Upturn the baked lid and support it on the ovenproof bowl. Moisten the back of the lid and place the smaller circle on top. Return to the oven for five hours until completely hardened.

5 Paint the bowls and lid, blending your chosen colours with black or white to dull the colours. Lightly dab the bowls with metallic paints, using a sponge. Allow to dry, then apply five coats of varnish. Glue jewellery stones to the metal decorations.

Wood, Wire and Tinwork

Wood, wire and tin are all everyday materials that can be obtained quite readily. With the recent revival of interest in folk art, wood and tin particularly have had a remarkable resurgence of popularity, and many artefacts, particularly those made from recycled materials, are now being produced in craft workshops throughout the country. Wood, wire and tin can all be formed into products either following a traditional or a contemporary style, and their versatility makes them a popular medium for many craftspeople.

The nature of the materials means that some of the projects require you to wear protective clothing, and some solvents can be very strong, so always work in a well-ventilated area and ensure that children do not get too close.

The projects in this section provide comprehensive instructions if you are a newcomer, but they also aim to inspire the more experienced to experiment and develop the true potential of these exciting craft forms.

Materials and Equipment

To complete the projects in this book, you can obtain most of the materials and equipment from craft suppliers and hardware shops. For tin plate, metal foils and sheet metals, you will need to visit a metal supplier or, if you wish to opt for recycled materials, a metal merchant or scrap yard dealer. Sheet metal, whether cut or uncut, is extremely sharp and should only be handled when protective leather gloves and a work shirt are worn. The following lists some of the materials you will need for working with wood, tin and wire.

Epoxy resin glue comes in two parts. Only mix up as much glue as you need at one time as it dries very quickly and is wasted otherwise. Once the glue has set firm, which takes about 24 hours, the join is very strong.

Fine wire is used to join pieces of metal together and as a decoration.

A flux is used during soldering to make the area to be soldered chemically clean. As the flux is heated, it runs along the metal, thus preparing the surface so the solder runs smoothly and adheres properly.

Hammers come in a variety of sizes, so always choose the appropriate hammer to suit the project.

Metal foils are thin sheet metals that usually come on rolls in 15 cm/6 in and 30 cm/12 in wide strips. Metal foil is so thin that it can be cut with a pair of household scissors.

Pliers are useful for holding wire and tin when you are cutting them and also for turning over edges.

Protective clothing such as leather gloves and a work shirt should be worn when cutting metals and wire and sawing wood. A mask and goggles are also needed for soldering. Children should be kept away from this work.

Saws are vital for cutting wood. The most useful varieties are a fretsaw, a coping saw and a jigsaw.

Solder is an alloy, or mixture, of metals. Solder is used to join two pieces of metal together by providing a filler of liquid metal between the surfaces. Always follow the manufacturer's instructions carefully when using solder. Solder is applied with a **soldering iron.**

Materials and Equipment

Tin plate is generally used in place of pure tin sheet, which is very expensive. Tin plate is mild sheet steel that has been coated with tin. The tin plating is very bright and will not tarnish in the open air or in humid conditions. Sheet metals come in different thicknesses, or gauges. The higher the gauge, the thinner the metal.

Tin snips and **shears** are needed to cut sheet metal. Try to find a pair with a spring mechanism to open and close the blades.

White spirit is useful for removing excess flux after soldering.

Wire cutters are invaluable for cutting lengths of wire to size.

Wood glue is very strong PVA (white) glue. It is white but becomes clear once it has dried.

Opposite and below *You'll need quite a few specialist tools for wire and tinwork. But whatever the medium, each project gives clear guidance on the equipment required.*

Amish Sewing Box

This simply painted box, plain and practical, catches the spirit of Amish crafts.

You Will Need

Materials

plain wood box
emulsion (latex) paints: duck-egg blue, brick-red and beige
clear water-based varnish
acrylic paints: raw sienna and burnt umber
white knob

Equipment

paintbrushes
cloth
screwdriver

1 Paint the inside of the box with two coats of duck-egg blue. Paint a base coat of red on the outside of the box and beige on the front drawer.

2 Tint the varnish with a small squeeze of raw sienna and burnt umber and paint the outside of the box. Apply it with a thick-bristled brush, using pressure to leave strokes visible.

3 Apply the same varnish over the beige base coat on the drawer and while it is still wet, use a dry thick-bristled brush to lift some of the glaze to imitate woodgrain.

4 Apply a coat of tinted varnish to the inside, and while it is still wet, wipe off patches of it with a damp cloth to imitate wear and tear. Varnish over the whole box.

5 Screw on the white knob. If you have bought a new one, try making it look a bit scruffy by scratching on the surface and rubbing it with some burnt umber to age it.

PUNCHED TIN PANEL

Tin-punching is a satisfying and stylish way to transform a panelled door. The graphic outline of the citrus slices and the pitted texture of the peel make the fruits appropriate motifs for this treatment.

YOU WILL NEED

MATERIALS

tracing paper
small cupboard with panelled door
3 mm/⅛ in tin sheet, to fit inside door panel
sheet of card
masking tape
strong clear glue

EQUIPMENT

pencil
scissors
hammer
steel punch

1 Trace the template from the back of the book, enlarging to fit your door panel. Lay the tin sheet on some card and attach the traced design using masking tape.

2 Starting with the square boxes around the fruit, hammer the steel punch every 2 mm/$\frac{1}{12}$ in to make a small dent. Hammer the larger dents to either side of the centre lines. Hammer small dents along all the fruit and leaf outlines.

3 Remove the tracing paper and fill in the whole fruit shapes with dents. Fill in the outer rims of the lemon slices with small dents.

4 Spread strong glue over the back of the tin and on the cupboard panel. Leave until tacky, then glue in position.

Ornamental Tree

This tiny ornamental tree will perfume your room with the invigorating aroma of lemon oil.

You Will Need

Materials

florist's medium stub wires
brown florist's tape
modelling clay
yellow acrylic paint
fine brass wire
green crepe paper
tracing paper
thin card
PVA (white) glue
4 small wooden beads
dark green gloss paint
sand or gravel
cotton wool
pure lemon oil
orange and lemon peel

Equipment

wire-cutters or old scissors
paintbrushes
pencil
scissors

1 Trim 15 pieces of stub wire to a length of 23 cm/9 in. Bind them all together with brown florist's tape for the first 12 cm/4¾ in, then bind each projecting end in turn. Divide the wires into pairs, and bind each pair part way up. Bend them out from the trunk, then inwards to shape the tree.

2 Make tiny lemons from clay, spike them on to wire and paint yellow. When dry, replace the wire supports with a loop of fine brass wire, covering the join with green crepe paper.

3 Trace the template from the back of the book, enlarging if necessary, and transfer to card. Make up the box by folding along the lines. Glue, then glue a bead to each corner. Paint dark green. Make a card tube to fit the trunk and glue into the centre of the box. Fill the box with sand or gravel and top with cotton wool.

4 Cut the leaves out of green crepe paper. Attach the lemons and leaves to the branches. Drip lemon oil on to the cotton wool and cover with orange and lemon peel.

Wooden Sheep Sign

Painted signs were a common sight outside shops and taverns in eighteenth-century towns. Here, you can create your own distinct sign.

You Will Need

Materials

tracing paper
5 mm/¼ in plywood, 90 x 60 cm/36 x 24 in
off-white emulsion (latex) paint
acrylic paints: burnt umber, deep grass-green and black
coarse-grade sandpaper
clear matt water-based varnish
artist's acrylic paints: raw umber and raw sienna

Equipment

pencil
coping saw or jigsaw
paintbrushes
stencil brush

1 Trace the template from the back of the book, enlarging to fit your piece of wood. Cut it out with a coping saw or an electric jigsaw.

2 Paint the sheep off-white, using random brushstrokes in all directions.

3 Mix some burnt umber into the off-white to obtain two shades of beige, then apply these with the stencil brush. Paint the grass and the black legs, adding highlights to the legs in dark beige.

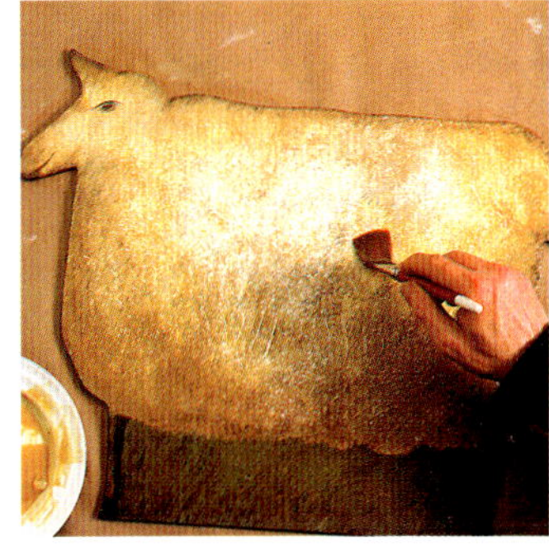

4 Use the darker beige to create the texture of fleece, applying the undiluted paint with a brush. Sand back the paint to reveal a patchy background. Paint an eye and a happy mouth. Apply a coat of varnish tinted with raw umber and raw sienna, and then a coat of clear varnish to finish.

Exotic Table Decorations

Make a selection of whole fruit in this design, as well as an ornamental tree in a tub. These table decorations will look lovely underneath a glass bowl or hanging from drinks glasses.

You Will Need

Materials	Equipment
tracing paper	*pencil*
PVA (white) glue	*dried-out ballpoint pen*
aluminium foil	*old scissors*
coloured varnish, or clear varnish tinted with artist's oil colours	*fine paintbrush*
fine wire	

1 Trace the templates from the back of the book, enlarging if necessary. Glue two sheets of foil together, shiny sides outwards. Lay the tracing over the foil and use a pen to draw round the outlines.

2 Cut out the foil shapes using old scissors, then cover with another sheet of tracing paper to protect the foil. Indent the details on the fruit and leaves with the dried-out ballpoint pen.

3 Using a fine paintbrush, paint the foil shapes with coloured varnish. Allow to dry.

4 Crease the leaves along their central veins and wind the stems around a length of fine wire. Glue them to the fruit. Wire the trunk of the tree.

Love and Kisses Soap Dish

A novel idea to brighten up the bathroom – a soap dish made of ordinary gardening wire, spelling out the message with a heart and crosses (kisses). This couldn't be simpler to do, and it will even keep the soap from making a mess into the bargain! If you wish, the soap dish can be attached to the wall by inserting a screw through the pencil-size hoop.

You Will Need

Materials	Equipment
thick, plastic-coated gardening wire	*wire-cutters*
	pencil
	pliers

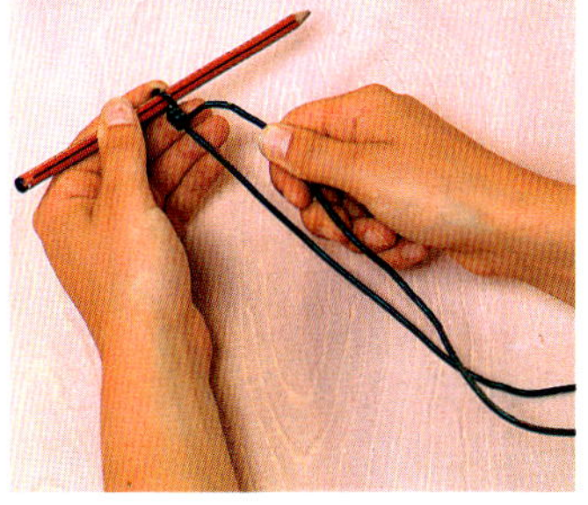

1 Cut an 88 cm/35 in length of wire and wrap it, at the halfway point, around the pencil. Make a coil, by twisting the pencil a couple of times.

2 Using about 16 cm/6¼ in of wire on each side of the coil, make a heart shape, and then finish off by twisting the wire into a coil again.

3 Using the wire ends left, hook them together and join the ends by crimping them with pliers. Make this loop into an even oval, which will form the rim of the soap dish.

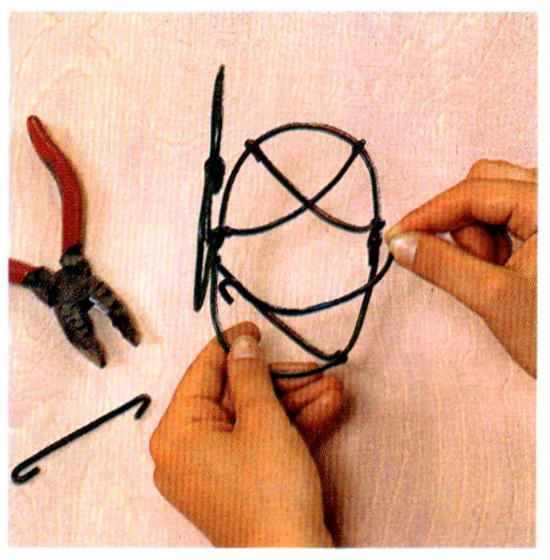

4 Cut four 14 cm/5½ in lengths of wire. Hook over the outside of the oval, making two crosses. Attach a shorter length across the centre.

WOODBURNING

Patterns burnt into wood were a traditional feature of Scandinavian folk art. Nowadays, the specialist tool for the technique is very easily manipulated and gives plenty of scope for creating a pattern to suit every taste.

YOU WILL NEED

MATERIALS

tracing paper
chalky-based transfer paper
masking tape
woodburning kit, with chisel- and flat-ended tools
clear satin water-based varnish
burnt sienna artist's acrylic paint

EQUIPMENT

hard and soft pencils
paintbrush

1 Trace the template from the back of the book, enlarging to fit your box. Place the transfer paper between the tracing and the box, tape in place and transfer the design, using a soft pencil.

2 Set the woodburner at medium, and follow the lines for the stems and leaf outlines. Use the chisel-ended tool and keep it moving or lift it off the surface as it will burn a deeper hole if held static.

3 Outline the fruit with the flat tool. Fill in the leaf outlines with a pattern of dots using the chisel-ended tool with a prodding movement.

4 Apply two coats of water-based satin varnish tinted with a squeeze of burnt sienna paint, followed by one coat of clear varnish.

GALVANIZED TRIVET

A practical accessory that is made from galvanized wire, and so will coordinate with and complement your stainless steel kitchen utensils and your pots and pans.

YOU WILL NEED

MATERIALS

2 mm/0.078 in galvanized wire

EQUIPMENT

pliers
broom handle

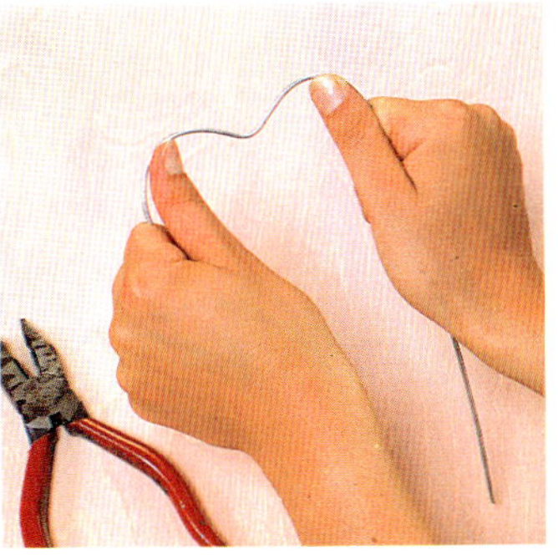

1 Take a 50 cm/20 in length of wire. Using pliers, make a heart shape by bending the wire in the centre, to form the dip in the top of the heart. At the ends, make hooks to join the wires together.

2 Make a coil by tightly and evenly wrapping more wire around a broom handle, about 50 times. Make hooks in the ends in the same way as you did before.

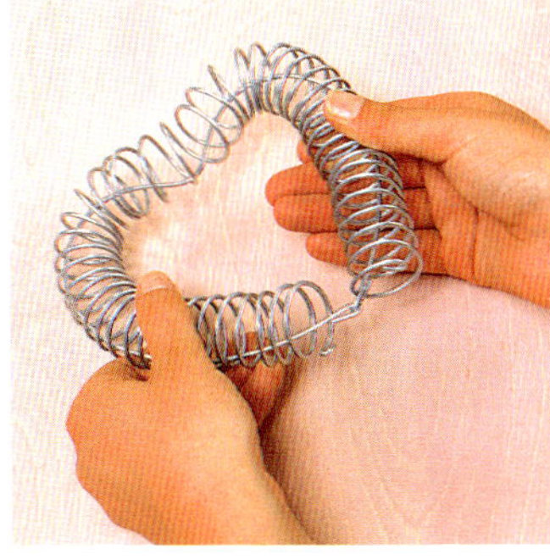

3 Thread the coil over the heart. Connect the ends of the heart by crimping the hooked ends together with pliers. You will need to manipulate the coil to make it sit evenly around the heart shape, before joining and crimping the ends together with pliers.

Tin Candleholder

Tin-punching is an ideal technique to use for creating beautiful candleholders, such as this one. The effect is graphic and yet delicately detailed, and the metallic effect will reflect the warm glow of the candlelight. Take care not to leave burning candles unattended.

You Will Need

Materials

tracing paper
aluminium or tin sheet
magazine or newspaper
epoxy resin glue
candle

Equipment

pencil
magic marker
protective gloves
tin snips or sharp scissors
magazine or newspaper
large, strong needle
tack hammer
metal ruler
wire brush

1 Trace the template from the back of the book, enlarging if necessary, and transfer the outline to the metal. Wearing gloves, cut it out, using tin snips or sharp scissors.

2 Lay the template on a magazine or newspaper to protect the work surface. Using a large, strong needle and a hammer, punch the pattern into the metal sheet.

3 Fold the two outer metal panels inwards along the dotted lines, using a metal ruler to crease the sheet cleanly. Do the same with the triangular flaps at the bottom.

4 Overlap the extra lip to secure the triangular shape, and glue it in place. Scratch the surface all over with the wire brush. Put the candle in the bottom of the container.

Tin Can Insects

There's more than one way to recycle empty cans: these light-hearted designs turn cans into insects to crawl up your garden walls. Use beer or lager cans that have the same logos on the front and back so that your insects look symmetrical. Take care not to cut yourself on the sharp edges of the cans.

You Will Need

Materials

tracing paper
large steel drinks (soda) can, top and bottom removed
masking tape

Equipment

pencil
scissors with small points
large paintbrush with a tapered handle
small long-nosed pliers

1 Trace the template on this page, enlarging if necessary. Cut up the side of the can opposite the bar code and open out flat. Place the template in position and secure with tape. Cut round the template carefully with sharp scissors.

2 Place the body of the insect over the tapered handle of a paintbrush, with the fattest part nearest the head. Shape the body by bending it around the handle. Fold the lower wings very slightly under the body and bend the upper wings forward, folding them slightly over the top part of the body.

3 Using some long-nosed pliers, twist the antennae back on themselves and curl the ends to complete.

Pierced Tin Shelf

Tin-piercing is a wonderfully cheap and effective form of decoration. Here, it is combined with a traditional quilting pattern to make a small shelf from a recycled cake tin.

You Will Need

Materials

sheet of paper, to fit tin base
old baking tin
scrap wood

Equipment

scissors
magic marker
tin snips
pliers
tack hammer
fine, sharp nails

1 Make a pattern for the arch by folding the paper in half and cutting a curve from one half. Select one of the tin's sides and draw the arch above it, using the paper as a guide.

2 Snip 5 mm/¼ in into the raw edges at 2.5 cm/1 in intervals and use pliers to fold it firmly and crimp it until no sharp edges remain exposed.

3 Draw your pattern on to the arch. The pattern used here is an old quilting pattern, but a folk-style embroidery pattern would be just as suitable.

4 Place the tin on a flat piece of scrap wood and use the hammer to tap the nails through the tin and along the dotted lines. The perforations should be quite close to each other without causing the holes to join.

Candle Collars

This is a clever way of making candles look extremely decorative and original.

You Will Need

Materials

tracing paper
thin card
masking tape
40 gauge/0.003 in copper foil
wooden block
fine jeweller's wire
glass beads

Equipment

soft and sharp pencil
scissors
bradawl
ballpoint pen

1 Trace the template on this page, enlarging if necessary. Transfer to thin card and cut out. Tape the template to some copper foil. Draw around the template using a sharp pencil to transfer the design.

2 Remove the template and cut around the outside of the collar. Pierce the centre of the collar using a bradawl. Insert the scissors through the hole and carefully cut out the centre of the collar.

3 Place the collar, face down, on a sheet of thin card. Redraw over the lines of the outer and inner circles with a ballpoint pen. Press dots randomly into the surface of the foil between the two rings. Draw veins on each petal.

4 Place the collar, face up, on some wood. Pierce a hole below the centre of each petal. Thread wire through the first hole in the collar, bending the end back to secure. Thread beads on, twisting the wire at the end to hold in place.

Painted Chest

The chest used in this project is a mixture of Old and New World influences. The shape is English, but the painted decoration was inspired by an old American dowry chest. You can use this pattern to decorate any chest you like.

You Will Need

Materials

blanket chest
shellac (optional)
emulsion (latex) paints: dusky-blue and regency-cream
tracing paper
antique pine acrylic varnish

Equipment

paintbrushes
pencil
pair of compasses
ruler
graining comb
cloth

1 If you are starting with bare wood, apply a coat of shellac to seal the surface.

2 Paint the chest with dusky-blue. Trace the templates from the back of the book, enlarging them to fit your box. Use the templates as a guide to position the panels. Draw the panels with a pair of compasses and a ruler.

3 Paint all the panel pieces with cream emulsion (latex) paint.

4 Apply a thick coat of varnish to one panel only.

5 Quickly comb the varnish in a pattern, following the shape of the panel. Make one smooth combing movement into the wet varnish, then wipe off the comb to prevent any build-up of varnish. Complete one panel before repeating steps 4 and 5 for the other panels.

6 Apply a coat of varnish to the whole chest. Immediately, take a just-damp cloth, screw it into a ball and use it to dab off random spots of the varnish.

Storage Canister

Transform canisters by spraying them with paint and painting cheerful sunflowers all over them.

You Will Need

Materials

plain metal storage canister
matt blue spray paint
acrylic paints: yellow, orange, brown and cream
acrylic sealer spray

Equipment

medium and fine paintbrushes
paint-mixing container

1 Wash the canister to remove any grease and dry thoroughly. Spray the can and lid with the blue paint, building the colour up with several fine layers and allowing each one to dry before applying the next, to prevent the paint from running.

2 Using the acrylic paints, paint in the sunflowers. For each one, paint a yellow circle about 3 cm/1¼ in in diameter and then evenly space the petals around the edge. Repeat the motif, placing it evenly around the canister, until the whole surface is covered. Allow to dry and then apply another layer of paint.

3 Add more colour to the petals, to give a feeling of depth. Paint the centres brown. Paint in the seeds with circles of brown, highlighting with cream. When the paint is dry, spray the canister and lid with an acrylic sealer, to protect the surface. The canister will withstand gentle cleaning, but not the dishwasher.

Wall Sconce

These fashionable room accessories were once essential to every household, and nowadays they restore a bit of the romance that electricity has taken out of life.

You Will Need

Materials

old piece of wood, such as driftwood
brass and black upholstery nails
wood glue
fine nails

Equipment

saw
hammer

1 Saw through the wood, making two sections to be joined at right angles. Begin the pattern by hammering the upholstery nails in a central line; the pattern can then radiate from it.

2 Form a pattern of arrows, crosses and diamonds, using the contrast between the brass and black nails to enhance the design.

3 Apply a coat of wood glue to the sawn edge of the base. Hammer fine nails through the back into the base.

Copper Frame

This frame combines two metal foils to create a stunning effect. The embossed shapes and simple nail patterns look very striking indeed.

You Will Need

Materials

sheet of thin copper foil, 1 cm/½ in wider than frame
softwood frame, with sides at least 7 cm/2¾ in deep
brass escutcheon pins, 1.5 cm/¾ in and 1 cm/½ in
sheet of thin aluminium foil
metal polish

Equipment

large, soft cloth
ballpoint pen
scissors
bradawl
tack hammer
white china marker
soft cloth

1 Spread out the cloth and put the copper foil on top. Lay the frame upside down on the foil and draw around the outer and inner edges with a ballpoint pen.

2 Mark on an inner frame 1.5 cm/¾ in deep, to allow for turning around the rebate of the frame. Cut out the outer corners and the middle of the foil with scissors.

3 Fold the foil around the outer edges of the frame and make holes with a bradawl. Hammer the longer pins through the holes. Fold the foil around the rebate, mark and pin it with the short pins.

4 Draw simple flower and leaf shapes on the back of the aluminium foil with the china marker. Cut out the shapes with scissors.

5 Place the shapes on the soft cloth and draw decorative patterns on the back of them with a ballpoint pen.

6 Place the flowers and leaves around the frame and prick through both the metals and the wood using a bradawl. Using the long pins, nail the shapes on to the frame through the pricked holes.

7 Further decorate the frame with more long pins hammered in to form star shapes. Finish off by gently rubbing the whole frame with a soft cloth and metal polish.

Christmas Decorations

These twinkly Christmas decorations were inspired by Eastern European architecture and folk art. Stamped and die-cut artefacts were very popular in many European countries throughout the nineteenth century, when there would have been a tin-worker in every village.

You Will Need

Materials

tracing paper
thin card
36 gauge/0.005 in aluminium foil
fine wire

Equipment

soft and sharp pencils
scissors
embroidery scissors
magic marker
ruler
dressmaker's wheel
ballpoint pen
wooden block
bradawl

1 Trace the templates from the back of the book, transfer to thin card and cut out. Cut a small piece of foil and place the template on it. Draw around the outline with a sharp pencil. Using embroidery scissors, cut out the foil shape. Cut it carefully to ensure that there are no rough edges.

2 Using the picture as a guide, mark the basic lines of the design on the back of the decoration using a magic marker and ruler. Place the decoration face down on card. Trace over the lines with a dressmaker's wheel to emboss a row of raised dots at the front. Trace a second line of dots inside the first, in the decoration's centre.

3 Using the picture as a guide, draw the details of the house on the back of the decoration with a pen.

4 Place the decoration face up on a small block of wood. Using a bradawl, make a hole in the top of the decoration, then tie a length of fine wire through the hole to make a hanger.

Sunflower Magnet

This sunflower fridge magnet will brighten up the kitchen on the darkest of mornings. In winter, you could consider making a whole row of them, as a reminder of the pleasures of the summer garden.

You Will Need

Materials

5 mm/¼ in thick birch-faced plywood sheet
medium- and fine-grade sandpaper
wood glue
white undercoat paint
acrylic paints: yellow, red, green, chocolate-brown and gold
gloss varnish
small magnet
epoxy resin glue

Equipment

pair of compasses
pencil
coping saw or fretsaw
medium and fine paintbrushes
paint-mixing container

1 With a pair of compasses, draw a circle on the plywood for the centre of the flower. Draw in the petals, leaf and stem freehand. Draw another circle the same size on the plywood and cut the shapes out.

2 Sand any rough edges off the flower shape. Sand the circle's edge to a curve. Then glue the circle to the centre of the flower with wood glue.

3 Paint with undercoat. Allow to dry and then sand lightly. Paint in the flower details with acrylic paints. Mix a golden-yellow and paint the petals. Paint the stem and leaves green. Paint the centre brown. When dry, add darker detail on the petals, veining on the leaves and gold dots on the centre. When dry, apply a coat of varnish. When the varnish is dry, stick the magnet on the back of the flower.

Gilded Candlestick

Candlelight gives a magical glow to a room, and this shimmering candlestick will really heighten the atmosphere. Both silver and gold are used here, to dramatic effect. The sunflower motif is a relief design built up with layers of gesso, and the depth of the relief enhances the light and shade effect.

You Will Need

Materials

turned-wood candlestick
red oxide primer
3-hour oil size
aluminium leaf transfer book
acrylic gesso
Dutch gold leaf transfer book
black watercolour paint
methylated spirit-based varnish

Equipment

medium and fine paintbrushes
large stencil brush
paint-mixing container
rag

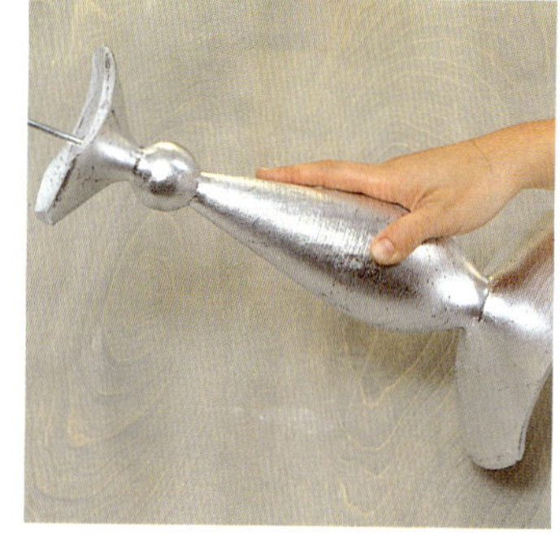

1 Prime the candlestick all over with red oxide and allow to dry. Then paint it with size and allow to dry for three hours. When the size is "squeaky", it is ready for gilding. Begin gilding the candlestick with aluminium leaf, rubbing it with a dry stencil brush, so it adheres to the size. Repeat until covered.

2 Paint a fine layer of acrylic gesso, freehand, in a sunflower shape. Allow to dry. Build up the relief with three or four layers of gesso.

3 Paint lines of gesso in the centre, to make a lattice pattern. Allow to dry.

4 Paint the sunflower with red oxide primer, to seal the surface and to act as a base for the gilding. Allow to dry.

5 Paint the sunflower with size and allow to dry.

6 Once the size is "squeaky", lay a sheet of Dutch gold leaf on the flower.

7 Rub it with the stencil brush, using the bristles to push the metal into the grooves, so it adheres.

8 Put some black paint on to a rag and rub it into the lattice to darken it, giving it an effect of greater depth. Finally, give the whole candlestick a coat of varnish.

Grasshopper on a Stick

Plant this bold, bright grasshopper in your garden or conservatory, and let it add a splash of colour among the foliage.

You Will Need

Materials

tracing paper
9 mm/3/8 in pine slat, 5.5 x 23 cm/2 1/4 x 9 in
2 pieces of 5 mm/1/4 in birch plywood, each 10 x 24 cm/4 x 9 1/2 in
sandpaper
wood glue
5 mm/1/4 in dowel, 48 cm/19 in long
white undercoat paint
enamel paints

Equipment

pencil
fretsaw
double-sided tape
craft knife
5 mm/1/4 in drill
medium and fine paintbrushes
empty wine bottle

1 Trace the templates from the back of the book, enlarging if necessary. Draw the body on the slat and cut out. Stick the plywood pieces together with tape and cut out the legs, sawing through both pieces at once. Cut out the antennae from plywood. Use a craft knife to whittle the edges. Sand all the rough edges.

2 Drill a hole in the underside of the body. Glue the legs and antennae in position on the body and stick the dowel in the hole. Paint with white undercoat and allow to dry, standing in an empty wine bottle. Colour the grasshopper with paints.

Gilded Candleholder

The gentle glow of candles has an obvious affinity with starlight, and this twelve-pointed star is gilded and studded with copper to reflect the light. Painted in warm, festive colours, it would make a lovely addition to a traditional Christmas table.

You Will Need

Materials

5 mm/¼ in birch plywood sheet
1 cm/½ in pine sheet
sandpaper
wood glue
white undercoat paint
acrylic paints: dark green, red and gold
matt varnish
6 copper disc rivets, 2 cm/¾ in

Equipment

pair of compasses
pencil
ruler
fretsaw
paintbrushes
spike
wire-cutters

1 Using a pair of compasses, draw a large circle on the plywood. With the same radius, mark the six points of the star around the circle and join with a ruler. Draw a smaller circle on the pine and mark out the second star in the same way. Draw a circle in the centre to fit your chosen candle size.

2 Cut out the two star shapes and sand any rough edges. Stick together with wood glue to form a twelve-pointed star. Paint with white undercoat and sand lightly when dry. Cover with a base coat of dark green acrylic paint, then paint on the design. Seal with a coat of matt varnish.

3 Using a spike, make six holes for the copper disc rivets. Trim the stems of the rivets with wire-cutters and push into the holes.

PAINTED TIN

This project does not require you to learn the somewhat specialized brushstrokes used in traditional tin-painting, although the colours and antiquing will ensure that it blends in well with any other painted pieces.

YOU WILL NEED

MATERIALS

metal primer
large metal tin with a lid
emulsion (latex) paints: black, brick-red and maize-yellow
tracing paper
masking tape
shellac
clear varnish
raw umber artist's acrylic paint
clear satin varnish

EQUIPMENT

paintbrushes
hard and soft pencils

1 Prime the tin, then paint the lid black, and the tin brick-red with yellow stripes.

2 Trace the template on this page, enlarging if necessary. Cross-hatch over the back of it with a soft pencil.

3 Tape the pattern in position on the tin and draw over it with a hard pencil to transfer the design.

4 Fill in the main body of the "3" in yellow.

5 Fill in the shadow of the "3" in black.

6 Varnish the tin with shellac to give it a warm glow.

7 Tint the varnish with some raw umber paint and apply it to the tin. Then apply a coat of clear satin varnish to seal the surface.

3

Lantern

This tin can lantern is reminiscent of Moroccan lanterns that have similar curlicues and punched holes. A cold chisel and heavy hammer are used to cut ventilation holes out of the metal on the lantern roof.

You Will Need

Materials

large tin can
thin aluminium sheet
sheet of chipboard
scrap of thin tin
flux
fine wire

Equipment

tin opener
magic marker
protective gloves
tin shears
pliers
file
pair of compasses
pencil
protective goggles
cold chisel
hammer
nail or centre punch
soldering mat
soldering iron and solder
protective mask
wire-cutters

1 Using a tin opener, remove one end of the tin can. Make an aperture for the door by marking a rectangle on to the front of the tin. Wearing gloves, cut out the rectangle.

2 Turn over the door edges with pliers to make the aperture safe. File away any remaining rough edges.

3 To make the lid, draw a semi-circle on a scrap of aluminium sheet. The radius should be equal to the diameter of the tin. Cut out and file the edges smooth.

4 Lay the lid on some chipboard. Wearing goggles, cut ventilation holes in the lid using a cold chisel and hammer. File any rough edges.

5 Using a hammer and nail or centre punch, punch holes around the top edge of the lantern and around the bottom of the curved edge of the lid. File away any rough edges around the holes.

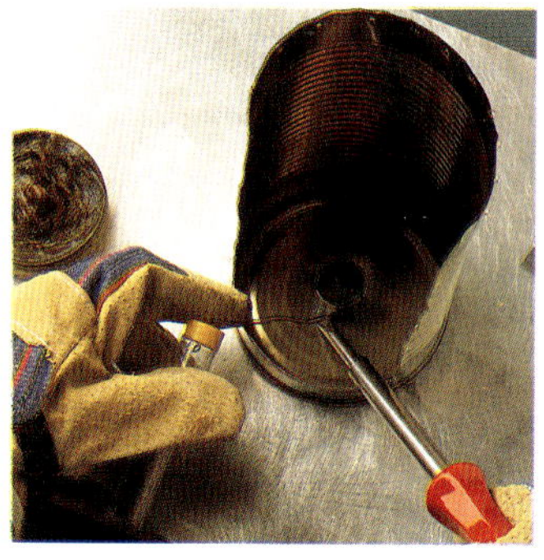

6 To make the candleholder, cut a strip of tin. File the edges and curve the tin around to make a circle. Place the lantern on a soldering mat. Apply flux to the join. Wearing a mask and goggles, solder the holder inside the lantern.

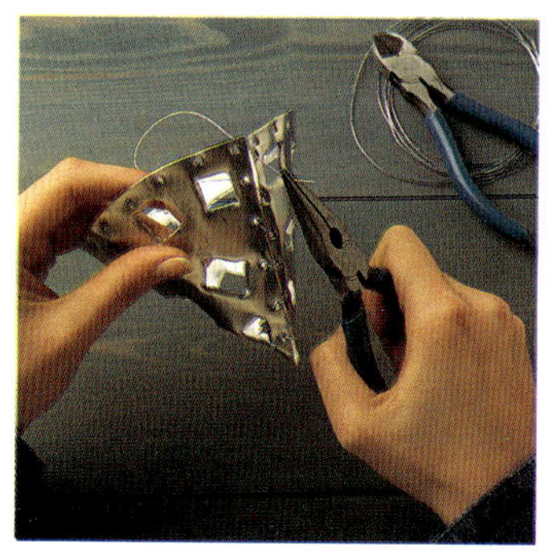

7 Curve the lid around to make a cone. Using a pair of pliers, thread fine wire through the holes in the lid to join the sides together.

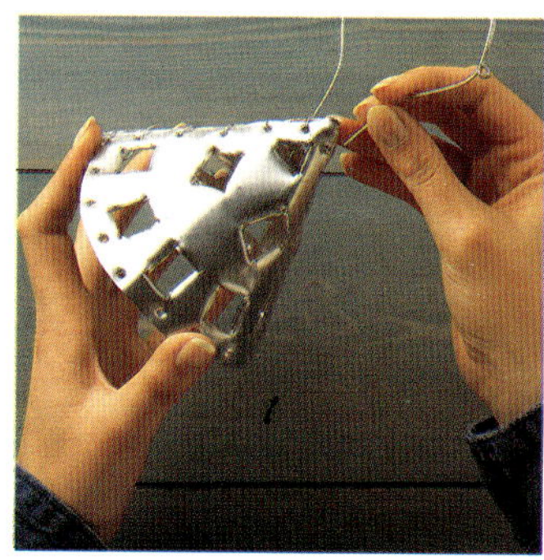

8 For the handle, cut a length of fine wire, then cut two shorter pieces. Make a loop in either end of the shorter pieces, then centre them on either side of the longer wire and solder in place. Curve them, then thread the ends through the holes in the top of the lid and twist them into tight spirals inside.

9 Attach the lid to the lantern using fine wire. Pull the wire tight using pliers.

10 For the door, make a decorative rectangular frame from lengths of wire. The frame should be slightly taller and wider than the aperture. Lay the frame on a soldering mat and solder all the sections together. When the door is complete, curve it to the shape of the lantern.

11 To make hinges, bend two short lengths of wire into "U" shapes. Bend each end of the "U" into right angles. Solder one end of each hinge to the lantern. Place the door inside the hinges so that it rests on them and doesn't drop down. Solder the other end of the hinges to the lanterns.

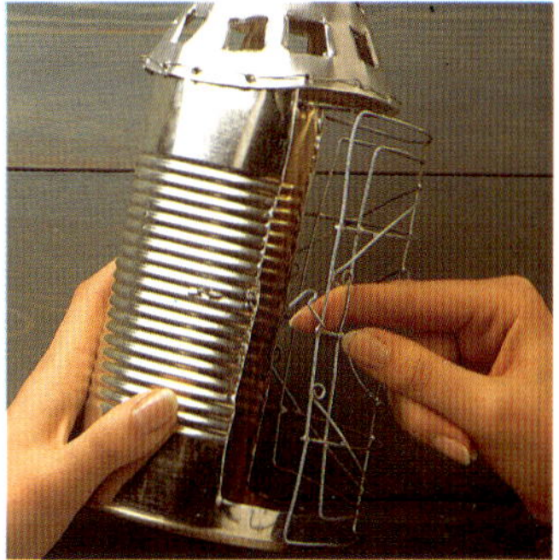

12 For the latch, make a hook and a "U"-shaped catch from short lengths of wire. Solder the catch to the side of the lantern and attach the hook to the door frame.

Wooden Dish

This wooden dish would be good for serving candies or nuts. It's very easy to make, if you take the time to measure, draw, and cut accurately.

You Will Need

Materials

5 mm/¼ in birch-faced plywood sheet
2.5 cm/1 in pine slat
double-sided tape
tracing paper
wood filler (optional)
sandpaper
wood glue
white undercoat paint
acrylic paints: red, green, yellow, white and brown
matt varnish

Equipment

pencil
fretsaw or coping saw
ruler
drill, with medium bit
paintbrushes
paint-mixing containers

1 Attach the plywood to the back of the pine with the double-sided tape. Trace the template on this page, enlarging if necessary. Place the template on the pine and draw around it. Cut out the heart shape from the plywood and pine with the fretsaw or coping saw.

2 Detach the plywood heart. On the pine heart, mark a line 5 mm/¼ in from the edge (make a smaller template and draw around it). Drill a hole for the saw blade. If you can't do this easily, saw through from the side and repair the cut with a little filler. Cut around the inner outline and detach the smaller heart. Sand the two pieces smooth.

3 Line up the plywood heart exactly with the pine one, as a base. Glue it in place and allow to dry. Sand around the edges again. Paint with white undercoat and allow to dry. Lightly sand again, with fine-grade sandpaper, and decorate with acrylic paints. When dry, finish with a coat of varnish.

Painted Garden Sticks

These cheerful sun and moon faces are very simple to make and will really brighten up the garden. Use them to enhance the festive atmosphere when you are having a barbecue or garden party. You could also put them into a border or bed, or use them to give height and structure to plants in a container.

1 Draw the sun and moon shapes freehand on tracing paper and transfer the outlines to the plywood. Cut out the shapes with the saw and sand the edges smooth. Drill a hole in the edge of each shape for the sticks.

2 Paint the sticks and shapes all over with undercoat. Allow to dry. Sand lightly with fine-grade sandpaper. Glue the sticks in place.

3 Decorate the sticks with acrylic paints and allow to dry thoroughly. Finish with a coat of varnish.

You Will Need

Materials

tracing paper
5 mm/¼ in birch-faced plywood sheet
medium- and fine-grade sandpaper
garden sticks or canes
white undercoat paint
PVA (white) glue
acrylic paints: red, yellow, brown, blue and white
gloss varnish

Equipment

pencil
coping saw or fretsaw
drill
medium and fine paintbrushes
paint-mixing container

Decorating Glass and Ceramics

Painting glass and ceramics is a straightforward craft that can be as simple or complex as you like. Using a wide range of special paints in different colours and finishes, you can produce a truly varied and dynamic set of glassware, crockery and decorations for around your home, or to give as gifts. Start by experimenting with a single plain tile, then progress as your confidence grows to decorate a whole tea service.

The important thing to remember about this craft, is that the surface to be treated must be totally clean and free from grease. Once that has been seen to, you can set to the task of transforming the object to an individual style of your choice. Don't be constrained by the templates and motifs offered here – just follow the steps carefully for the technique, then develop your own personalized style.

Materials and Equipment

You probably already have most of the materials and equipment you need for painting glass and ceramics among your household supplies. However, materials such as paints do have to be specially purchased.

As well as considering the aesthetic qualities of a particular type of paint, you should also consider the practicalities; whether, for instance, it can withstand the level of wear and tear it will receive. You should also consider any safety implications, and always read the manufacturer's instructions before applying paint to a surface. This is of the utmost importance if the end product is to be used for food or drink.

A variety of paints can be used on glazed and fired surfaces and specially formulated paint ranges are available from specialist suppliers for application on glassware and ceramics. These include the following.

Solvent-based cold ceramic and glass paints are specially designed for use on ceramics and glass. They are called "cold" because they are not fired. The solvent evaporates, once applied, to leave the colour in place as painted. When painted on to a non-porous surface, such as glazed white tiles, they can be wiped off with a solvent. They take about 24 hours to dry.

Water-based ceramic paints are special paints that are brighter than their solvent-based counterparts, come in a wide range of colours and can be mixed to achieve yet more colours. They have a thermal resin acrylic which, when heated, renders the paint indelible. Though water-based, the paints should not be diluted more than 20 per cent with water. Once the painted object is dry, the object can be baked in the oven to fix the paints. Always follow the manufacturer's instructions.

Acrylic paints A wide range of these can be used on ceramics and glass, though they are not specifically designed for such use. They include rich, opaque colours available in glossy, matt or a pearly finish. Acrylic paints adhere well, but are for decorative use only and are best coated with at least one coat of polyurethane varnish.

Enamel paints work well on glass and ceramics, and they give a hard, smooth covering. However, some of them do contain lead and so are unsuitable for any piece of tableware. They are very durable, with a great range of colours.

Polyurethane varnish and glazes come in matt or gloss finish. Always read the manufacturer's instructions before use and use in a well-ventilated room. Apply the finish evenly, using a large, flat brush and stroking in one direction. The more coats you apply, the more durable and washable the surface, but keep each coat thin, allowing a minimum of four hours' drying time between coats. Polyurethane varnish is unsuitable for surfaces that may come into contact with food or the mouth.

Right *A selection of tools and materials you'll need to create your own decorative glass and ceramic projects.*

Materials and Equipment

Lemon Tiles

You could paint this fresh, graphic design on individual tiles to make focal points on the wall or create a repeating design by setting decorated tiles in groups or rows. Reserve some tiles to paint with a simple "filler" design like the checks used here. Use solvent-based ceramic paints that do not need to be fired.

1 Trace the template on this page, enlarging it to fit your tiles exactly. Copy it on to paper and decorate the border with squares, if liked.

2 Place a sheet of carbon paper on the tile, then the paper template, and secure with masking tape. Draw over the outlines with a sharp pencil to transfer the design.

3 Mix up enough ceramic paint in each colour to complete all the tiles you need, adding ceramic paint medium to give transparency. Paint the tiles, allowing each colour to dry before applying the next.

You Will Need

Materials

tracing paper
plain white ceramic tiles
paper
carbon paper
masking tape
ceramic paints
transparent ceramic paint medium

Equipment

pencil
ruler (optional)
scissors
paintbrush

Japanese Glass Vase

Transform a plain vase with some highly effective and attractive stamping in a calligraphic style.

You Will Need

Materials

high-density foam, 25 x 10 x 5 cm/10 x 4 x 2 in
black acrylic enamel paint
washed plain glass vase

Equipment

set square
felt-tipped pen
craft knife
plate

1 Using a set square and pen, draw lines 1 cm/½ in apart on the foam. Cut along the lines with a craft knife, then part the foam and cut through.

2 Spread an even coating of paint on to a plate. Curl up a strip of foam and dip it into the paint.

3 Curl the foam strip into an open-ended shape. When the curve looks right, press it on to the vase. Lift it off straight away to avoid smudges.

4 Press a straight strip of foam into the paint, then use it to continue the line around the side of the vase.

5 Complete the calligraphic pattern with a series of these straight lines. Applying the pressure unevenly will give a more authentic effect.

Soap Dish

Inspired by the colours of bright glycerine soap, this dish, with its green, yellow, black and white aquatic theme, adds a fresh and humorous note to a bathroom.

You Will Need

Materials

glazed dish with sides
ceramic paints: yellow, black and bright green
tracing paper
carbon paper
masking tape

Equipment

paintbrushes
hard and soft pencils

1 Paint the base of the dish yellow. Using a fine paintbrush, paint around the inside edge of the base, then use a larger brush to fill the middle. Spread the paint thinly. Fix the paint following the manufacturer's instructions.

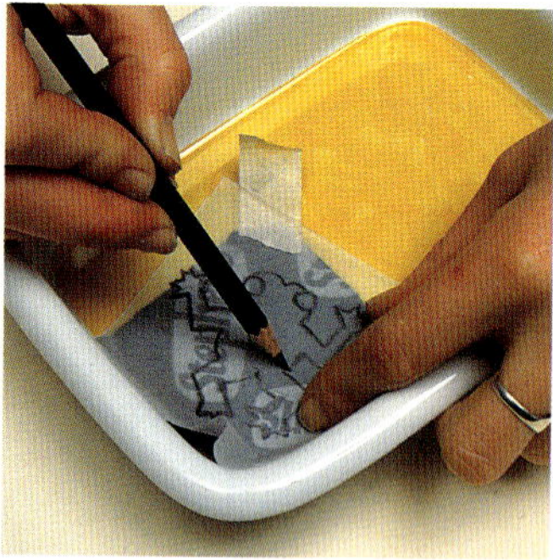

2 Trace the template on this page, enlarging if necessary. Place some carbon paper on the underside of the tracing, position on the dish and tape down. Trace around the frog three times to create a triangle of frogs.

3 Using a fine paintbrush, paint the frogs black from the outline in, spreading the paint thinly to achieve a watery effect. Fix the paints as before.

4 Paint the inner sides of the dish green. Start from the yellow edge, working the strokes along and up and stopping where the sides curve above the rim. Allow to dry. Paint green dots randomly over the yellow base.

5 Paint the outer sides of the dish green. Paint along the edge under the top rim, working the strokes along and down, and tackling a small area at a time. Allow to dry. Fix the paints as before.

6 Using a fine paintbrush, paint a black outline around the frogs, leaving small gaps of yellow here and there. If you like, paint circles with central black dots for a frog spawn effect.

7 Using a soft pencil, mark a stripe motif at the four corners on the rim, then complete the rim pattern one section at a time, following the photograph. Paint the stripe motif in black. Allow to dry, then fix the paints as before.

Gilded Fruits

The colours of the fruit really glow in transparent glass paints. Relief gold outliner defines the design like the leading in a stained-glass window.

You Will Need

Materials

glass bowl
gold glass-painting outliner
solvent-based glass paints: red, green and yellow

Equipment

methylated spirit
paper towels
packing material or bean-bag
paintbrushes

1 Wash the bowl in hot, soapy water and dry thoroughly. Wipe over the surface with methylated spirit to remove any remaining traces of grease.

2 After a few practice runs, draw the design carefully with the gold outliner. It is easiest to do this in sections, leaving each section to dry for at least 12 hours before moving on to the next.

3 Prop the bowl on its side, supported by packing material to keep the section that you are painting horizontal so that the paint does not run. Apply the glass paint thickly to avoid streaky brushstrokes.

4 Leave each section to dry overnight before beginning the next. If you are a beginner, stick to single blocks of colour. More experienced glass painters could try blending two or more colours into each other to achieve an attractive effect.

Candle Jar

A straight-sided jar is a good shape to choose if you haven't tried painting glass before, as the flow of the paint is easiest to control on a flat, level surface. As the candle burns down inside the jar, the jewelled colours of the design will really start to glow.

You Will Need

Materials

glass jar, with a candle
gold glass-painting outliner
solvent-based glass paints: red, green and purple

Equipment

methylated spirit
paper towels
paintbrushes
white spirit

1 Wash the jar in hot, soapy water and dry thoroughly. Wipe over the surface with methylated spirit to remove any remaining traces of grease.

2 Lay the jar down on its side. After a few practice runs on an old jam jar, draw the design carefully with the gold outliner. Allow this to harden for at least 12 hours before starting to colour your design.

3 When painting the background, apply the glass paint thickly to avoid streaky brushstrokes. Be careful not to allow the paint to run down the sides of the jar: if it does, wipe off immediately with paper towels and white spirit. Complete the design and leave it to dry for at least 12 hours before starting on the next side.

Low-relief Jug

Ceramics with low-relief decorative motifs are ideal for beginners to paint. Like children's colouring books, the shapes are all set out for you to colour in, and as there are no clearly defined outlines, minor mistakes are not noticeable. Reproduction Victorian white relief pattern and contemporary Portuguese pottery make the ideal base for this work.

You Will Need

Materials

white glazed low-relief jug
ceramic paints: acid-yellow, golden-yellow and light, medium and dark green
polyurethane varnish

Equipment

paintbrushes

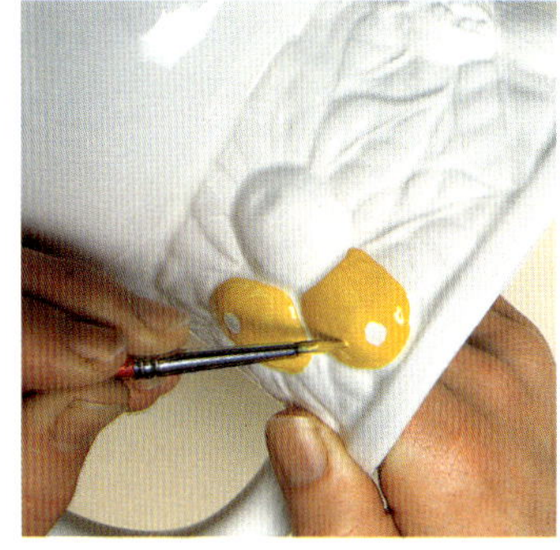

1 Paint some lemons on the jug in acid-yellow. Vary them to give one group two acid-yellow lemons, the next group one, and so on. Leave a narrow white line around each lemon and leave the seed cases and small circles at the base of the fruit white. Allow to dry.

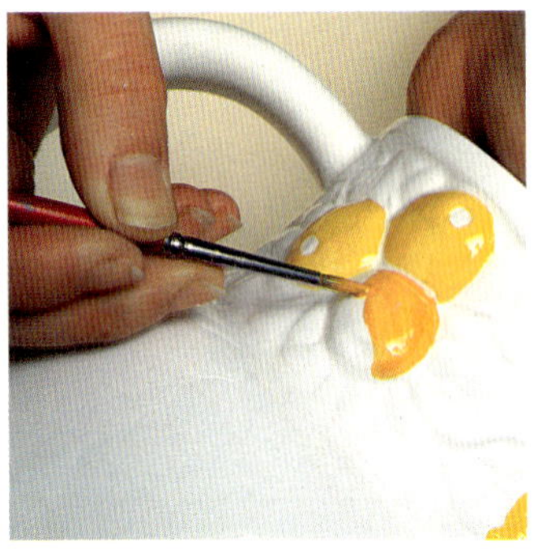

2 Work your way around the relief pattern, painting the remaining fruit a rich golden-yellow. Leave a narrow white line around each fruit. Allow to dry thoroughly.

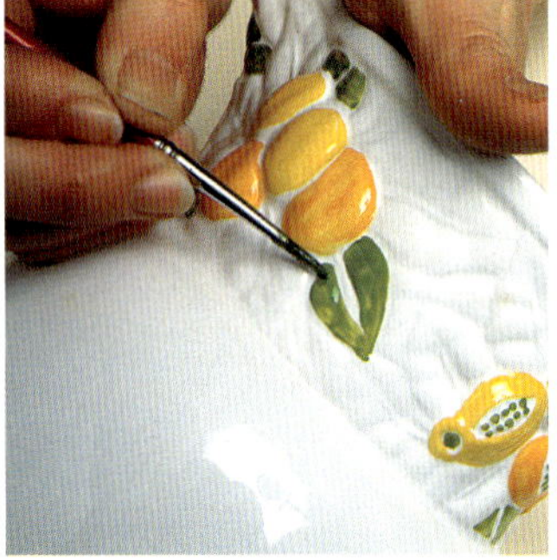

3 Use the three shades of green for the leaves. Start with the palest green, painting roughly a third of the leaves, evenly spaced apart. Leave the central mid-rib of each leaf white and a narrow white line around each leaf. Allow to dry.

4 Paint a third of the leaves medium green, again spacing them evenly around the jug. Paint the narrow base of the jug green, and allow to dry once more.

5 Paint the remaining leaves dark green and allow to dry. Fix the paints according to the manufacturer's instructions.

6 Paint the rim or the handle in acid-yellow, leaving a narrow white line at the lower line. Once dry, varnish the jug.

Gilded Bottle

A corner of a star forms the motif on this lovely, glowing bottle.

You Will Need

Materials

flat-sided glass bottle or jar
gold glass-painting outliner
solvent-based glass paints: red, blue, green and yellow

Equipment

methylated spirit
paper towels
paper
paintbrushes

1 Wash the bottle or jar in hot, soapy water and dry thoroughly. Wipe over the surface with methylated spirit to remove any remaining traces of grease.

2 Lay the bottle or jar on its side. Practise with the gold outliner on a piece of paper first, then draw on the design from the back of the book. Allow to dry for 12 hours.

3 Apply the glass paint between the outlines, brushing it on thickly to avoid streaky brushstrokes. Leave the bottle or jar, lying on its side, to dry for at least 36 hours before starting the next side.

Maritime Tiles

Four plain ceramic tiles combine to make a striking mural design, reminiscent of Japanese crafts in its graphic simplicity and clear, calm blue and white colour scheme. There are many different brands of ceramic paint available. Some are fixed by baking in the oven, while others can just be left to dry.

You Will Need

Materials

tracing paper
masking tape
4 white glazed tiles, 15 x 15 cm/6 x 6 in
ceramic paints: mid-blue, dark blue and black

Equipment

soft and hard pencils
china marker
small and fine paintbrushes
paint-mixing container

1 Trace the template from the back of the book, enlarging if necessary. Tape the tracing to the tiles, positioning it centrally. Transfer the outline to the tiles with a hard pencil.

2 Trace over the outline again with the china marker. Draw the border freehand, and add any extra details to the fish. Follow the finished picture as a guide.

3 Using the ceramic paints, fill in the fish shape. First, paint the main part of the fish in mid-blue.

4 Paint the detail and the border with dark blue. Highlight the scales with black. Fix the paint following the manufacturer's instructions. The tiles should withstand gentle cleaning.

Italianate Tiles

These Florentine-style tiles are based on ceramic decoration of the Renaissance. They are painted with easy-to-use enamel paints that are fixed in the oven. A single tile could be a focal point in a bathroom, but when several are arranged together, interesting repeat patterns are formed. Adapt the colours to fit in with your own decor.

You Will Need

Materials	Equipment
tracing paper	*soft and hard pencils*
washed white square tiles	*paintbrushes*
masking tape	*paint-mixing container*
enamel paints: mid-green, dark blue-green, rust-red and dark blue	

1 Trace the template on this page, enlarging it to fit your tiles. Trace off the main motif (and the border if you wish) and rub over the back of the tracing with a soft pencil. Position the tracing on each tile, secure with masking tape, and draw over the outline with a hard pencil.

2 Paint the leaf in mid-green enamel paint and allow to dry. You may need to mix colours to achieve the shades you wish. Using a dark blue-green, paint over the outline and mark in the veins. Paint a dot in each corner of the tile in the same colour.

3 With a fine brush, paint a border of rust-coloured leaves and a slightly larger leaf in each corner. Paint a curved scroll to either side of the large leaf in dark blue. Repeat with the remaining tiles. When the paint is dry, fix it following the manufacturer's instructions.

Whisky Glass

The fleur-de-lys was the heraldic emblem of the kings of France from the twelfth century. Use the template to make two sizes of fleur-de-lys. Paint each motif in a different combination of colours, matching them with small motifs on the opposite side.

You Will Need

Materials

whisky glass
black cerne relief outliner
tracing paper
masking tape
solvent-based glass paints: red, blue and yellow

Equipment

methylated spirit
paper towels
pencil
fine black pen
paintbrushes
craft knife

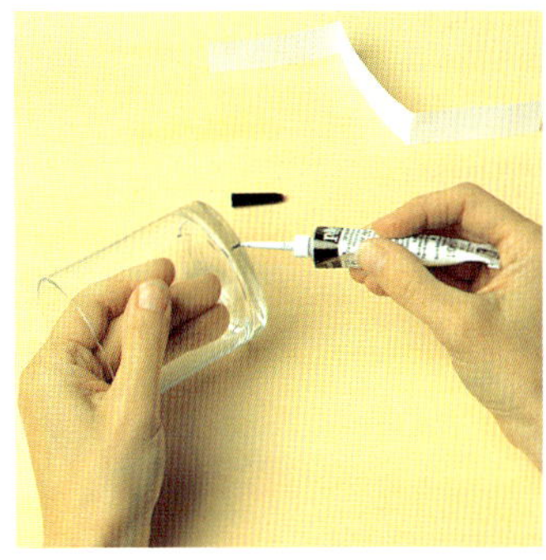

1 Wash the glass in hot, soapy water and dry thoroughly. Wipe over the surface with methylated spirit to remove any remaining traces of grease. Divide the base of the glass into three equal sections and mark them with cerne relief.

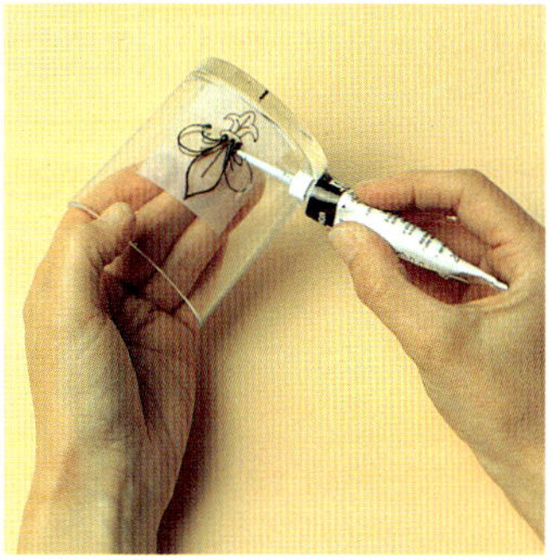

2 Trace the template from the back of the book, enlarging if necessary, and tape it inside the glass. Draw the design with the black pen in each of the three sections. Leave each section to dry for at least 12 hours before moving on to the next. Outline small motifs opposite in this way.

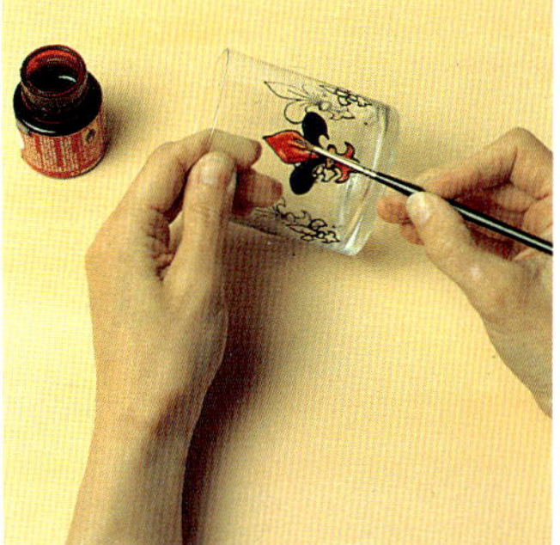

3 Colour the first large motif, using different colours for each section, and allow to dry overnight before turning the glass for the next motif. Paint each small fleur-de-lys in colours matching the motif on the opposite side of the glass. When you have finished, scrape off the reference marks on the base and allow the paint to dry before washing.

Decorated Tea Service

If you are bored with your plain tea cups and saucers, why not cheer yourself up with some pretty stamped patterns in vibrant colours?

You Will Need

Materials	Equipment
tracing paper	*pencil*
paper or thin card	*eraser*
spray adhesive	*craft knife*
white china tea service	*cutting mat*
ceramic paints: orange, blue and black	*piece of glass*

1 Trace the template from this page, enlarging it if desired, and transfer to paper or thin card. Spray the template with adhesive and stick it on the end of an eraser.

2 Cut around the outline of the star, making sure that the points are sharp.

3 Cut horizontally into the eraser, to meet the outline cuts, and remove the excess. The star shape must have points of even lengths, so make a test print and adjust any obvious flaws with a craft knife before you work on the china.

4 Spread an even coating of orange paint on to the glass and press the star stamp into it. Make a test print to ensure that the stamp is not overloaded, then begin stamping widely spaced stars. The inked stamp will tend to slide on the glazed surface, so compensate for this by dotting it on and removing it directly.

5 Stamp blue stars in the same way, leaving space for the final colour.

6 Stamp black stars in the spaces so that the three colours form an all-over pattern. Allow to dry, then fix the paints according to the manufacturer's instructions.

Sun Jug

A good way to brighten up a plain jug is to use china paints to apply a vivid and bold motif. This cheerful sun face would be particularly welcome on the breakfast table. The colours could be adapted to suit your other china.

You Will Need

Materials

tracing paper
washed white ceramic jug
masking tape
ceramic paints: black, bright yellow, ochre, blue, red and white

Equipment

soft and hard pencils
scissors
fine paintbrushes
hairdryer (optional)

1 Trace the template from the back of the book, enlarging if necessary. Cut it out roughly and rub over the back with a soft pencil. Make several cuts around the edge of the circle, so that the template will lie flat against the jug, and tape it in place. Draw over the outlines with a hard pencil to transfer the design.

2 Using and mixing the paints according to the manufacturer's instructions, paint the sun. Go over the outline for the features in black first of all and allow the paint to dry completely; a hairdryer can speed up the drying process. Paint the main face and the inner rays in bright yellow and then paint the cheeks and the other parts of the rays in ochre.

3 Paint the background in blue and then add fine details to the sun face, to give it a sense of depth. Finish off by painting a white dot as a highlight in each eye. Fix the paints according to the manufacturer's instructions.

HANDPAINTED FLORAL TILES

This is a great idea for decorating plain ceramic tiles, which could then be framed and hung on the wall.

YOU WILL NEED

MATERIALS

tracing paper
masking tape
washed white glazed tiles
ceramic paints: green, yellow, red and blue

EQUIPMENT

soft and hard pencils
scissors
paintbrushes
paint-mixing container

1 Trace the template from the back of the book, enlarging if necessary. Turn the paper over and rub over the outline with a soft pencil. Tape the transfer to the tile. Draw over the main flower outline with a hard pencil, to transfer the motif to the tile.

2 Using a medium brush and thin layers of paint, colour in the leaves and petals. Fix the paints according to the manufacturer's instructions.

3 With a fine brush and blue paint, draw in the outline and detail of the petals, leaves and stalk. Paint tiny dots in the centre of the flower. Transfer the four corner motifs in the same way and with a fine brush, paint them blue. Fix the paint as before.

Star-sign Bottle

Create a container fit for a magic potion using glowing glass paints to enhance a gilded design. This beautiful bottle would look stunning catching the light on a bathroom windowsill, but make sure the contents don't obscure the jewel-like colours.

You Will Need

Materials	Equipment
flat-sided glass bottle	*methylated spirit*
gold glass-paint outliner	*paper towels*
scrap paper	*paintbrush*
solvent-based glass paints: red, blue, green and yellow	

1 Wash the bottle in hot, soapy water and dry thoroughly. Wipe over the surface with methylated spirit to remove any remaining traces of grease.

2 Practise using the gold outliner on paper before drawing the outline design (as seen in the picture) on one side of the bottle. Allow to dry for at least 24 hours.

3 Apply the glass paint between the outlines, brushing it on thickly to achieve an even coating. Leave the bottle on its side to dry for at least 24 hours.

4 Using the gold outliner, draw the astrological symbols (see template section) around the design. Allow to dry completely before repeating the design on the other side of the bottle.

Majolica-style Tiles

Majolica is glazed or enamelled earthenware, noted for its bright colours. These tiles imitate the style very effectively, making use of ceramic paints on crisp, white ceramic tiles.

You Will Need

Materials

tracing paper
4 white square ceramic tiles
ceramic paints: dark blue, yellow and red

Equipment

pencil
fine paintbrushes
paint-mixing container

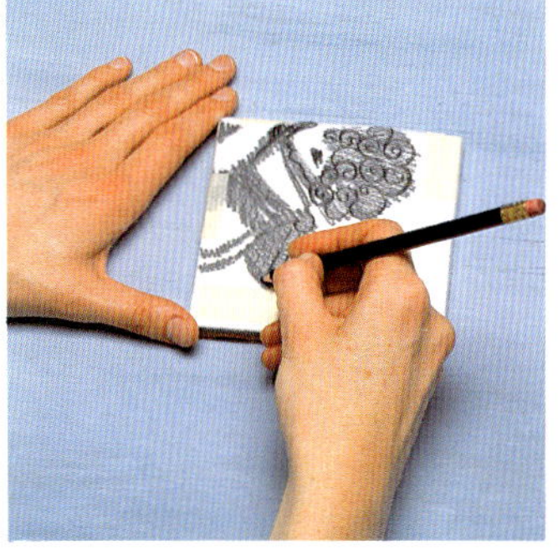

1 Trace the template from the back of the book, enlarging it to fit your tiles. Transfer a quarter of the design on to each tile.

2 With a fine brush and dark blue paint, paint over the main outline on each tile. Fix the paint according to the manufacturer's instructions.

3 Fill in the wings, hair and drapery with yellow. Allow the colour to dry. Mix the colours to add darker tones, using the finished picture as a guide. Fix the paints again, to prevent the colours smudging.

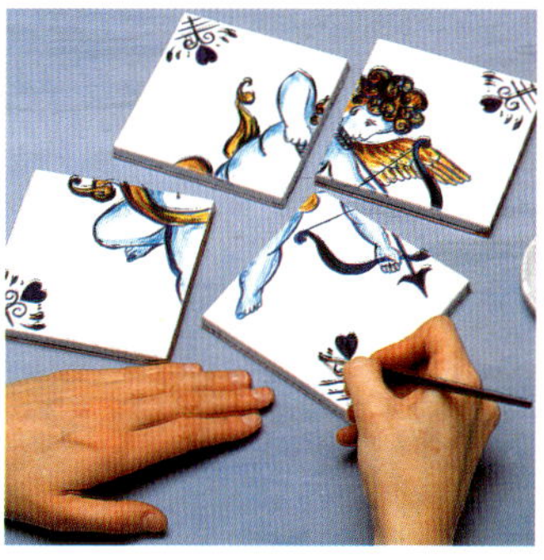

4 With diluted blue paint, mark in the shadows on the cupid's face and body. Go over any areas that need to be defined with more blue paint. Paint the corner motifs freehand and then fix for the final time.

Frosted Jug

If you love the effect of frosted glass but don't like the rather banal designs often found in shops, this technique is for you. You can use the same technique to make a set of glasses to go with the jug.

You Will Need

Materials	Equipment
paper	*pencil*
sticky-backed plastic	*scissors*
washed glass jug	*soft paintbrush*
etching fluid cream	*rubber gloves*

1 Draw a cupid and star freehand on to paper and cut out. Trace around the shapes on to sticky-backed plastic and cut out.

2 Peel the backing off the plastic and stick the shapes around the jug.

3 Follow the manufacturer's instructions to paint the etching fluid cream on to the outside of the jug, avoiding the handle. Leave to stand for about ten minutes.

4 Wearing rubber gloves, wash the cream off the jug in warm water and leave it to dry. If there are any unfrosted patches on the glass where the cream hasn't taken, simply repeat step 3. When you are satisfied with the frosted finish, peel off the shapes.

Rosebud Jug

If you are a beginner at painting on glass, you might find it easier to trace the template (see back of book) on to paper and fit the paper inside the jug. Then trace the design with the outliner.

You Will Need

Materials

tracing paper
glass jug
old jam jar
gold glass-painting outliner
solvent-based glass paints: red and green

Equipment

methylated spirit
paper towels
pencil
packing material or bean bag
paintbrush
white spirit

1 Wash the jug in hot, soapy water and dry thoroughly. Wipe over the surface with methylated spirit to remove any remaining traces of grease.

2 Controlling the flow of the outliner can be tricky, so have a few practice runs on an old jam jar. Draw your design on to the jug. This is easiest to do in sections and each section should be left to harden for at least 12 hours before you begin the next.

3 To fill in the design, prop the jug up on its side on the packing material or bean bag. Try to keep the area that you are painting horizontal, to stop the paint from running. Carefully paint in a section, applying the glass paint thickly, to prevent streaky brushstrokes. Remove any excess paint with the brush. Leave each section to dry overnight before turning the jug to do the next section. Clean the brush with white spirit each time.

Mosaic Dragonfly Plaque

Very effective mosaics can be made using broken china, then fixing the pieces with ceramic adhesive and grouting just as you would when laying tiles. The old, chipped plates you were going to throw out may be just the colours you need.

You Will Need

Materials

tracing paper
plywood, 51 x 51 cm/ 20 x 20 in
PVA (white) glue
acrylic primer
dark green acrylic paint
electric cable
selection of china
tile adhesive
coloured tile grout

Equipment

pencil
fretsaw or coping saw
bradawl
paintbrush
sandpaper
cable strippers
tile nippers
rubber gloves
nail brush
cloth

1 Trace the template from the back of the book, enlarging if necessary. Transfer it to the plywood. Cut out the dragonfly and make two holes at the top of the body with a bradawl. Seal the front surface with diluted PVA (white) glue and the back with acrylic primer. Allow to dry. Sand the back surface and paint green.

2 Strip some electric cable and cut a short length of wire. Push this through the holes on the dragonfly and twist together securely.

3 Cut the china into regular shapes using tile nippers. Dip each piece into the tile adhesive, scooping up a thick layer, and press down securely. Allow to dry overnight.

4 Press the grout into the gaps between the china. Allow to dry for five minutes, then brush off the excess. Leave for another five minutes, then polish with a cloth.

Mosaic Shield Plaque

This plaque uses simple square tiles to build up the design. By carefully mixing light and dark shades, you can give the impression of the curved edge of a shield without having to cut the glass pieces.

You Will Need

Materials

5 mm/¼ in medium-density fibreboard, 23 x 30 cm/ 9 x 12 in
tracing paper
PVA (white) glue
glass mosaic squares, 2.5 x 2.5 cm/1 x 1 in
white grouting
2 screw eyes
picture wire, 20 cm/8 in

Equipment

pencil
ruler
paintbrush
damp cloth
soft, dry cloth

1 Draw a line 2.5 cm/1 in in from each edge of the board. Rule a line down the centre of the board. Draw a horizontal line 11.5 cm/4½ in from the top, then mark in a gentle curve in each lower quarter. Trace a shield shape on to tracing paper as a base for working out the design. Take time to find a satisfying arrangement of colours.

2 Paint a thick layer of glue in a top quarter of the shield and stick on your chosen tiles. Surround these with a single row of white around the outside edge, and a darker colour along the centre lines. Repeat with the remaining quarters of the shield.

3 Leave overnight for the glue to harden, then fill in the spaces between the tiles with white grouting. Wipe off the surplus with a damp cloth and, when dry, polish with a soft cloth. Fix the screw eyes into the back and attach the wire for hanging.

Sequinned Rose Bottle

This ingenious technique could be used to decorate any kind of container, but it is particularly suited to a tall, narrow bottle, which might otherwise be hard to work on. The rose motif shown here would make a very suitable decoration for a special gift bottle of fragrant rosewater!

You Will Need

Materials

glass bottle
tights
matching thread
invisible thread
sequins
bugle beads
glass beads

Equipment

needle
dressmaker's scissors
beading needle
fabric marker

1 Place the bottle in the toe of one leg of the tights. Thread a needle, wrap it around the neck of the bottle, secure it and trim away the excess fabric.

2 Thread the beading needle with invisible thread and work the rose motif: firstly, thread a sequin and then a bugle bead, bring the needle down and then up next to the first stitch and continue working like this.

3 Draw the stripes with the marker and fill them with sequins and glass beads, in the same way.

Painted Vase

Painted glassware was a popular folk art from Europe, with bright figures used to adorn bottles of spirit and drinking tumblers from France to Hungary. Try to find old glasses in junk or antique shops for this project as imperfections won't show.

You Will Need

Materials	Equipment
tracing paper	*pencil*
glass	*scissors*
masking tape	*cloth*
enamel paints: red, green, yellow, blue and black	*paintbrushes*
enamel paint thinner	*paint-mixing containers*
	elastic band

1 Trace the template from the back of the book, enlarging it to fit inside your glass. Cut out and secure it with masking tape.

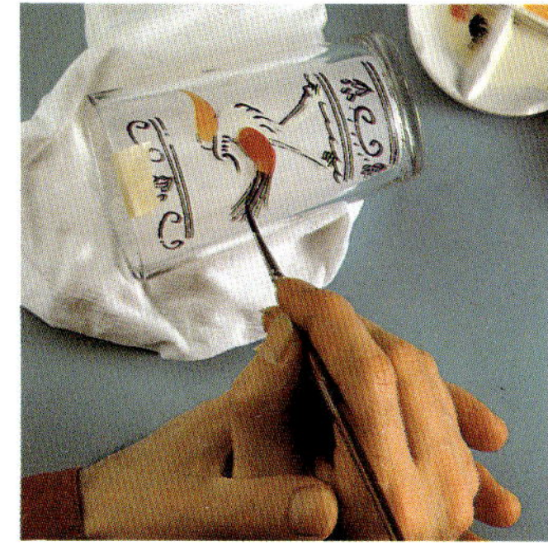

2 Rest the glass on a cloth and support your painting hand with your other hand as you paint. Make sure the paints are thinned enough to make them flow nicely as you paint the pattern on.

3 Add the dots and motifs to suit your glass. Allow to dry, then place an elastic band around the glass to guide you as you paint stripes of colour.

4 Introduce some individuality by adding embellishments of your own, perhaps just a few squiggles, some dots or even your initials.

Fruit Bowl

This is a freehand project, and the loosely drawn oranges, leaves and flowers do not demand sophisticated artistic skill. You can substitute apples, pears, pineapples or lemons for the oranges.

You Will Need

Materials

white-glazed bowl
ceramic paints: orange, lilac, lime-green, dark green, burgundy and black
polyurethane varnish

Equipment

black magic marker
paintbrushes

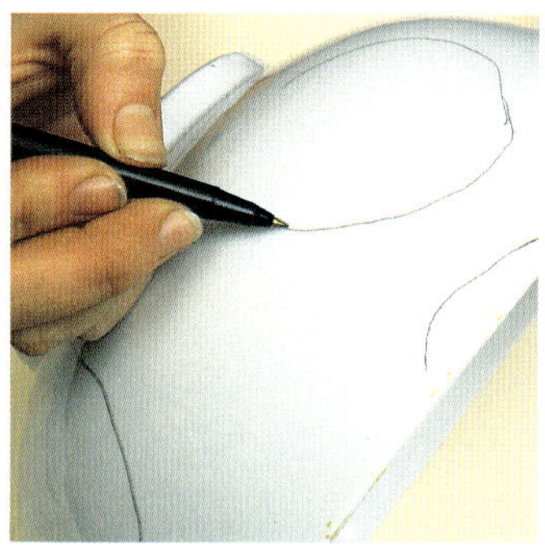

1 Draw four or five whole oranges on to the bowl, leaving space for the leaves and flowers. Draw four or five cut-off oranges along the top rim and base.

2 Paint the oranges, spreading the paint thinly. Allow to dry.

3 Draw flowers peeping out from behind the oranges, as shown, and paint them lilac, leaving the centres white.

4 Draw leaves, one small and one large, for each orange. Space them so there are no big gaps in the background. Draw half leaves going off the bowl.

5 Paint the small leaves in lime-green and the large leaves in dark green.

6 Paint the background burgundy, leaving a thin white outline around the motifs. Spread the paint thinly so the brushstrokes remain visible for textural variety.

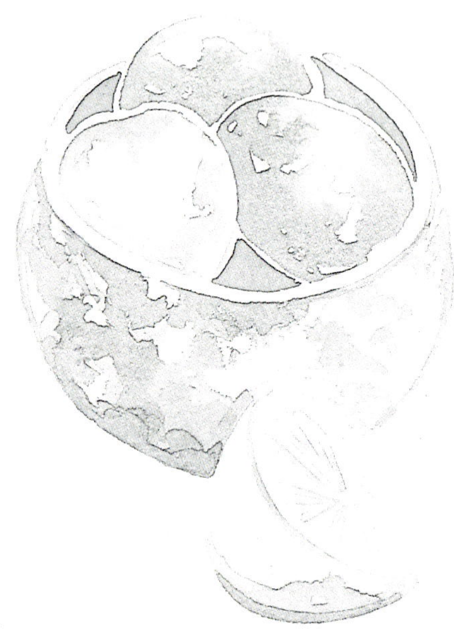

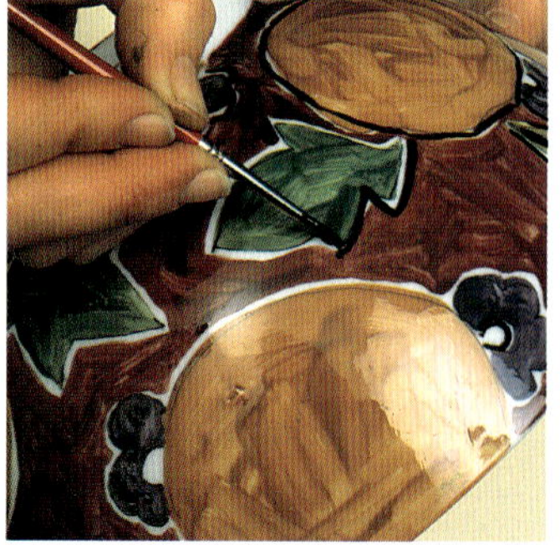

7 Paint loosely around the motifs in black. Vary the pressure on the brush so the line is sometimes thick and sometimes thin. Paint the mid-ribs in the leaves and the circular centres in the flowers.

8 Paint the rim at the bottom in dark green, spreading the paint thinly to emphasize the hand-painted quality of the design. Allow to dry, then varnish the bowl.

Holly Platter

Display this festive painted plate heaped high with Christmas tree balls, repeating the chosen colour scheme, or a mixture of tree balls and pine cones, spray-painted in metallic colours or left natural. For a children's party, heap the platter with sweets and wrapped chocolate coins.

You Will Need

Materials

white-glazed plate
masking tape
paper or thin card
ceramic paints: green, red, maroon and gold
gold spray
polyurethane varnish

Equipment

pencil
craft knife
cutting mat
paintbrushes

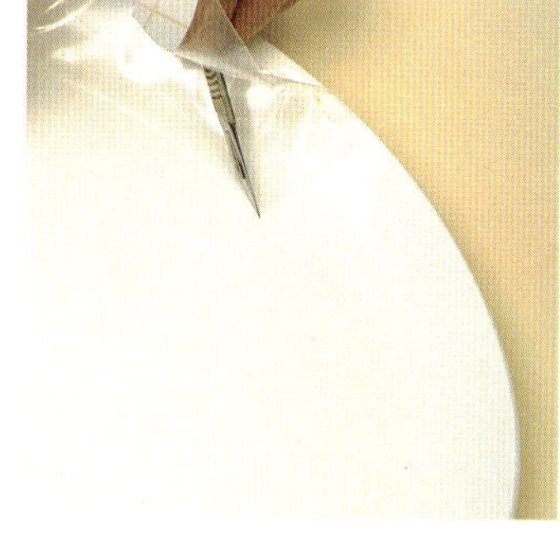

1 Mask off the centre of the plate with masking tape, leaving the outer rim clear.

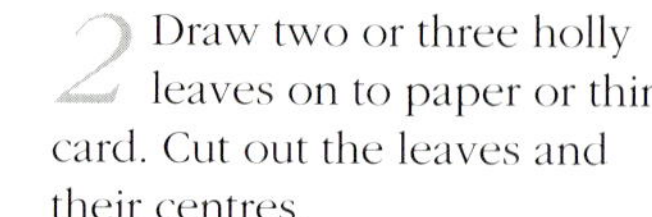

2 Draw two or three holly leaves on to paper or thin card. Cut out the leaves and their centres.

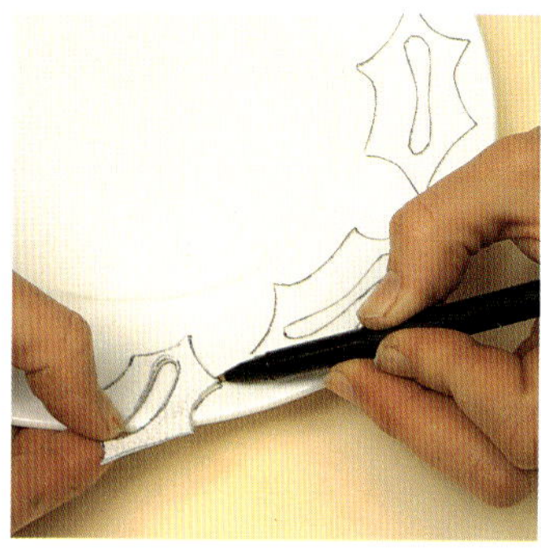

3 Lay the leaf stencils to fit around the rim of the plate, leaving space for a border, if liked. Mark on where the first stencil starts, then trace the leaves on to the plate.

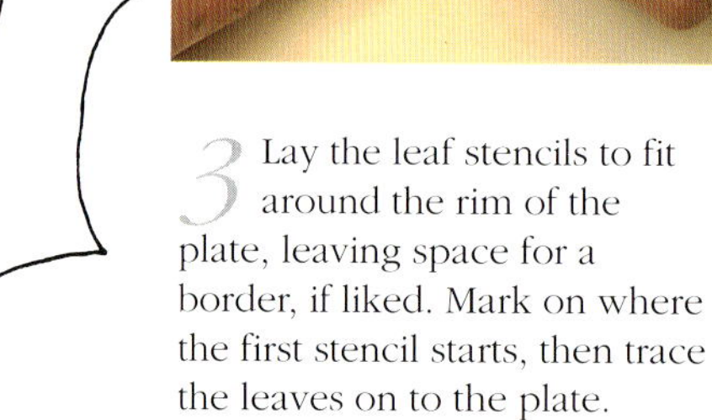

4 Add some straight and curved stems to the leaves. Some can be single, and others should join to form sprigs. Fill the gaps with berries.

5 Paint the leaves and stems green, leaving the central mid-rib white. Allow to dry, then add touches of green to highlight. Allow to dry, then paint the berries red.

6 Paint the background maroon, using a fine brush to go around the motifs first.

7 Paint a gold outline around the leaves and berries and along one side of the stems. Try to leave as much white outline as possible. Use the edge of a craft knife to remove the masking tape from the plate.

8 Lightly spray the plate gold, then paint a narrow red band around the rim, if liked. Allow to dry, then coat with a layer of varnish.

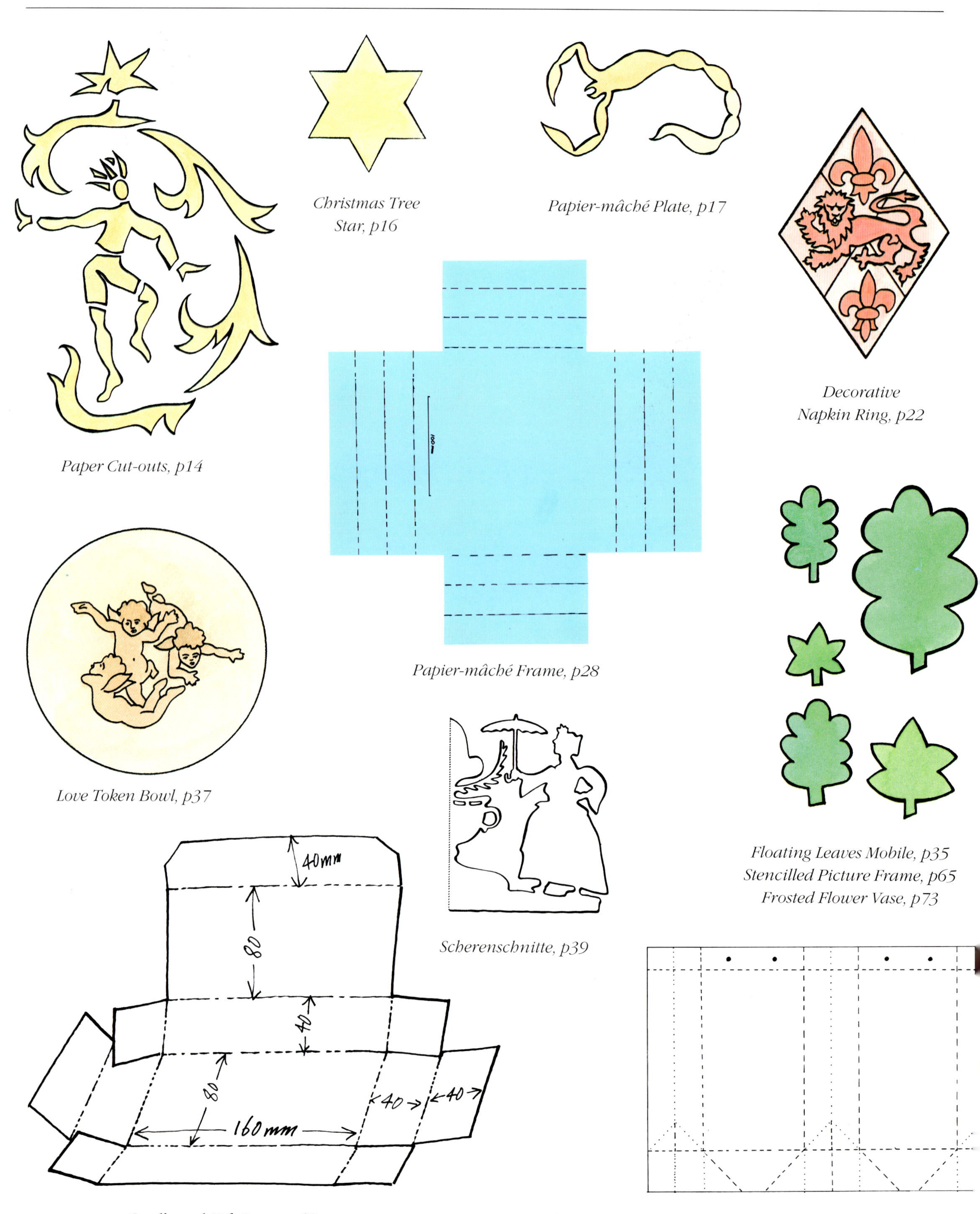

Paper Cut-outs, p14

Christmas Tree Star, p16

Papier-mâché Plate, p17

Decorative Napkin Ring, p22

Papier-mâché Frame, p28

Love Token Bowl, p37

Floating Leaves Mobile, p35
Stencilled Picture Frame, p65
Frosted Flower Vase, p73

Scherenschnitte, p39

Cardboard Gift Boxes, p40

Carrier Bags, p42

Stencilled Sprig Curtain, p48

Creepy Crawly Handkerchief, p52

Stencilled Sea Wall, p60

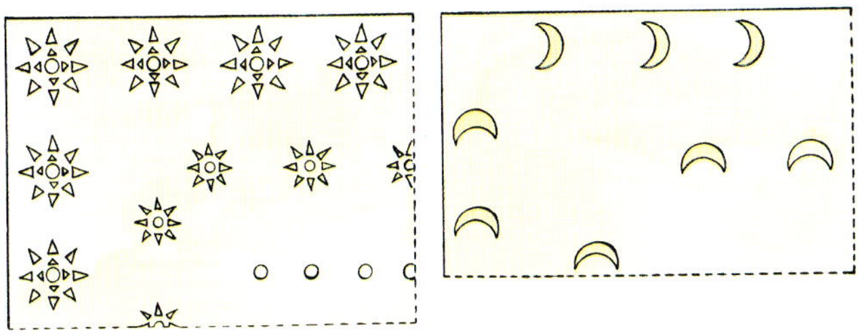

Suns and Moons Napkin, p49

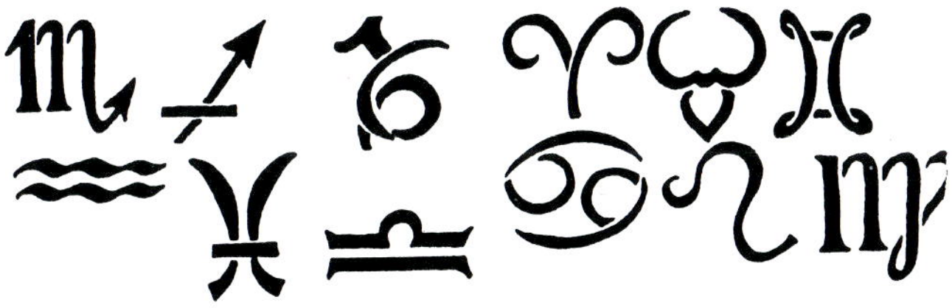

Zodiac Café Curtain, p56

Fleur-de-lys Tiles, p61

Mexican Citrus Tray, p66

Cupid Linocut, p67

Medieval Cork Tiles, p68

Gilded Wall Border, p70

Art Nouveau Rose Box, p72

Country-style Shelf, p74

Lemon Slice Napkins, p84

Beaded Orange Purse, p86

Embroidered Insect Display, p82

Fleur-de-lys Shoe Bag, p85

Sparkling Ivy Garland, p88

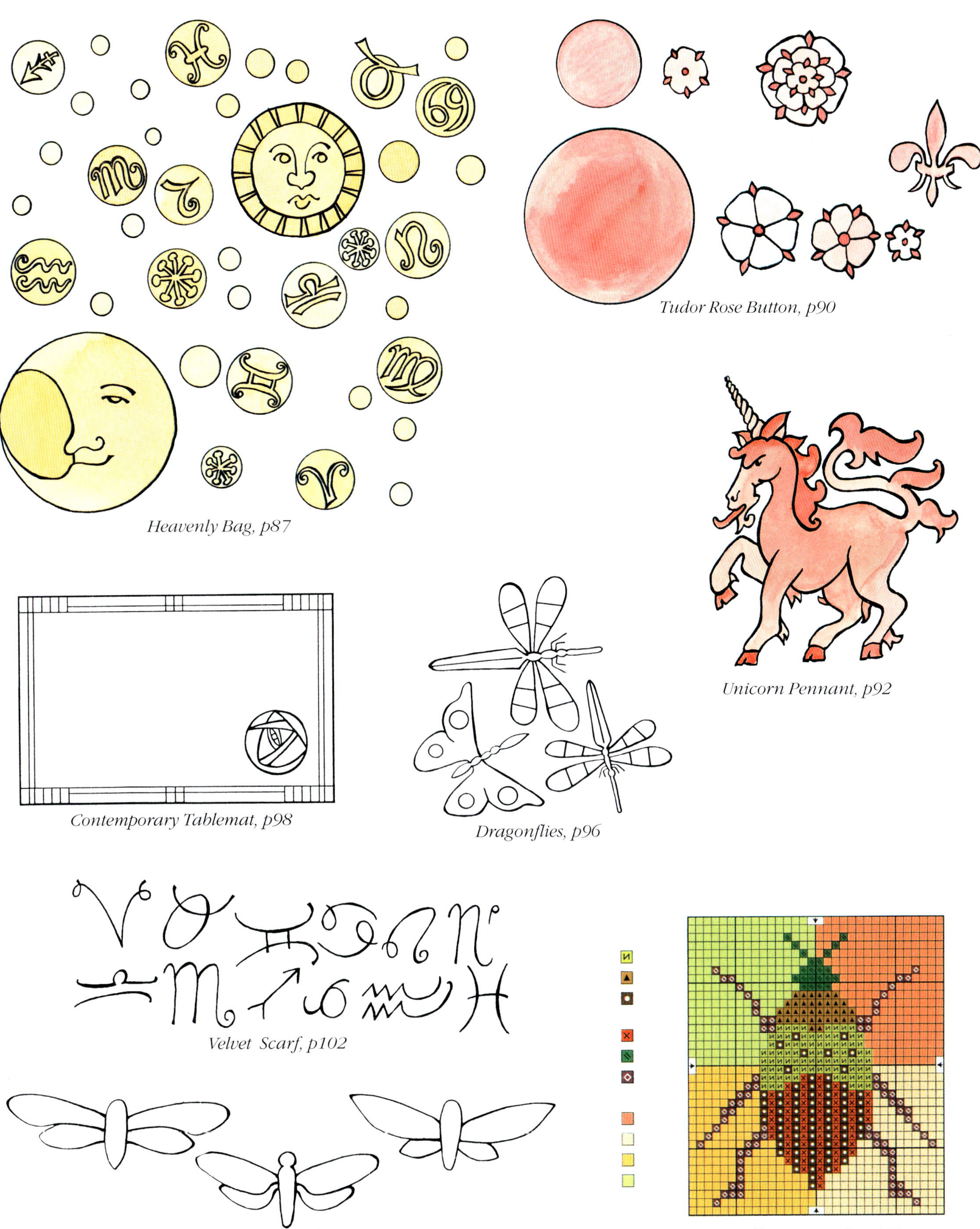

Heavenly Bag, p87

Tudor Rose Button, p90

Unicorn Pennant, p92

Contemporary Tablemat, p98

Dragonflies, p96

Velvet Scarf, p102

Silver Moth Scarf, p103

Needlepoint Beetle, p108

Baby Suit, p100
Bridal Heart, p105

Decorative Pincushion, p106

Cupid Camisole, p107

Oak Leaf Potholder, p116

Heraldic Tablemat, p117

Appliquéd
Sunflower Card, p120

Star Patchwork Sachet, p121

Matisse Outfit, p118

Rose Appliqué Bag, p124

Fleur-de-lys Tieback, p126

Cradle Quilt, p128

Appliqué Throw, p122

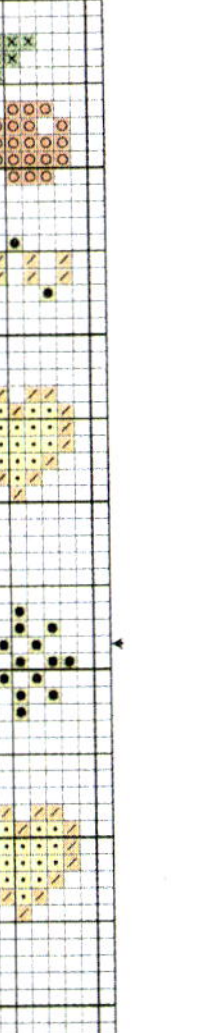

Orange Sampler, p127

Star-spangled Banner, p132

Star-spangled Scarf, p131

Oranges Tea Towel, p136

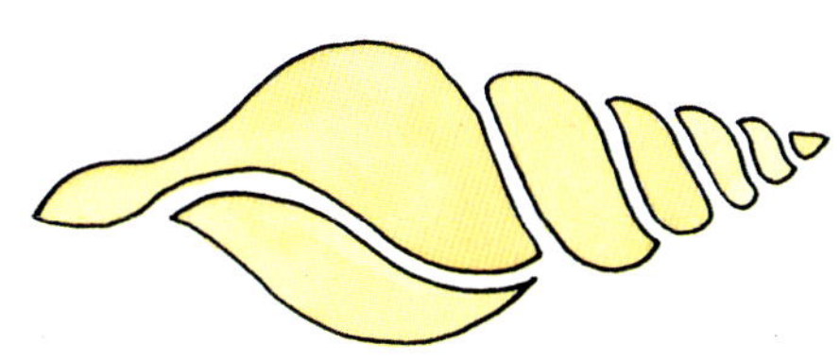

Seashell Beach Bag, p130

Appliqué Star Card, p139

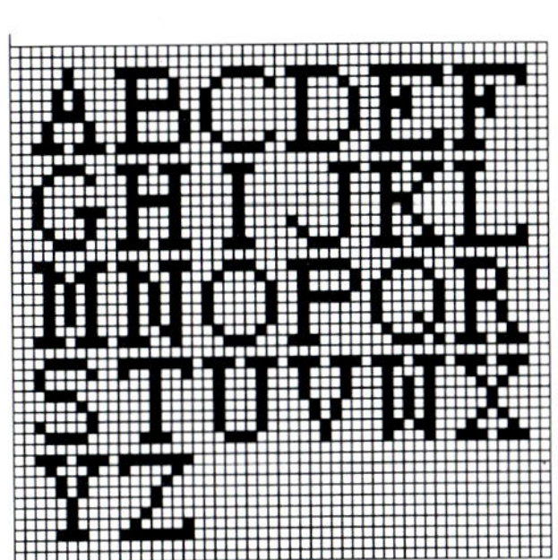

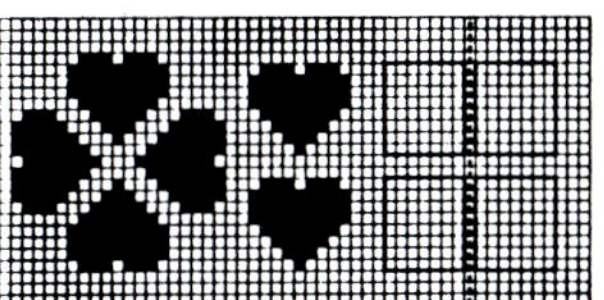

Shaker Towel, p137

Appliqué Notebook, p140

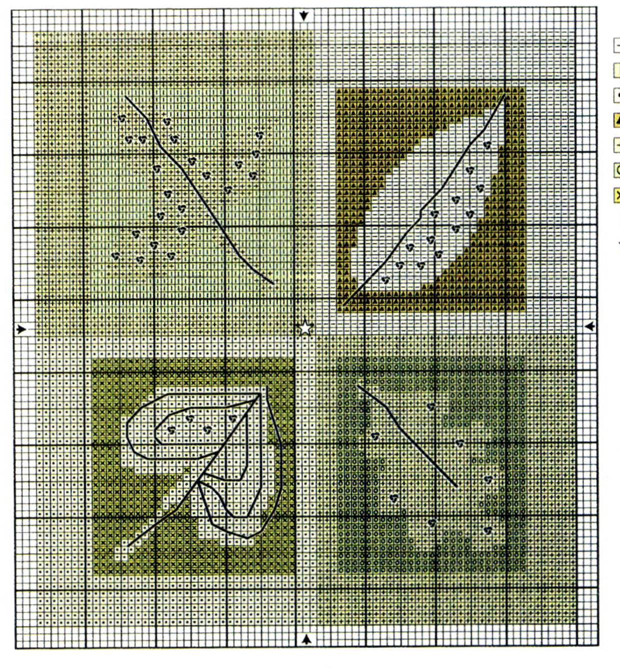

Needlepoint Mat, p138

Hand Towel and Washcloth, p141

Appliquéd Sheet and Pillowcase, p142

Child's T-shirt, p143

Initial Cushion, p144

Wheatsheaf, p150

Gingerbread Hearts, p151

Star Frame, p155

Hanging Shapes, p152

Antique Wall Tile, p160

Display Case, p162

Folk Angel, p166

Winged Heart, p170

Love Bug, p172

Wall Decoration, p173

Gingerbread Cupids, p176

Cornucopia, p174

Checkered Heart, p175

Punched Tin Panel, p185

Ornamental Tree, p186

Exotic Table Decorations, p188

Wooden Sheep Sign, p187

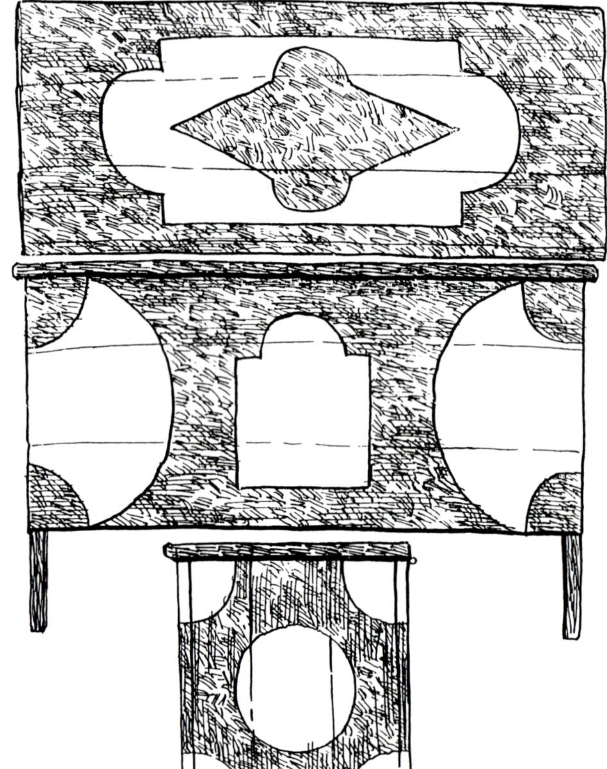

Painted Chest, p196

Tin Candleholder, p192

Woodburning, p190

Christmas Decorations, p202

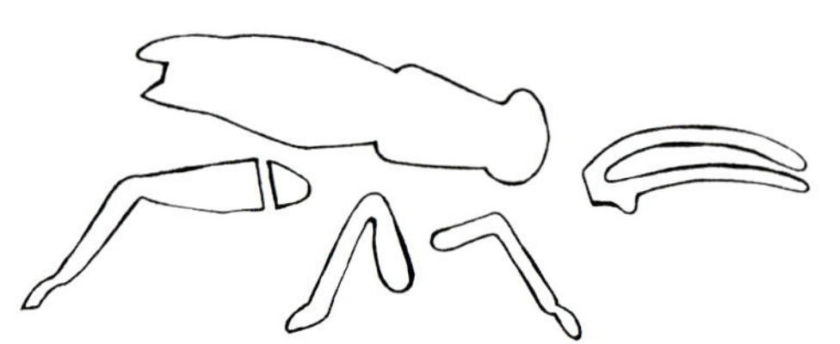

Grasshopper on a Stick, p206

Gilded Bottle, p226

Maritime Tiles, p227

Whisky Glass, p229

Sun Jug, p232

Handpainted Floral Tiles, p233

Mosaic Dragonfly Plaque, p238

Rosebud Jug, p237

Majolica-style Tiles, p235

Painted Vase, p241

INDEX